ATARI ST

TRICKS & TIPS

Valuable collection of software tools and programming hints

By Rolf Brückmann
Lothar Englisch
Jörg Walkowiak
and Klaus Gerits

A Data Becker Book

Published by

Abacus Software

Fourth Printing, November 1988
Printed in U.S.A.
Copyright © 1985, 1987, 1988

Copyright © 1986, 1987, 1988

Data Becker GmbH
Merowingerstraße 30
4000 Düsseldorf, West Germany
Abacus
5370 52nd Street SE
Grand Rapids, MI 49508

ATARI, 520ST, ST, TOS, ST BASIC and ST LOGO are trademarks or registered trademarks of Atari Corp.

GEM, GEM Draw and GEM Write are trademarks or registered trademarks of Digital Research Inc.

IBM is a registered trademark of International Business Machines.

ISBN   0-916439-47-X

Table of contents

Chapter 1

ST BASIC

ST BASIC

Two languages are packaged with the ST—BASIC and LOGO. BASIC is the most widely used language for personal computers, of course. We won't talk about all of ST BASIC's commands. You can find out more about that in other books, such as the **ST BASIC Training Guide** from Abacus. Instead, we'll introduce some the features that are unique or peculiar to this version of ST BASIC.

If you're already familiar with BASIC on other personal computers, then you should have little trouble adapting to ST BASIC. The syntax of ST BASIC is very similar to the Microsoft BASIC on the IBM PC.

On the other hand, ST BASIC has some very impressive capabilities. In particular, ST BASIC has a very flexible interface to the GEM (Graphics Environment Manager) and to the VDI (Virtual Device Interface). These provide a convenient way to make use of many powerful ST features.

1.1 The special ST BASIC commands

Below is a short description of the commands unique to ST BASIC.

FOLLOW, UNFOLLOW

The FOLLOW command outputs the value of simple variables when the contents of that variable change during the program run. This makes it much easier to search for programming errors. The UNFOLLOW command turns off the output of variable values. The syntax for UNFOLLOW is:

```
FOLLOW a,angle%,text$
.
. (other BASIC statements)
.
UNFOLLOW text$
```

BREAK, UNBREAK

The BREAK and UNBREAK commands are also used for program debugging. The BREAK command halts the execution of the program when the corresponding line number is reached. At this time the following is displayed:

```
b nnn
Br
```

The b signifies the BREAK, and nnn is the line number at which the BREAK was encountered. Br signifies that you are in break mode. Program execution continues if you press the <RETURN> key.

BASIC is still in the BREAK mode. If the corresponding line number is encountered again (in a loop, for example), program execution is halted again. You can disable this with the UNBREAK command. Example:

```
BREAK 120,512,2013
UNBREAK
```

TRON, TROFF

The TRON and TROFF commands are also used for program debugging. They may only be used in command mode.

TRON turns tracing on for the entire program. All line numbers are displayed as they are encountered during program execution.

TRON i-j turns tracing on for a specific range of lines. All line numbers with values falling between i and j are displayed as they are encountered during program execution.

TROFF turns off tracing for the entire program.

TROFF -100 turns off tracing for a specified range of lines.

TRACE, UNTRACE

The TRACE and UNTRACE commands are additional commands for debugging, similar to TRON and TROFF. But in addition to displaying the line number of the statement being executed, the contents of that line are also displayed. The syntax is identical to TRON and TROFF.

BLOAD

The BLOAD command loads the contents of a file to a particular range of memory. You can use the BLOAD command to load machine language programs or screen images. The syntax is:

    BLOAD *filename, addr*

Here, *filename* is the name of the file to be loaded. *addr* is a memory address and is not checked for validity. You are free to load a file to any memory location. Remember that if you fail to specify a load address, a fatal error will occur. In this case, the contents of the file is loaded to the default address 0. This overwrites the important exception vectors and you'll have to reboot the ST.

BSAVE

The BSAVE command saves a range of memory to a file. You can use this command to save a screen image or a machine language program.

The syntax is:

    BSAVE *filename, addr1, addr2*

filename is the name under which the memory range is to be saved. *addr1* is the starting memory address and *addr2* is the number of bytes to be saved.

Examples:

    BSAVE "screen.bin",&h78000,&h7d00

    BSAVE "mprog.bin",&h7fd00,768

In the first example, the screen contents of the 520 ST screen of are saved to the file called `screen.bin`. In the 1040 ST, the screen memory is located at `&hf8000`.

Immediately following screen memory are 768 bytes of unused memory. This area may be used for short machine language routines, since it's not used by the operating system or BASIC. The second example saves the contents of this unused memory area.

CALL

There are two ways of calling machine language programs from ST BASIC. The first way is to use the `CALL` command. The parameters for `CALL` specify the address of the desired routine and the values which are to be passed to it. The address of the routine must be a variable.

```
address = &h7fd00
CALL address

address = &h7fd00
value1 = 33.33
value2% = 100
z$ = "test"
CALL address(val1,val2%,100,z$,"empty string")
```

In the first example the routine is called without parameters. The machine language routine may modify all registers. The value of the stack pointer must be restored to its value upon entry to the routine. This is because the routine itself must be ended with `RTS`. If the stack pointer is not restored, your program will probably crash..

The second example demonstrates how parameters are specified in the `CALL` command. The parameters must be enclosed in parentheses and separated from each other by commas. All variable types are allowed as parameters. The parameters are converted to signed 32-bit integers. Therefore a value of 33 is passed through `val1`. For strings (`z$`, `"empty string"`) the address of the string is passed, also represented as a 32-bit value.

How can the data be accessed in the machine language program? When the machine language program is called, registers A0, A7, and D0 are used. A0 contains the address of the routine. You may think that this is superfluous, because the address of the routine is normally known. You just might be surprised. Later we will show how helpful the contents of A0 can be.

Register D0 contains the number of values passed. It's contained in the lower 16 bits. This value is also very important for some applications, especially if the routine can be called with a variable number of parameters. The use of a 16-bit counter is more than sufficient. Such an enormous number of parameters cannot be placed in one BASIC line.

Register A7, the user stack pointer, contains the return address to the BASIC interpreter. Additional information is also placed on the stack. For example, you can transfer the number of parameters into register Dx with the instruction MOVE.W 4(SP),Dx.

With the instruction MOVE.L 6(SP),Ax you get the start of a table. In this table are as many long words (32-bit values) as parameters in the CALL command. In these long words are the values or addresses of the strings.

PEEK

PEEK is a function that returns the contents of memory. In ST BASIC, PEEK can return 8-bit, 16-bit or 32-bit values.

Normally PEEK returns a 16-bit value. For example, PEEK(0) returns the contents at the memory locations 0 and 1. The value at memory location 0 is the low-byte, and the value at memory location 1 is the high byte.

The command DEF SEG may be used so that subsequent calls to PEEK return an 8/16/32-bit value depending on the DEF SEG setup.

To return a 32-bit value, you can use PEEK in conjunction with the DEFDBL declaration. DEFDBL is always used in conjunction with DEF SEG, PEEK or POKE.

POKE

POKE is the counterpart of PEEK. The POKE command places a value at a specific memory location. In ST BASIC the value may be 8 bits, 16 bits or 32 bits long.

POKE normally places a 16-bit value in memory. POKE &1000, &2468 will place the hexadecimal value &68 in memory location &1000 and &24 in memory location &1001.

After DEF SEG, subsequent POKE commands place 8/16/32-bit values in memory.

Using POKE in conjunction with the DEFDBL function places 32-bit values in memory.

DEF SEG

The DEF SEG command sets the segment address for the commands PEEK and POKE. DEF SEG or DEF SEG=0 sets the segment to the physical address 0 in memory. This is the default condition after power-up.

If a value greater than 0 is entered, the segment for PEEK and POKE is set to this address. The following example will clarify this point. To access the ST's screen memory you could do the following:

```
value = PEEK(&h7fd00)
```

Alternatively, you can set the segment for the desired address. Then the address specified for PEEK and POKE are to be viewed as relative to the start of that segment.

```
DEF SEG=&h7fd00 : REM Address following is
value = PEEK(0) : REM relative to &7FD00
```

Remember that in the first example, the contents of addresses &h7fd00 and &h7fd01 are returned (16-bit-values). In the second example, the contents of address &h7fd00 are returned (8-bit value).

GOTOXY xpos,ypos

The GOTOXY command positions the cursor on the screen. An output command (PRINT or WRITE) then starts at this location. The cursor position specified in this manner also determines the location of the INPUT command.

The X and Y coordinates are relative to the upper left-hand corner of the screen. Constants can also be used in place of the variables, of course.

Unfortunately, the GOTOXY command to one of the several defective ST BASIC commands. The X position is not evaluated correctly. The specified value is (incorrectly) increased by two. This can lead to rather confusing results. If, however, one of the scroll bars is clicked after the output, the contents of the output window are reprinted and this time in the proper positions. You should therefore use caution when working with this command. Screen masks cannot be easily constructed at the current time.

Try this example to see the problem yourself. After the program is finished, click the output window scroll box to verify that the updated positions have changed.

```
10 GOTOXY 10,10:PRINT "Here is position 10,10"
20 PRINT "12345678901234256789"
```

Here is an example using GOTOXY in conjunction with the INPUT command:

```
GOTOXY x.pos,y.pos:INPUT value
```

INKEY$

The INKEY$ function reads the keyboard and returns the ASCII value of the key pressed. In the current version of ST BASIC, the INKEY$ does not work properly. Characters are not read from the keyboard. This is probably because of the fact that, before the execution of each command, a test is made to see if the keys <CONTROL> and G or <CONTROL> and C are pressed. In this case the program is either ended (<CONTROL>C) completely or interrupted (<CONTROL> G).

However, the internal keyboard buffer is regularly emptied by this test. The INKEY$ function is then so fast that during the processing, no new key presses appear in the keyboard buffer. The function will then always return with no key value. You can use the INPUT$ or the INP function to replace the INKEY$ function in many cases, however. We will describe both.

INPUT$

The INPUT$ function is available only in a few BASIC dialects (such as the IBM PC). With this function, one or more characters can be read from the keyboard or from a file. The most interesting feature of this command is that (almost) no interpretation of control characters is made. The syntax is:

```
     text$ = INPUT$(10)

     a$(i) = INPUT$(10,1)
or
     a$(i) = INPUT$(10,#1)
```

In the first case, 10 characters are read from the keyboard without displaying these keys on the screen. The keys <RETURN>, <ENTER>, <CONTROL> G, and <CONTROL> C can be pressed without interrupting the input. The only terminating condition besides reaching the specified number of characters is the input of <CONTROL> Z. This character, with an ASCII value of 26, is usually used in files as the identifier for the end of the file. The input of 10 characters is rarely necessary (such as for the invisible entry of a password). However, if the number is reduced to one, this command becomes a replacement for the following statement which does not function correctly in ST BASIC:

```
10 a$=INKEY$:IF a$="" then 10:' doesn't work on ST
```

The special keys of the ST keyboard, the function keys and cursor keys, do not return ASCII values. These keys cannot be read with the INPUT$ function.

In the second and third examples, 10 characters are read from a previously opened file and placed in a variable. If you work with data records of a set length, the otherwise special characters like comma, semicolon, quote, and CR (<ENTER> key) can be read without difficulty. For many applications, it's also useful for a file to be read character by character. This is possible by specifying the number of characters to be 1 as the parameter of the INPUT$ function.

INP, OUT

On earlier generation computers with Z-80 or 8080 processors, the INP command and the OUT command are often used to address the I/O ports built into these processors. But since the MC68000 used in the ST has no port addressing, we have to figure out what these commands do in the ST, and what results they yield.

In the BIOS of the ST there are three function calls with the names BCONSTAT, BCONIN, and BCONOUT. Almost all of the system input and output to the screen, printer, RS-232 interface, MIDI interface, and keyboard processor is performed with these three calls. In assembly language, these calls are used with the number of the desired device to be accessed.

The following assignments apply:

Number	**Device/interface**
0	Centronics interface/printer
1	RS-232 interface
2	Console (keyboard and screen)
3	MIDI port
4	Keyboard processor

These same numbers are used with the INP and OUT commands. You can therefore address all of the interfaces directly from BASIC. For example, the command,

```
OUT (0),65
```

outputs the value 65 (ASCII value of the letter A) on the printer. You might prefer to use the command:

```
LPRINT "A"
```

Doing so seems to work just as well. But try to send the character LF with ASCII value 10 to the printer by means of LPRINT. You will soon notice its effect. The ST, or more exactly ST BASIC, sends the character sequence CR/LF, the ASCII characters 13 and 10—which is completely unnecessary. This sequence is not used at all when printing graphics with Epson printers and their compatibles. Neither the bit pattern nor the given number of graphic bytes agrees with what is expected when this sequence is received.

It gets even worse. Since the ST sends the character sequence CR/LF after every 72 characters, we get some really messed up graphics.

But don't worry. The OUT command will solve the problem in this case very nicely.

Other devices besides the printer can be accessed with the OUT command. The other interfaces are also available to us. The RS-232 interface can be fully utilized from BASIC. You can also read from the RS-232 port with the INP function. With it, a terminal program can be written for the ST in BASIC with relatively little effort.

The INP and OUT commands using device number 2 allow writing of BASIC programs under the GEM environment. The entire screen is then available. For input, the INP(2) behaves like using the function INPUT$. INP(2) has a decisive advantage, however. The function and cursor keys also return unambiguous values and can therefore be read.

The MIDI interface, both input and output, can be programmed using device number 4. Readers with appropriate instruments, such as electronic organs or synthesizers, can control their devices with ST BASIC. This is assuming that you know the protocol used for MIDI. With this knowledge, it is relatively simple to control the devices with a BASIC program.

The last possible device on our list is the keyboard. As you know, the ST has an intelligent keyboard. It contains its own processor which reads the keys, the mouse and joysticks. In addition, the keyboard processor contains a clock. Values can only be sent to the keyboard processor, since the "answer" is usually discarded by the operating system. INP(4) always returns the value 16.

VARPTR

VARPTR is a function that returns an address. A variable or file number is passed to the VARPTR function as the argument:

```
OPEN "I",1,"xyz.dat"
? VARPTR (#1)
```

In this example we can make no reasonable interpretation of the return value. This version of ST BASIC does not correctly support VARPTR using a file number.

```
a$ = "TEST"
ad = VARPTR (a$)

a = 10
adr = VARPTR (a)
```

In these two examples, the interpretation is relatively simple. Let's look at the first case.

After the VARPTR function is used, the variable ad contains the address of the string a$. The string descriptor itself consists of six bytes. The first byte of the string descriptor contains a flag whose function will be explained shortly. The second byte in the descriptor specifies the length of the string. Since the maximum value contained in a single byte is 255, the maximum length of a string is 255. The third through sixth bytes contain the address at which the string itself is located in memory.

But if you check these values with the example above, you will be amazed at the string address. The "address" turns out to be the string itself. All strings which are one to four characters long are stored directly in the "address" of the string descriptor. Try changing a$ = "TESTER" and check its address.

This also clarifies the meaning of the flag, the first byte of the descriptor. If a zero is entered here, the string is less than five characters—therefore placed in the descriptor itself. If the hexadecimal value 10 is entered here, however, the contents of positions three through six are the actual memory address of the string.

Using the VARPTR function for numerical variables returns the memory address at which the number is to be found. Real numbers are stored in four bytes. Integers (such as A%) are stored in two bytes. We will take a closer look at integer arrays later, since they are well suited for protecting small machine language programs in memory.

SOUND

The SOUND command of ST BASIC is quite capable and very easy to use. The sound chip in the ST is the YM-2149. This IC is compatible to the well-known AY-3-8910, which is used in various other computer systems (such as MSX computers). This chip offers a broad range of capabilities for creating sounds over three different voices. In addition, an external noise source can be combined to allow the creation of special effects (like drums or explosions).

The SOUND command has a maximum of 5 parameters, specified as numerical values. The syntax is as follows:

    SOUND *voice,volume,note,octave,duration*

The value of *voice* can be 1, 2, or 3 according to the desired voice.

The value of *volume* is 1 and 15; 1 is soft and 15 is full volume. This value is stored according to the voice in bits 0-3 of register 8 (voice 1), 9 (voice 2), or 10 (voice 3).

The variable *note* allows values between 1 and 12. Since an octave consists of 12 steps, notes can be played directly.

The *octave* can be between 1 and 8, meaning that the ST can create sounds over eight octaves.

The *duration* can accept values between 1 and 255. The duration is measured in 20 milliseconds. If you specify a duration of 50, a tone lasting about 1 second is produced.

The following table shows the assignment of notes to numbers for the variable *note*:

1	C	2	C#	3	D
4	D#	5	E	6	F
7	F#	8	G	9	G#
10	A	11	A#	12	H

The concert pitch A (440 Hertz) can be created with the SOUND command:

    SOUND 1,15,10,4,255

Octave 4 is the one normally designated as octave zero. Smaller octave values result in deeper tones; higher values create higher tones.

WAVE

With the SOUND command alone you can program very nice single-voice melodies, but they become more interesting and polyphonic with the WAVE command. This command gives us many more sound capabilities. It is also harder to understand. It took us a lot of work to understand the construction and the parameters. For complete understanding, an exact knowledge of the hardware construction of the sound chip is useful.

Like the SOUND command, the WAVE command also has five parameters. The first parameter is comparable to the *voice* parameter of the SOUND command. With it, the voice that creates the tone can be selected. The possible values are somewhat different here, however.

The best way to understand WAVE is to take a closer look at a special register in the sound chip. This is register 7, called the multi-function register. If bit 0 of register 7 is set, voice 1 is turned off. If bit 1 is set, voice 2 is turned off. If bit 2 is set, then voice 3 is turned off. A cleared bit creates the tone programmed for the voice.

Bits 3 to 5 are responsible for switching noise to the three voices. Here too, the function is enabled with a cleared bit, while a set bit turns the sound off for the corresponding voice.

Bits 6 and 7 are responsible for programming the data direction of the two universal 8-bit ports integrated into the sound chip. But as these two bits have no function in sound creation, we will not discuss them further here.

The bits 0 to 5 can be manipulated with the first parameter of the WAVE command. If the parameter is viewed as a binary value, the individual bits of the parameter have exactly the reverse function. If the value 1 is passed as the parameter, bit 0 of register 8 is cleared, causing voice to be turned on. All other bits of register 7 are set, turning all of the other functions off. If, for example, this parameter is 37 (%100101 in binary), voices 1 and 3 are turned on and voice 2 is turned off. In addition, the noise source is switched into voice 3. If the first parameter is zero, all the voices and noise sources are switched off.

The second parameter of WAVE affects three registers of the SOUND chip at the same time. These are the registers 8, 9, and 10. Not all bits are affected, only bit 4. Bit 4 in the three registers named determines if the volume of the three voices is affected by the specification of SOUND (contents of bits 0 to 3 of the three registers; see SOUND) or through a hardware waveform.

The hardware waveform is a special feature of the sound chip. By using the waveform, the volume of the tone is changed periodically or even just once. The waveform offers many possibilities for changing the sound of a tone.

The second parameter must also be viewed as a binary value. The following list shows the meaning of the bits in the WAVE command:

Bit number	Function
1 cleared	volume voice 1 from bits 0-3 reg 8
1 set	volume voice 1 via waveform
2 cleared	volume voice 2 from bits 0-3 reg 8
2 set	volume voice 2 via waveform
3 cleared	volume voice 3 from bits 0-3 reg 8
3 set	volume voice 3 via waveform

The value range is thereby set to 0 through 7. If the value 0 is passed as the second parameter, the volume of all three voices is determined by the volume given in the SOUND command. For a value of 5, the volume of voices 1 and 3 are manipulated by the hardware waveform, while voice 2 runs via the volume set in bits 0 to 3 of register 9.

The third parameter of the WAVE command has a close relationship to the second parameter. This parameter selects one of the 9 different waveforms. The possible values can lies between 0 and 15, but some values create identical waveforms. The possible results are difficult to describe with words. Accordingly, the values and their corresponding waveforms are found in Figure 1.

The fourth parameter also manipulates registers in the sound chip directly, as well as their relationship to the waveform. The sound chip contains two 8-bit registers whose contents affect the period of the waveforms. The value of this parameter ranges from 0 to 65535. The larger the value, the longer the period of the waveform. For extremely small values (<1000), the waveforms are at such a high frequency that an additional audible frequency results. This can be used for various special effects.

The fifth parameter determines the length of the tone to be created. It is only effective in the program mode if another SOUND or WAVE command follows. In the direct mode or from the editor, the tone continues until a key is pressed, i.e. until the next mouse click.

Figure 1

Programmable Sound Generator Waveforms

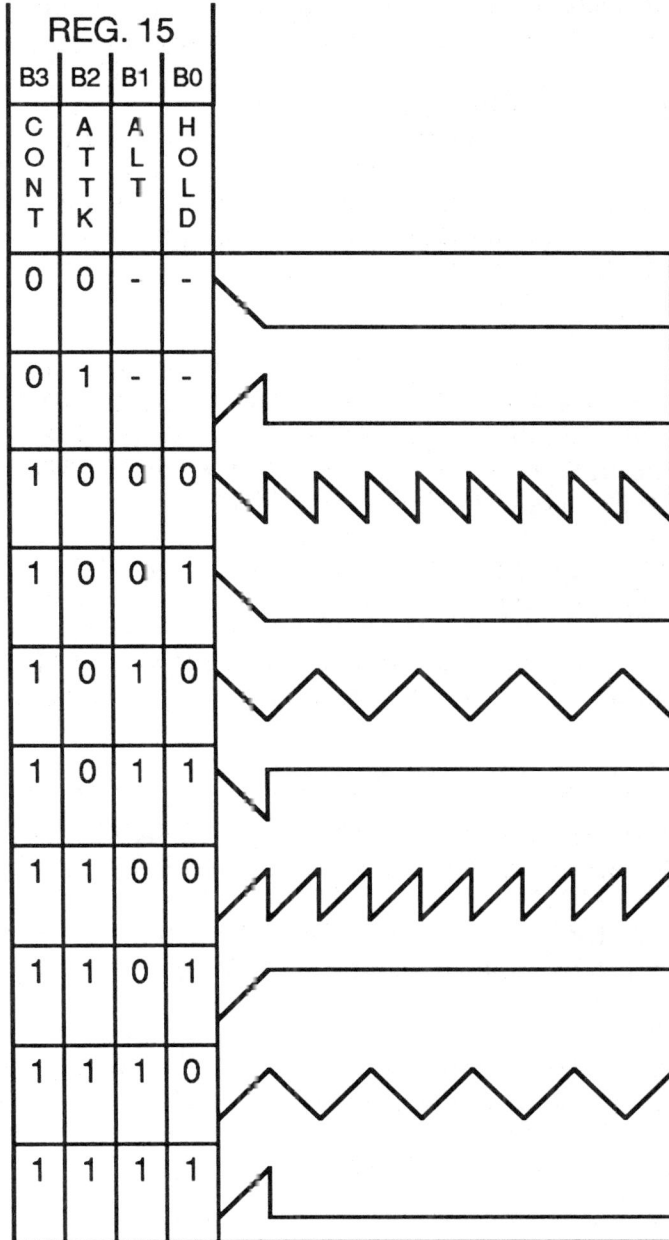

REG. 15			
B3	B2	B1	B0
CONT	ATTK	ALT	HOLD
0	0	-	-
0	1	-	-
1	0	0	0
1	0	0	1
1	0	1	0
1	0	1	1
1	1	0	0
1	1	0	1
1	1	1	0
1	1	1	1

LINEF

The `LINEF` command is the simplest graphic function of ST BASIC. With this command, arbitrary points or lines can be drawn on the screen. Four parameters are required to specify the starting and ending coordinates of the line. A line width of one point is preset. Later we will show how to change not only the line width, but also the line pattern and appearance of the starting and ending points.

```
LINEF 10,10,50,40
```

The line is drawn from coordinate 10,10 to coordinate 50,40.

CIRCLE

The `CIRCLE` command is for creating draw circles or arcs on the screen. Either three or five parameters are required. Three parameters are required to draw simple circles. The first two parameters determine the X and Y coordinates of the center of the circle, and the third parameter is the radius in screen units. The fourth and fifth parameters are required only to draw arcs. These then specify the start and end angle in degrees. Note that the angle is specified in tenths of a degree.

The following command would create a half circle with a radius of 100 points:

```
CIRCLE 320,199,100,0,1800
```

Enter this line to see the zero point for the angle specification as well. The circle is always drawn counterclockwise from the 3 o'clock position.

Also, the line width is also set to one pixel for the `CIRCLE` command. We'll show you how to change the line width later.

You'll notice that the circle isn't really a circle at all. `CIRCLE` can only draw a polygon that approximates the shape of the circle. If you use a radius of 30 you can see that the resulting shape is not a circle, but an octagon. If you need a "real" circle, you have to calculate the values yourself and draw it with the `LINEF` command.

PCIRCLE

The PCIRCLE command also draws a "circle" or arc. The required parameters are identical to those of the CIRCLE command. This circle, however, is filled with a color or pattern. The color and pattern are set with the COLOR command.

ELLIPSE

In addition to the circle shape, ST BASIC has a command to draw an ellipse or partial ellipse. For this reason the ELLIPSE command has either four or six parameters. The first two parameters specify the X and Y position of the origin, while the following two parameters specify the radius of the ellipse in the X and Y direction. The (optional) parameters 5 and 6 specify the angle of a segment to be drawn. These last parameters are the same as for the CIRCLE command.

```
ELLIPSE 320,200,100,30,450,2700
```

PELLIPSE

The "P" in front of the name again designates that the resulting shape will be filled with the current color and pattern. The parameters are identical to those of the ELLIPSE command.

COLOR

The COLOR command sets the character color, the color of the fill pattern, the color of lines drawn with LINEF, and the pattern used when filling screen sections. A total of five parameters are required.

The first parameter specifies the color for subsequent text output. Only the values 0 and 1 are possible with monochrome monitors. If 0 is used as the parameter, the text will be "invisible" i.e. in the background color. With a color monitor, the value of this parameter depends on the display mode. In low-resolution mode (320x200), the value range is from 0 to 15. In medium-resolution mode (640x200), the values range from 0 to 3.

The second parameter specifies the color for the next PCIRCLE, PELLIPSE, and FILL command. The values correspond to those of the first parameter.

The third parameter determines the color of the lines drawn.

The fourth parameter determines the style used when something is filled:

Value	Fill
0	no fill
1	solid fill
2	patterns
3	hatching patterns
4	user-defined pattern

Currently, the last pattern (4) is defined as the Atari logo, $\int\!\mid\!\setminus$.

The fifth parameter determines the selection of the pattern (0-24) or hatching (0-12). If this value is 0, no pattern is drawn, independent of other settings.

FILL

The FILL command allows you to fill arbitrary areas. The settings for fill are made with the COLOR command. The first two parameters for FILL specify the X and Y coordinates of a point within the area to be filled.

The third parameter is optional. It's a color number representing the screen coordinate that limits the boundaries for the filling. If this parameter is omitted, then the fill is bounded by any color except the background color.

FULLW

This command is one of several commands for manipulating windows. With the FULLW command, any one of the four windows can be set to maximum size. The four windows present in BASIC are accessible via the following numbers:

0	EDIT window
1	LIST window
2	OUTPUT window
3	COMMAND window

By entering:

```
FULLW 2
```

the output window is set to the full available screen area. The other three windows are covered up by the output window.

CLEARW

This command clears any of the four windows. It is comparable to the CLS command of Microsoft BASIC, but refers to a special window in ST BASIC. The command,

```
CLEARW 2
```

clears the output window. The position of the output cursor is not affected by this command, so the command GOTOXY 0,0 should generally follow a CLEARW 2 command. This places the cursor in the upper left corner.

CLOSEW

Windows can be closed with the CLOSEW command. They then disappear from the screen completely. The numbers of the windows correspond to those in the other window instructions.

OPENW

With this command, closed windows (CLOSEW) can be opened again. This command functions only when at least one other window is open. It appears to be an error in this version of ST BASIC.

Summary

This brings us to the end of our description of the special commands of ST BASIC. The other commands and functions of ST BASIC are equivalent to those in other BASIC dialects. Since there is a great deal of literature covering the standard functions and commands, we will not go into them.

We have intentionally postponed a discussion of two special, very powerful commands. They are the GEMSYS and VDISYS commands. But since these commands are so complicated and powerful, we have set aside a special section for them. You will really be surprised by what you can do with them from ST BASIC.

1.2 BASIC and GEM

We've already seen some of the features that make ST BASIC a very complete implementation of the BASIC language. In addition, ST BASIC has commands that allow easy access to the powerful features of GEM.

GEM, the Graphics Environment Manager, is the visually-oriented user interface to the operating system. Rather than typing commands into the computer, the user can perform the equivalent of the command by manipulating "pictures" on the screen with the mouse.

GEM provides a comprehensive set of services for application programs. If an application is written to use these standard services, then it's possible to move that application to any computer that supports GEM.

How can this be possible? It's because the ST has a 68000 processor. The IBM PC uses an 8088 processor. GEM runs on both the ST and the IBM PC. If an application is written in a high-level language such as C to run on the IBM PC with GEM, then it need only be recompiled to run on the ST. In practice, small program changes are usually necessary, since hardware-specific aspects of the computer may creep into the application. But the concept of application portability is a very attractive feature of a GEM.

We'll now take a closer look at GEM by studying its two main components. These are the AES, or Application Environment Services, and the VDI, or Virtual Device Interface.

The AES manages the visual features that are characteristic of GEM applications: windows, pull-down menus, icons, etc. All of these are high-level and complex functions which are generally unsuitable for use from BASIC. There are exceptions, however, as we will see shortly.

The VDI provides the fundamental graphic primitives for displaying text and graphics or inputting data from the keyboard or mouse. The VDI is subdivided into the GDOS (Graphic Device Operating System) and the device drivers. Of particular importance is the device driver. This part of GEM is hardware-dependent and must be adapted for each output device. In the current release of GEM for the ST, the only available device driver is for the display monitor. Additional device drivers will certainly become available in time.

1.2.1 The VDISYS command

The VDI performs dozens of different functions. You can use the VDISYS command to access these functions from ST BASIC.

As part of the VDISYS command, several parameters are passed to GEM. The parameters consist of five arrays or memory areas in which values are stored. The arrays are named CONTRL, INTIN, INTOUT, PTSIN, PTSOUT. These names are reserved variable names is ST BASIC. Apparently the authors of ST BASIC found the features of the VDI so powerful that they reserved those variable names. The reserved variable names represent the address of the arrays, not the array itself. You can see the address of the arrays by entering:

```
? contrl;intin;intout,ptsin,ptsout
```

To be precise, the named arrays are not the actual arrays used by the VDI. Rather, the contents of the named arrays are transfered to the VDI.

Since ST BASIC makes it very convenient to access the array contents, using the VDI calls are simple. Here's an example:

```
POKE CONTRL    ,(command number)
POKE CONTRL+ 2,(number of parameters in ptsin)
POKE CONTRL+ 4,(number of parameters in ptsout)
POKE CONTRL+ 6,(number of parameters in intin)
POKE CONTRL+ 8,(number of parameters in intout)
POKE CONTRL+10,(sub-function command number)
POKE CONTRL+12,(device handle, between 1 and 10)
REM
POKE INTIN    ,(first parameter)
POKE INTIN + 2,(second parameter)
POKE INTIN + 4,(third parameter)
:
to
:
POKE INTIN + n,(last parameter)
REM
POKE PTSIN    ,(first parameter)
POKE PTSIN + 2,(second parameter)
POKE PTSIN + 4,(third parameter)
:
```

```
to
:
POKE PTSIN + n, (last parameter)
REM
VDISYS
REM
```

In this example, the individual parameters are POKEd into the corresponding array elements. Since the individual elements are all 16 bits wide, a single POKE places the value into the array element. This also explains the steps of two in the POKEs. The elements in the CONTRL array, CONTRL+4 and CONTRL+8 are not POKEd. After the call these these elements are PEEKed to determine how many parameters were returned in INTOUT and PTSOUT. The following example will make this clearer:

Normally, the mouse cursor is invisible. We can call the VDI to make it visible. As previously mentioned, the VDI performs many different functions. Each function is uniquely identified by a function code. The function code for enabling the mouse cursor is 122. For a complete list and in-depth description of these calls see the **GEM Programmer's Reference** from Abacus.

The name for function code 122 is SHOW MOUSE. We POKE the function code 122 into one element of the CONTRL array. SHOW MOUSE expects no parameters to be passed in the PTSIN array, so we POKE the value 0 into CONTRL+2. One parameter is expected in the INTIN array, so we POKE the value 1 into CONTRL+6. SHOW MOUSE does not have any subfunctions, so CONTRL+10 is set to zero.

CONTRL+12 contains the *device handle*. When ST BASIC is started, this element is set to a value of 2 to indicate the screen. Since any value between 1 and 10 is allowed for the device handle for output to the screen, you do not have to change this element. For a value between 11 and 20 output is sent to a plotter (if a suitable device driver were present). For a value between 21 and 30, the output is sent to a printer. These, then, are the values for the CONTRL array.

Now to the INTIN array. The counterpart to SHOW MOUSE is a function called HIDE MOUSE, which disables the mouse's cursor. When HIDE MOUSE is called, the VDI stores the number of HIDE MOUSE calls in an element of INTIN. If SHOW MOUSE is called with a value other than zero in INTIN, one is subtracted from the stored number. The cursor does not necessarily become visible after the call.

If INTIN has a value of zero, the number of HIDE MOUSE calls is ignored and the mouse cursor is enabled regardless.

The complete example looks like this:

```
1        rem 1_2_1
10       poke contrl,122
20       poke contrl+2,0
30       poke contrl+6,1
40       rem
50       poke intin,0
60       rem
70       vdisys
80       rem
```

After the call you'll find a value of zero in CONTRL+4 and CONTRL+8. This signals that the function has not returned any values in INTOUT or PTSOUT arrays.

1.2.2 Using VDI calls from BASIC

Most VDI calls can be used from ST BASIC. Some calls are unnecessary or superfluous since they have counter parts as BASIC commands. It's much more complicated to draw a line with VDISYS than with the LINEF command. Similarly, text output is simpler with PRINT than with VDISYS.

Try the examples that follow and decide for yourself whether you can make use of a given function.

First we'll look at some special effects with text.

Text effects

VDI function 106 changes the appearance of the characters for text display.
Here's an example:

```
10      rem 1_2a   text effects
100     fullw 2:clearw 2
110     a$    = "this is normal,        intin = "
120     a$(0) = "this is bold,          intin = "
130     a$(1) = "this is light,         intin = "
140     a$(2) = "this is italic,        intin = "
150     a$(3) = "this is underline,     intin = "
160     a$(4) = "this is outlined,      intin = "
170     gotoxy 6,3
180     ?a$;i
190     for i=0 to 4
200     gotoxy 6,5+2*i
210     poke contrl    ,106
220     poke contrl+ 2,0
230     poke contrl+6 ,1
240     poke intin     ,2^i
250     vdisys
260     ? a$(i);2^i
270     next
280     poke contrl    ,106
290     poke contrl+ 2,0
300     poke contrl+6 ,1
310     poke intin     ,0
320     vdisys
330     a=inp(2)  : rem wait for keypress
```

This example demonstrates the different special effects. In addition, special
effects may be mixed. For example, setting a value of 9 in INTIN produces
"**bold/underlined**." In lines 280 to 320 the normal display mode is
re-enabled by setting INTIN to zero. Unless you do this, all subsequent
text is displayed with the special effects.

27

Change character size

The size of the text can also be changed. A total of six character heights are possible. Since this also changes the character width, there are some problems outputting the three larger character heights.

The PRINT command assumes a character width of 8 pixels. Since the characters can be wider than 8 pixels, the right portion of the character is cut off. The three smaller character heights can be used without problems.

Here's an example of changing the character height:

```
1       rem 1_2_2b   change character height
10      fullw 2:clearw 2
20      a$(0) = "very small        , intin = "
30      a$(1) = "small             , intin = "
40      a$(2) = "normal            , intin = "
50      a$(3) = "large             , intin = "
60      a$(4) = "larger            , intin = "
70      a$(5) = "gigantic          , intin = "
80      a(0)=1:a(1)=9:a(2)=10:a(3)=16:a(4)=18:a(5)=20
90      gotoxy 6,3
100     for i=0 to 5
110     gotoxy 6,5+2*i
120     poke contrl   ,107
130     poke contrl+ 2,0
140     poke contrl+6 ,1
150     poke intin    ,a(i)
160     vdisys
170     ? a$(i);a(i)
180     next
190     poke contrl,107
200     poke contrl+ 2,0
210     poke contrl+6 ,1
220     poke intin,10
230     vdisys
240     a=inp(2) : rem wait for keypress
```

We can solve the character width problem through programming. More about this in our next example.

Graphic Text Output

VDI function 8 outputs text. The string of text may contain special effects and may be used to correctly display enlarged characters that are only partially displayed with the PRINT command.

The text to be displayed is placed into the INTIN array. Each character of the text string occupies the lower byte of the array element (each is 2 bytes wide). In this example, the text string is placed into the array in lines 220 to 240. The last character of the text string **must** have a zero value, line 250.

The display location (on the screen) is passed through the PTSIN array. The display location are actual screen coordinates, not a relative location within the window. The VDI does not recognize windows; the AES manages them. The display location is relative to the upper-left corner of the character to be displayed. A value that positions some of the text off the screen should be avoided.
Here's the program:

```
10       rem 1_2_2c  graphic text output
100      a$(0)  = "small"
110      a$(1)  = "somewhat larger"
120      a$(2)  = "normal"
130      a$(3)  = "still larger"
140      a$(4)  = "very large"
150      a$(5)  = "gigantic"
160      a(0)=1:a(1)=9:a(2)=10:a(3)=16:a(4)=18:a(5)=20
170      yp(0)=50:yp(1)=62:yp(2)=80:yp(3)=100:
         yp(4)=125:yp(5)=160
180      fullw 2:clearw 2
190      for c=0 to 5
200      a=a(c):a$=a$(c)
210      gosub setheight
220      for i=1 to len(a$(c))
230      poke intin+(i-1)*2,asc(mid$(a$(c),i,1))
240      next
250      poke intin+(i-1)*2,0
260      poke contrl   ,8
270      poke contrl+ 2,1
280      poke contrl+ 6,len(a$(c))+1
290      poke ptsin    ,100
300      poke ptsin+2  ,yp(c)
310      vdisys
```

```
320     next c
330     a=10
340     gosub setheight
350     a=inp(2) : rem wait for keypress
360     end
370     setheight:
380     poke contrl   ,107
390     poke contrl+ 2,0
400     poke contrl+6 ,1
410     poke intin    ,a
420     vdisys
430     return
```

Lines 210 and 370 illustrate another feature of ST BASIC: labels. You may use labels throughout a BASIC program. A label **must** be defined at the start of a line and be followed by a colon. Program text may follow the colon.

One of the nicest features of labels is that they are valid replacements for line numbers. So the commands GOTO, GOSUB, ON GOTO, ON GOSUB, and RESTORE may be used with labels. Line 340 shows such a replacement.

Line 350 waits for a keypress, which will end the program.

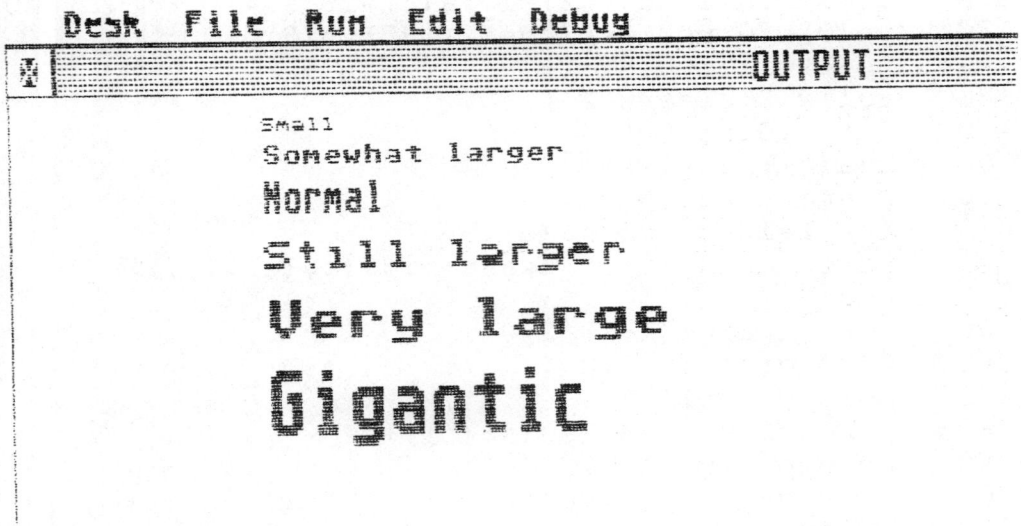

Change direction of text output

You can change the angle of text output using VDI function 13. Only angle steps of 90 degrees may be specified, and these are given in units of tenths of a degree. A 90-degree angle is therefore specified as 900 units. The angle is passed to VDI function 13 through INTIN (line 320).

After you've displayed the text at the desired angle, you must set the angle back to zero, since all subsequent output is affected by the change.

```
10      rem 1_2_2d  change direction of text output
100     a$ =" round and round"
110     fullw 2:clearw 2
120     for angle = 0 to 3
130     gosub txt.angle
140     for i=1 to len(a$)
150     poke intin+(i-1)*2,asc(mid$(a$,i,1))
160     next
170     poke intin+(i-1)*2,0
180     poke contrl   ,3
190     poke contrl+ 2,1
200     poke contrl+ 6,len(a$)+1
210     poke ptsin    ,300
220     poke ptsin+2  ,200
230     vdisys
240     next angle
250     a=inp(2)  :  rem wait for keypress
260     angle =0:gosub txt.angle
270     end
280     txt.angle:
290     poke contrl   ,13
300     poke contrl+ 2,0
310     poke contrl+6 ,1
320     poke intin    ,angle*900
330     vdisys
340     return
```

Set line type

We've already mentioned that the characteristics of the drawing lines can be changed. VDI function 15 is used to set the line type. You can choose from among seven different line types by setting the parameter in INTIN. The following example displays the different line types available:

```
1        rem 1_2_2e  set line type
10       fullw 2:clearw 2
20       i=20
30       for pattern= 1 to 7
40       gosub set.pattern
50       for c=1 to 20
60       linef 20,c+i,500,c+i
70       next c
80       i=i+30
90       next pattern
100      a=inp(2) : rem wait for keypress
110      end
120      set.pattern:
130      poke contrl    ,15
140      poke contrl+ 2,0
150      poke contrl+ 6,1
160      poke intin     ,pattern
170      vdisys
180      return
```

In this program, all 7 line types are displayed, each 20 times. Line type 7 appears as a solid line, but can be changed to a user-defined line type. The next example shows you how to do this.

Define line type 7

VDI function 113 is for defining line type 7. The bit pattern for the user-defined line type is stored in INTIN as a 16-bit word. The leftmost bit of the word corresponds to the leftmost pixel of the line segment.

```
10      rem 1_2_2f  define line type 7
100     fullw 2:clearw 2:i = 10
110     poke contrl    ,113
120     poke contrl+ 2,0
130     poke contrl+ 6,1
140     poke intin     ,&haaaa : ' pattern
150     vdisys
160     poke contrl    ,15
170     poke contrl+ 2,0
180     poke contrl+ 6,1
190     poke intin     ,7 : ' pattern
200     vdisys
210     for c=1 to 20
220     linef 20,c+i,500,c+i
230     next c
240     a=inp(2)
```

In this example we used a bit pattern %1010101010101010, which is equivalent to the hexadecimal number &hAAAA. Try defining your own line types. If the line is drawn vertically, note where the leftmost bit of the word appears.

Change line width

To vary the width of a line, you use VDI function 16. This saves you the
trouble of using multiple LINEF or CIRCLE commands to make a thicker
line.

The parameter representing the thickness is set in INTIN. Allowable values
are the odd numbers beginning with 3. A value of 2 represents one pixel,
the default value.

```
10      rem 1_2_g  change line width
100     fullw 2:clearw 2
110     i=20
120     linef 20,c+i,500,c+i
130     i=i+24
140     f = 3 to 25 step 2
150     gosub set.width
160     linef 20,  i,500,  i
170     i=i+25
180     next c
190     c=2:gosub set.width
200     a=inp(2): rem wait for keypress
210     end
220     set.width:
230     poke contrl    ,16
240     poke contrl+ 2,1
250     poke contrl+ 6,0
260     poke ptsin     ,c
270     poke ptsin + 2,0
280     vdisys
290     return
```

This program draws the different line thicknesses from 1 pixel to 25 pixels
in width. You might want to call the last line a bar, since it's quite thick!

Change appearance of end points

VDI function 108 sets the appearance of the endpoints of a line. If you have run the previous program, you can see that the endpoints of the line are cut off square. This is the standard setting for line representation.

But the end points can be drawn with rounded ends. For drafting or technical work, the lines can be drawn with arrowheads at the ends. It's a lot of work in BASIC, especially for the larger line thicknesses. But the VDI makes it much easier to do.

This function also works with the CIRCLE and ELLIPSE commands. You can change the sample program in such a way to draw a CIRCLE segment (arc) instead of a line (lines 140 and 180).

VDI function 108 requires parameters to specify the appearance of the starting and ending points of the line. These are passed in INTIN and INTIN+2. The values of 0, 1 and 2 are valid. A value of 0 is the default at power up. A value of 1 specifies that the starting or ending point is an arrowhead. A value of 2 specifies that the starting and ending point is rounded.

The following example is based on the one previous, for setting the line thickness. Therefore, you can just modify the previous program where needed and don't have to re-type the whole thing.

After one pass, a keypress (anything but <ESC>) is expected. The picture is then drawn with new end points. Pressing the <ESC> key ends the program and sets the parameters back to the power-up values.

```
10      rem 1_2_2h   rem end points
100     start = 0:fin =0
110     gosub set.end
120     i=20
130     fullw 2:clearw 2
140     linef 20,c+i,500,c+i
150     i=i+24
160     for c = 3 to 15 step 2
170     gosub set.width
180     linef 20,  i,500,  i
190     i=i+35
200     next c
210     c=2:gosub set.width
```

```
220     a=inp(2)
230     if a=27 then fin = 0:start = 0:
        gosub set.end:end
240     fin = fin +1
250     if fin = 3 then fin = 0:start = start +1
260     if start = 3 then start = 0
270     gosub set.end
280     goto 120
290     end
300     set.width:
310     poke contrl    ,16
320     poke contrl+ 2,1
330     poke contrl+ 6,0
340     poke ptsin     ,c
350     poke ptsin + 2,0
360     vdisys
370     return
380     set.end:
390     poke contrl    ,108
400     poke contrl+ 2,0
410     poke contrl+ 6,2
420     poke intin     ,start
430     poke intin + 2,fin
440     vdisys
450     return
```

Reading the mouse position

You'll probably notice that there isn't a BASIC function for reading the position of the mouse. The VDI has a function for this: 124. It also lets you know if any of the buttons are pressed. VDI function 124 requires no parameters.

The call to this function returns a value in intin. A value of 0 indicates that no buttons were pressed. A value of 2 indicates that the right button was pressed. A value of 3 indicates that both buttons were pressed.

The mouse position is returned in the ptsout array. The X-position is found at element ptsout. The Y-position is found at element ptsout+2. Both positions are the actual screen positions, not a position relative to a window.

The following program is more complex than earlier ones. The program is used to build a screen menu. We have several programming tricks so you should study the code closely.

When you run the program, a small menu is displayed. Using the mouse, you can point to the individual menu items and select them by clicking the mouse button. The first three selections are disabled in this example. But if you select the fourth, the program is ended.

To emphasize which selection was clicked, it is displayed in bold while the others appear in fainter type (line 60). You can select the variables *active* or *inactive* according to your taste.

In this example, only the y-position of the mouse is needed to determine which menu item is selected. The value returned by the VDI is converted into an output line in line 110. To determine the y-position more easily, the REM command in line 110 should be removed. The y-position is then displayed in the upper lefthand corner for each change in the y-position.

```
1       rem 1_2_2i   read mouse position
10      a$(1)="Program load"
20      a$(2)="Program start"
30      a$(3)="Change Data"
40      a$(4)="Program end"
50      p(1)=7:p(2)=8:p(3)=9:p(4)=10
60      activ = 1 : inactiv = 2
70      fullw 2:clearw 2
```

```
80    gotoxy 5,5 : ? "Choose one :"
90    effect = inactiv : gosub text.effect :
      gosub 210
100   gosub mouse.button
110   outval = int((y.pos-108)/16) :
      rem gotoxy 1,1:?y.pos
120   gosub mouse.in : if button = 0 then 100
130   gosub mouse.out
140   if outval <1 or outval > 4 then 90
150   gosub 210
160   effect = activ : gosub text.effect
170   gotoxy 5,p(outval) : ? a$(outval)
180   if outval <> 4 then effect = inactiv
      else effect =0
190   gosub text.effect
200   if outval =  4 then select.ende else 100
210   for i=1 to 4
220   gotoxy 5,p(i) : ? a$(i)
230   next i
240   return
250   goto 100
260   '
270   mouse.in: rem ************************
280   poke contrl   ,122
290   poke contrl+2 ,0
300   poke contrl+6 ,1
310   poke intin    ,0
320   vdisys
330   return
340   '
350   mouse.out: rem ***********************
360   poke contrl   ,123
370   poke contrl+2 ,0
380   poke contrl+6 ,0
390   vdisys
400   return
410   '
420   mouse.button: rem *******************
430   poke contrl   ,124
440   poke contrl+2 ,0
450   poke contrl+6 ,0
460   vdisys
470   button=peek(intout)
```

```
480    x.pos =peek(ptsout)
490    y.pos =peek(ptsout+2) - 38
500    return
510    '
520    text.effect: rem ********************
530    poke contrl   ,106
540    poke contrl+2 ,0
550    poke contrl+6 ,1
560    poke contrl+10,1
570    poke intin,effect
580    vdisys
590    return
999    '
1000   select.ende: rem *******************
1010   poke contrl,122
1020   poke contrl+2,C
1030   poke contrl+6,1
1040   rem
1050   poke intin,0
1060   rem
1070   vdisys
1080   end
```

Desk   File   Run   Edit   Debug

OUTPUT

Choose one :

Program load
Program start
Change Date
Program end

Set Writing mode

There are several *write modes* built into GEM. Normally, all output to the screen is done in *replace mode*.

In replace mode, if something is already displayed on the screen, any new text or output overwrites or replaces the old text or output.

In *transparent mode*, the background is not cleared when new text or output is displayed.

In the *XOR* mode, each pixel on the screen is reversed.

When you first run this program disable line 160 with a REM or its abbreviation ('). On a white background, there is no visible difference. Then when you run the program for the second time, enable line 160 by removing the REM. The results will clarify the different write modes.

```
0      rem 1_2_2j  set write mode
100     fullw 2:clearw 2:dim x$(4)
110     x$(1)="normal text,   replace mode"
120     x$(2)="text  in  transparent  mode"
130     x$(3)="text is  in  the  xor  mode"
140     x$(4)="text in reverse transparent"
150     color 1,1,1,2,2
160     fill 1,1 : rem out first run
170     for i=1 to 4
180     gosub set.wrt.mode
190     gotoxy 10,6+i: ?x$(i)
200     next
210     a=inp(2) : i=1
220     gosub set.wrt.mode
230     end
240     set.wrt.mode:
250     poke intin    ,i
260     poke contrl   ,32
270     poke contrl+2,0
280     poke contrl+6,1
290     vdisys
300     return
```

1.2.3 The GEMSYS command

The VDISYS call is used to access the functions of the Virtual Device Interface. As you'll recall, the other major portion of GEM is the Application Environment Services, AES. To access the AES, you use the GEMSYS command.

Parameters for this command are passed in various ways. These parameters may differ from those of the VDI. Also, the addresses of the parameter arrays are not readily available as with the VDISYS command. Instead, a table containing the address of the arrays is used. The table is accessed by the reserved variable name GB.

Table GB contains six addresses and is therefore 24 bytes long. The array names (used by Digital Research) are CONTROL, GLOBAL, INT.IN, INT.OUT, ADDR.IN and ADDR.OUT. We'll use these names in the following examples.

The CONTROL array works much like the CONTRL array in the VDISYS command. As a BASIC programmer you need not concern yourself with this array at all, because it's handled by a GEMSYS command in BASIC.

The second address in the GB table points to the GLOBAL array. This array contains various parameters which should not be changed. The values are also set by GEM.

The other four arrays function similarly to the VDISYS command. Note that the elements of the INT.IN and INT.OUT arrays are two bytes apiece (word), while the elements of the ADDR.IN and ADDR.OUT arrays are four bytes apiece (long word).

The AES performs dozens of functions. Under BASIC, it's not possible to use all of these functions. For example, the keyboard and mouse operations are handled by interrupt routines. These may not be performed in ST BASIC (in most cases the system will crash).

In order to make full use of the functions of the AES, you will have to use a language such as C, Pascal or Modula 2.

Despite the limitations, you can perform some AES functions from BASIC. This next example changes the name of the output window.

```
1       rem 1_2_3  name output window
10      gosub gem.arrays
20      x1=0:a$="This is our output window"
30      poke int.in ,3
40      poke int.in+2,2
50      x1=varptr(a$)
60      poke int.in+4,x1 / 2^16
70      poke int.in+6,x1 and &hffff
80      poke int.in+8,0
90      poke int.in+10,0
100     gemsys 105
110     end
120     '
50000 gem.arrays:
50003 a# = gb:int.in = peek(a#+8): rem old version
int.in   = peek(gb+8) *2^16 + peek(gb+10)
50007 return
```

The address of the int.in array is found and stored in the variable of the same name in line 50003. The variable x1 must be set up so as not to invalidate the result of the later VARPTR function. The text for the output window is contained in a$. You can put text of your choice here, as long as the string length doesn't exceed 20 characters.

Parameters are POKEd into the int.in array. The GEMSYS command is identical to the VDISYS command in this respect. Lines 60 and 70 pass the address of the string to the array. The VARPTR function finds this address (line 50). If you don't completely understand this parameterpassing, re-read the explanation of the VARPTR function in the previous section.

Interestingly, we don't POKE any values into the CONTROL array. We simply give GEMSYS the desired function number directly. ST BASIC calculates the values for the CONTROL array from this number and then places these into the array itself. This would also work well for VDISYS.

1.3 The speed of BASIC commands

Everyone is interested in how fast the ST will run in BASIC. But how are
you to measure the execution speed? ST BASIC has no way of measuring
time. Fortunately the problem can be solved relatively easily. The operating
system contains an interrupt-controlled counter in memory locations $4BA
to $4BD. The contents of these memory locations constitute a long word, a
32-bit value. The long-word value is incremented 200 times per second.
Thus the resolution of the timer is 5 milliseconds. However, most
commands are processed in a significantly shorter time. Therefore, to
measure the duration of a command, you can execute the command many
times in a loop and then divide the resulting time by the number of passes.
After subtracting the time for the FOR...NEXT loop, you'll have an
accurate time for the execution of the command.

We determined the execution time of many commands with the following
short program:

```
10      rem 1_3  measure execution time of cmd in 130
100     timer = &h4bc
110     time1 = peek(timer)
120     for i = 1 to 10000
130     let a = 1
140     next i
150     time2 = peek(timer)
160     time  = time2 - time1
170     time  = (time*5/10000)-.8495
180     ? "the command in 130 requires"time
        "milliseconds"
```

On the average, all ST BASIC commands require between about 0.6 and
1.9 milliseconds. The slowest is the PRINT command. The time to output a
single character is about 4.5 milliseconds. The exact duration of a PRINT is
not so easy to calculate. We did this by determining the time for the
GOTOXY command and noting it. We then determined the time for the line:

```
130 gotoxy 0,0:PRINT "a";
```

and subtracted the time for the GOTOXY. Note the semicolon at the end of
the PRINT output. Without the semicolon the characters CR and LF would
be printed after the "a".

The times increase dramatically if we remove the GOTOXY command and the semicolon. Then the screen scrolls on (almost) every output. If you really want to find out the time required for this, you should reduce the number of passes to 100 or 200 (lines 120 and 170). Otherwise the test run is very time-consuming.

The most interesting results are from the floating-point functions like SQR, SIN, and LOG. These functions are very fast. If we compare the times determined with those from other computers, we see an enormous increase in speed. The time for the SQR function on a Commodore 64 is about 54 milliseconds. On the ST the function requires only about 1 millisecond!

The surprising differences of times, compared to the other functions, is brought about because much of BASIC is written in C. Only the floating-point functions are written in assembly language. Floating-point routines were written by Motorola, the developer of the 68000.

1.4 BASIC and machine language

Do you have a need to mix BASIC and machine language? Most functions are available directly from BASIC. But it's the word *most* that made us decide to investigate further. Recall that the clock time is unavailable from BASIC. Yet the operating system has an accurate clock that runs in two-second steps. Here's a way to use the clock from BASIC.

1.4.1 "SAFE" places for machine language programs

We decided to write a machine language program for using the clock. But first we are faced with another problem. How do we combine a machine language program and a BASIC program and avoid problems?

The simplest solution is to place the machine language routine in an area of memory that's safe from BASIC. One choice is the "free" area above the screen memory. Screen RAM is organized to use the upper 32K of memory. On the 520ST, screen RAM is located at $78000. On the 1040ST, it is located at $F8000. The screen occupies 640 x 400 = 32,000 bytes. The remaining 768 bytes of the 32K area (32K = 32,768) is not used by the operating system. Assuming that it is small enough to fit, a machine language program can be POKEd into this area.

A program that uses this area must determine if the computer has 512K or 1024K and select the corresponding address. When a "free" area like this exists, many programs may want to use this memory for routines. If two programs try to use the same area simultaneously, then there's a good chance that there will be serious problems.

So where should machine language routines be located? One trick is to pack the machine language routine into a string variable. BASIC does not care if a variable A$ contains text like "Hi there everybody" or a machine language program. We'll demonstrate how you can transfer machine code to a string variable shortly.

To read the clock from a machine language program, you use the TRAP #1 instruction with a value of $2C on the stack. This call to the operating system returns the time in the D0 register. The value in D0 is coded in individual bits. To determine the time, you must decode the bits.

Here's the routine to read the clock:

```
000000    move.l    a0,a5           address of routine to a5
000002    move.w    #$2c,-(a7)      get function number clock time
000004    trap      #1              execute function
000008    addq.l    #6,a7           repair stack pointer
00000a    move.w    d0,$10(a5)      write clock time in memory
00000e    rts
000010    ds.w      1               space for time
```

If you assemble this routine and call it from BASIC using the CALL command, the address of the routine is found in register A0. The first instruction transfers the routine address to register A5—we'll need it later. Next the clock time is determined by calling the operating system using the TRAP #1 instruction. Then the stack pointer is restored to its original value. The time is returned in register D0, which is saved in memory. Register A5 is used to access this "save area," which is 16 bytes ($10) from the start of the routine.

By assembling this routine, you'll get the opcodes for the machine language instructions. Here are the opcodes for the routine above:

$2a,$48,$3f,$3c,$00,$2c,$4e,$41
$54,$8f,$3b,$40,$00,$10,$4e,$75

The next step is to get these values into a string variable. We can use the following BASIC statements to do this:

```
1         rem 1_4_1a  m/l in string
10        for i=0 to 17
20        read byte
30        clk$=clk$+chr$(byte)
40        next
50        data &h2a,&h48,&h3f,&h3c,&h00,&h2c,&h4e,&h41
60        data &h54,&h8f,&h3b,&h40,&h00,&h10,&h4e,&h75
70        data &hff,&hff
```

The last two values represent the area to store the clock time. If you do not reserve the area within the string variable, you will overwrite another variable stored in memory.

We've written the machine language routine and stored it in a "safe" place in memory. Now we must find a way to execute the routine.

To do this, we must know the address at which the string is stored. You may recall that the VARPTR may be used to determine the address of a string descriptor. In bytes 3 through 6 the descriptor is the address of the actual string. This is also the address of our machine language routine, of course.

```
80 addr = 0
90 addr = varptr (clk$)
```

The VARPTR function returns an address into the variable addr.

Line 80 is important, by the way. If the variable addr is not initialized, the results can be corrupted by initialization during the VARPTR function.

Now we call the machine language program to read the clock time. We use the CALL command.

```
100 call addr
```

After this command, the clock time is found in the rightmost two characters of the string variable clk$. You can access these "characters" using the RIGHT$ and LEFT$ function.

```
110 time$ = right$(clk$,2)
120 sec=(asc(right$(time$,1))+
    asc(left$(time$,1))*256)*2
125 print "Total seconds since 12:00 AM " sec
130 goto 100
```

This method of calling a machine language routine from BASIC has its drawbacks. A string variable is limited to 256-characters in length. Therefore the length of the machine language routine is limited too. Passing parameters through individual strings can be complicated. So we came up with alternative way to combine machine language and BASIC.

This method is the most flexible option for combining machine language programs in BASIC programs. The routine is placed in an integer array.

If you examine the structure of an integer array you will see that the individual elements of the array are located one after the other in memory. The element with the lowest index lies at the lowest address. Each element is two bytes in length—just right for the opcodes of the 68000. The size of a machine language program in an array is not as severely limited as it is with the string method. Programs can easily be 1000 bytes or longer.

```
1       rem 1_4_1b  m/l in integer array
10      dim clk%(8)
20      for i=0 to 8
30      read clk%(i)
40      next i
50      data &h2a48,&h3f3c,&h002c,&h4e41,&h548f
60      data &h3b40,&h0010,&h4e75,&h0000
```

As you see, we first dimension the array (line 10) and then place the program in it. This initialization is shorter than with the previous program because the data elements are now 16 bits each.

Once again we must determine the address of the routine by using the VARPTR function. The result of the VARPTR points directly to the first command of the routine. Therefore we can use the result as the jump address for the CALL command!

```
70      ad = 0
80      ad = varptr (clk%(0))
90      call ad
```

We can also get the result easily. It is contained in array element clk%(8).

```
100     ?clk%(8)
```

Parameters can also be passed to the routine in the same way. You simply enter the parameters into the appropriate array elements and the program fetches them from the selected memory locations.

1.5 The most expensive clock in your house

Some people might consider this program to be rather useless. We disagree, because the program demonstrates some fundamental programming techniques.

We have used several graphics capabilities of the ST in the following program with a short routine for reading the clock time. The following is a short description of some of the special features of the program:

Several variables are initialized in the first seven lines of the program.

Variable h0 is the size of the type for the digital display. If you stop the program, the ST will not automatically switch back to the normal type size. This is especially annoying during a test run when you've made a typing error in the program. For the test run, set this variable to a value of 10. This will set the type to its normal size.

Variables xm% and ym% determine the center of the dial.

Variables sec.p%, min.p%, hrs.p% determine the length of the three pointers.

Variable pi is the value π (3.14159), which is not directly available in ST BASIC.

Next, the type height is set, the array for the machine language program is set , and the dial is drawn.

The actual program begins in line 1130. Line 1135 checks for the mouse button. If a button is pressed, the character size is returned to normal. The machine language program places the seconds in clk%(20), the minutes in clk%(21), and the hours in clk%(22). After this, a comparison is made to see if the new value for the seconds is the same as the old value. As long as this is the case, a new pass through the loop is made. Not until the seconds have changed is the loop exitted.

The remainder of the program is relatively easy. You should have no trouble understanding it.

Figure 1.4-1

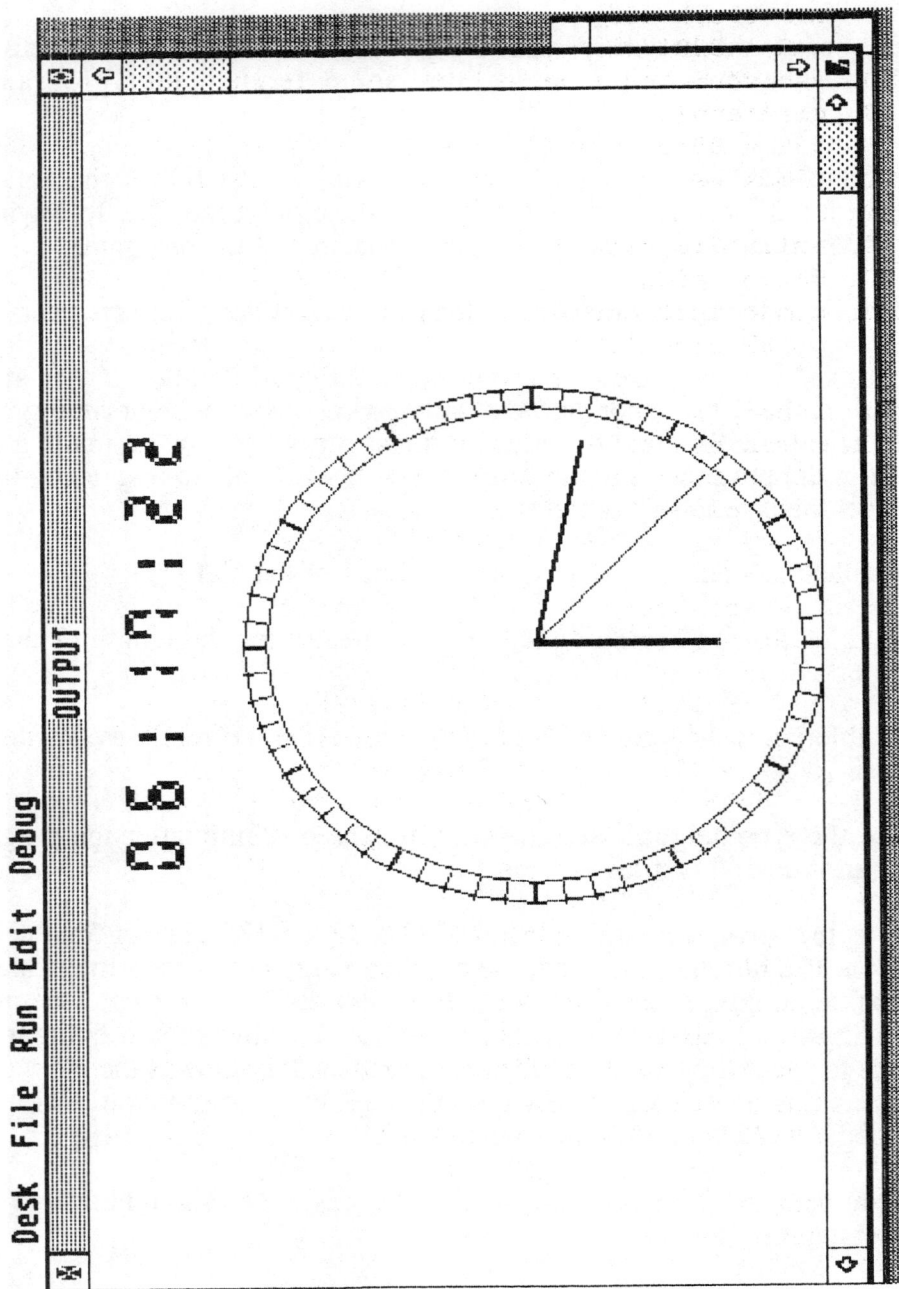

```
100      rem clock
1000     h0=25
1010     dim clock%(23)
1020     xm% = 320:ym% = 200
1030     sec.z% = 115 : min.z% =105 : std.z% = 80
1040     pi=4*atn(1)
1050     g89 = 89.9*(pi/180) : g90 = pi/2 : g91 = 90.1*(pi/180)
1060     clock  = 0
1070     '
1080     fullw 2:clearw 2
1090     gosub height
1100     gosub init.clock
1110     gosub clockface
1120     '
1130     loop: '   ************************
1135     gosub mouse.button
1140     clock = varptr (clock%(0))
1150     call clock
1160     if sec% = clock%(20)*2 then loop
1170     '
1180     ' erase hands ****************
1190     sec% = clock%(20)*2
1200     color 0,0,0,0,0
1210     dmy% = std% : std% = clock%(22)
1220     if dmy%<> std% then phi = phistd :r%=std.z%:gosub draw
1230     dmy% = min% : min% = clock%(21)
1240     if dmy%<> min% then phi = phimin :r%=min.z%:gosub draw
1250     phi = phisec : r%=sec.z%: gosub draw
1260     '
1270     '
1280     ' draw new hands ************
1290     color 1,0,1,1,1
1300     phisec = sec%*pi/30-g90: r%=sec.z%
1310     phi = phisec : gosub draw
1320     phimin = min%* 6 * (pi/180)-g90 : r%=min.z%
1330     phi = phimin : gosub draw
1340     phistd = std%* 30 * (pi/180)-g90 : r%=std.z%
1350     phi = phistd : gosub draw
1360     gosub digital
1370     goto loop
1380     '
1390     draw:    ' **********************
1400     linef xm% ,ym% ,xm%+r%*cos(phi) ,ym%+r%*sin(phi)
```

```
1410  if r%= sec.z% then return
1420  '
1430  linef xm%+1,ym%  ,xm%+r%*cos(phi)+1,ym%+r%*sin(phi)
1440  linef xm%  ,ym%+1,xm%+r%*cos(phi)  ,ym%+r%*sin(phi)+1
1450  linef xm%+1,ym%+1,xm%+r%*cos(phi)+1,ym%+r%*sin(phi)+1
1460  if r%= min.z%then return
1470  '
1480  linef xm%+2,ym%  ,xm%+r%*cos(phi)+2,ym%+r%*sin(phi)
1490  linef xm%  ,ym%+2,xm%+r%*cos(phi)  ,ym%+r%*sin(phi)+2
1500  linef xm%+2,ym%+2,xm%+r%*cos(phi)+2,ym%+r%*sin(phi)+2
1510  return
1520  '
1530  clockface:   '*******************
1540  circle xm%,ym%,120,120
1550  circle xm%,ym%,130,130
1560  for std%= 1 to 12
1570  phi = std%* 30 * (pi/180)-g90 : r1%=130 : r0%=120
1580  linef xm%+r0%*cos(phi),ym%+r0%*sin(phi),
      xm%+r1%*cos(phi),ym%+r1%*sin(phi)
1590  phi = std%* 30 * (pi/180)-g89 : r1%=130 : r0%=120
1600  linef xm%+r0%*cos(phi),ym%+r0%*sin(phi),
      xm%+r1%*cos(phi),ym%+r1%*sin(phi)
1610  phi = std%* 30 * (pi/180)-g91 : r1%=130 : r0%=120
1620  linef xm%+r0%*cos(phi),ym%+r0%*sin(phi),
      xm%+r1%*cos(phi),ym%+r1%*sin(phi)
1630  next std%
1640  for min%= 1 to 59
1650  phi = min%* (pi/30) : r1%=130 : r0%=120
1660  linef xm%+r0%*cos(phi),ym%+r0%*sin(phi),
      xm%+r1%*cos(phi),ym%+r1%*sin(phi)
1670  next min%
1680  return
1690  '
1700  digital: ' ***********************
1710  sec$=str$(sec%): if len(sec$)=2 then
      sec$=" 0"+right$(sec$,1)
1720  min$=str$(min%): if len(min$)=2 then
      min$=" 0"+right$(min$,1)
1730  std$=str$(std%): if len(std$)=2 then
      std$=" 0"+right$(std$,1)
1740  timdig$=right$(std$,2)+"Z"+right$(min$,2)+"Z"+
      right$(sec$,2)
1750  gosub printdig
```

```
1760   return
1770   '
1780   height:    ' ************************
1790   poke contrl    ,107
1800   poke contrl-2,0
1810   poke contrl-6 ,1
1820   poke intin,h0
1830   vdisys
1840   return
1850   '
1860   printdig: rem ********************
1870   poke contrl    ,11
1880   poke contrl-2 ,2
1890   poke contrl-6 ,10
1900   poke contrl-10,10
1910   poke contrl-12,2
1920   poke intin     ,1
1930   poke intin+2  ,1
1940   for i%=1 to 8
1950   poke intin - (i%*2+2),asc(mid$(timdig$,i%,1))-32
1960   next i%
1970   poke ptsin,210
1980   poke ptsin+2,80
1990   poke ptsin+4,220
2000   poke ptsin+6,0
2010   vdisys
2020   return
2030   '
2040   init.clock:    ' ********************
2050   data &h2a48,&h3f3c,&h002c,&h4e41,&h548f,&h3b40,&h0028
2060   data &h026d,&h001f,&h0028,&hea48,&h3200,&h0240,&h003f
2070   data &h3b40,&h002a &hec49,&h3b41,&h002c,&h4e75
2075   data &h0000,&h0000,&h0000,&h0000
2080   for i% = 0 to 23
2090   read clock%(i%)
2100   next i%
2110   return
2120   mouse.button: ' ****
2130   poke contrl,124: poke contrl+2,0: poke contrl+4,0
2160   vdisys
2170   button = peek(intout)
2180   if button <> 0 then h0=10: gosub height: end
2190   return
```

1.6 Automatic hardcopy

To get a hardcopy of the screen, you can press the <ALT> and <HELP> keys simultaneously. Memory location 1262 is a flag that tells the ST to print a screen hardcopy. Normally the memory location has a value of -1. Pressing <ALT> <HELP> increments the value and generates the hardcopy.

Knowing this, you can POKE memory location 1262 to get "automatic" hardcopy:

```
poke 1262,0
```

Alternatively, you can issue a VDI function 5 to perform hardcopy as follows:

```
contrl    ,5
contrl+ 2,0
contrl+ 6,0
contrl+10,17
```

By the way, the hardcopy can be interrupted by pressing <ALT> <HELP> while it's printing.

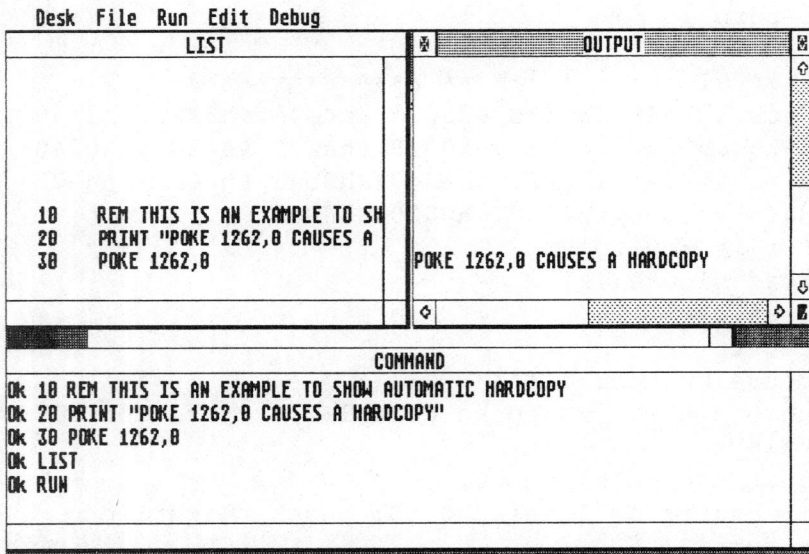

```
 Desk  File  Run  Edit  Debug
┌─────────────── LIST ───────────────┐  ┌──────────── OUTPUT ────────────┐
│                                     │  │                                │
│                                     │  │                                │
│                                     │  │                                │
│                                     │  │                                │
│    18    REM THIS IS AN EXAMPLE TO SH│ │                                │
│    28    PRINT "POKE 1262,0 CAUSES A │ │                                │
│    38    POKE 1262,8                │  │POKE 1262,8 CAUSES A HARDCOPY   │
│                                     │  │                                │
└─────────────────────────────────────┘  └────────────────────────────────┘

┌─────────────────────── COMMAND ───────────────────────┐
│Ok 18 REM THIS IS AN EXAMPLE TO SHOW AUTOMATIC HARDCOPY │
│Ok 28 PRINT "POKE 1262,8 CAUSES A HARDCOPY"             │
│Ok 38 POKE 1262,8                                       │
│Ok LIST                                                 │
│Ok RUN                                                  │
│                                                        │
└────────────────────────────────────────────────────────┘
```

CHAPTER 2

Utilities for the ST

Utilities for the ST

This chapter contains a very powerful set of utility programs. These are mostly machine language programs that change or extend the functions of the operating system. All are memory-resident, and will make it easier to work with the ST and other applications.

Each utility is preceded by a brief description of the program, its application and its capabilities. The source code for each program is written in 68000 assembly language.

Each is documented so that you can makes changes or enhancements according to your needs. But to do so, you'll require an assembler.

If you program only in BASIC, you can use the BASIC loader to create the program. A BASIC loader contains the machine language utility in the form of DATA statements. The BASIC loader uses a checksum to insure that input errors are eliminated. By running the BASIC loader, you create a program file on the disk that's normally created by the assembler and linker. Once you've run the BASIC loader for each utility, you can then start each of them by clicking the appropriate icon with the mouse.

2.1 Current time display

In the following utility we'll show you three programming techniques to use in your own programs. The first technique lets you execute a program periodically. The second technique shows you where in memory to place a short program so it's not destroyed later by other programs. The third technique shows you how to use the ST's system fonts.

This utility creates a digital clock in the upper righthand corner of the screen. It's displayed whenever you are working on the desktop or with GEM programs. In both of these cases, the top line of the screen is a status line and the last 10 characters are normally unused.

To work correctly, the clock time is continually redisplayed. To do this we use the ST's vertical blank interrupt (VBL). The VBL is called each time the computer has completed displaying a complete video picture. This happens 70 times a second with the monochrome monitor.

The VBL routine checks a jump table containing the addresses of user routines to be executed during the VBL. The table normally has 8 entries. A zero value indicates that the entry is not used. To execute a user routine, you must search the table and place the address of your routine into the first unused entry. From then on, this routine is executed 70 times per second during a VBL interrupt.

Now we have to find a place for the program itself. In order to explain the program, we'll repeat part of an earlier chapter.

If the program is smaller than 3 full pages (768 bytes), you can place the program above screen memory. After power-up the ST reserves the top 32K of memory for the screen display. On the 520 ST the screen occupies $78000 to $7FFFF.

You'll recall that the screen is a maximum of 640x400 pixels, which equates to 256,000 bits, or 32,000 bytes. A 32K area contains 32,768 bytes, so the last 768 bytes of screen memory are "left over." Screen memory occupies only the area from $78000 to $7FCFF, inclusive. The memory from $7FD00 to $7FFFF is not used for screen output. So this area can be used for a short routine.

To install the utility, an initialization routine must copy the program to this memory area and then set the VBL vector to point to this address.

The VBL table is part of the system variables. To access a system variable, the ST must be in the supervisor mode. Then we need to find an unused entry in the VBL list, save the address of this entry in register A2 and copy our utility to its proper location. The length of the utility is a counter. The destination address is the length of the utility *plus* 32000, the length of the screen. Now we can copy the utility to the top of the screen memory. Then we call the routine to initialize the time display and finally set the VBL vector to our routine and return to the desktop.

The `init` routine returns a pointer to the font which we will use to display the time. To do this we use a special part of TOS (*line A routine*) that returns a pointer to a vector array of the three system fonts in register A1. Next we get the address of the second font, the 8x16 pixel font which is the standard for monochrome display. We set the VBL counter to 1 which will start our routine after the next VBL.

A counter is used because we don't have to display the time 70 times a second. We decrement the counter each time through the routine and update the display only when the counter is zero. The display routine resets the counter. This routines gets the clock time from the processor and is identical to the corresponding BIOS function which returns the time in DOS format with a resolution of 2 seconds. The keyboard processor however keeps time exactly to the second in BCD format. This time is saved by the ST at address $A46 at the label `time` in the program listing. The three bytes, the hour, the minute and the second are in the 24-hour format but are written to the screen by the routine `wrtbcd`.

The routine `wrtchar` writes a character contained in register D0 to the top line of the screen. The cursor position is contained in the register D6 (a value between 0 and 79). The current position within the screen memory is determined from the cursor position and the base address of the screen memory. Then the address of the point, the offset of the next raster line, the number of scan lines and the height of the character are determined from the font header. In the routine at label `loop`, the data from the font definitions is copied to the screen, raster line by raster line, until an entire character is written. The program will work on a monochrome monitor without changes.

Why didn't we write the characters to the screen with the BIOS or GEMDOS routine? Why did we copy the system font data to the screen memory? The answer is that we are working within an interrupt routine. Using the BIOS or GEMDOS routines, a screen output can be interrupted and the cursor may be moved to a different position on the screen. To avoid this, we would have to save the cursor position, set the cursor to the top line, write the character to the screen and then set the cursor to its original position. If another font were being used, then our display time would become confused. By accessing the system fonts directly, we avoid these problems and perform the work at faster speeds.

Figure 2.1 shows the time display in the status line of the desktop.

Following is the assembly language listing of the program. If you do not have an assembler, the short BASIC program will create an equivalent machine language program to display the time. Running the BASIC loader creates a program file called TIME.PRG. You can start it as usual by clicking its icon.

Figure 2.1

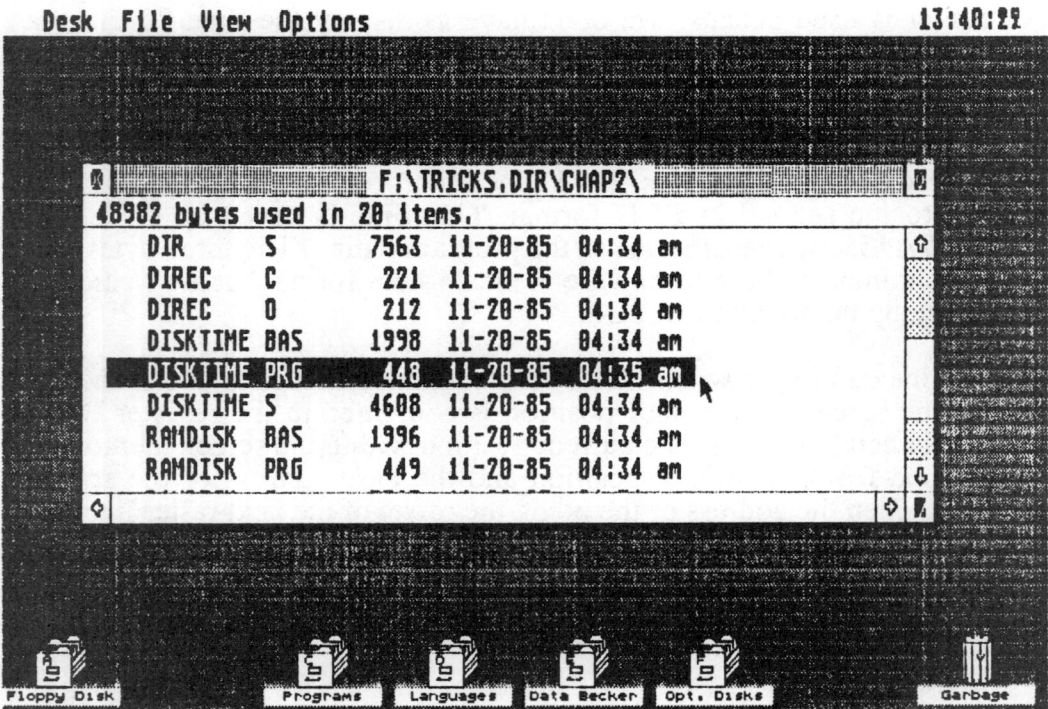

```
*      disktime program
*      join program in vertical blank lineup
*      Mono version, color version in comments
*      LE 2/8/85
*      Color Mod 7/23/86 by Greg Dykema

_v_bas_ad    equ      $44e      screen address
hz_200       equ      $4ba      200hz system timer

gemdos       equ      1
setexec      equ      5
bios         equ      13
keep         equ      $31
gettime      equ      23
super        equ      38        execute in supervisor mode
xbios        equ      14

             move.l   4(sp),a0      calculate program size
             move.l   #$100,d6
             add.l    12(a0),d6
             add.l    20(a0),d6
             add.l    28(a0),d6

             bsr      init                program init.

             clr      -(sp)
             move.l   d6,-(sp)      number bytes
             move     #keep,-(sp)
             trap     #gemdos

init         dc.w     linea
             moveq    #2*4,d0   font number #1*4,do color
             lea      fontptr(pc),a3
             move.l   (a1,d0),(a3)      mark font pointer

             move     #gettime,-(sp)
             trap     #xbios
             addq.l   #2,sp
             move     d0,d7

             pea      sup_rout(pc)
             move     #super,-(sp)      execute rest in
```

```
*                                         supervisor mode
          trap       #xbios
          addq.l     #6,sp
          rts

sup_rout:
          move       d0,d7
          and        #%11111,d0
          lsl        #1,d0            seconds in binary
          move       d0,second

          move       d0,d7
          lsr        #5,d0
          and        #%111111,d0
          move       d0,minute

          move       d7,d0
          moveq      #11,d1
          lsr        d1,d0
          move       d0,hour

          move       #$2700,sr        interrupts disabled

          move.l     hz_200,time
          add.l      #200,time

          pea        hz_int(pc)
          move       #$45,-(sp)       timer c interrupt
*                                     vector
          move       #setexec,-(sp)
          trap       #bios
          addq.l     #8,sp
          move.l     d0,hz_save       200hz vector mark
          rts

hz_int    movem.l    d0-d7/a0-a6,-(sp)      save regs

          move.l     time,d0
          cmp.l      hz_200,d0        one second yet?
          bne        no_show          no

          add.l      #200,time        next second
          addq       #1,second
```

```
            cmp       #60, second        check seconds
            bne       show_time
            clr       second
            addq      #1,minute          next minute
            cmp       #60,minute         check minutes
            bne       show_time
            clr       minute
            addq      #1,hour
            cmp       #24,hour           check hours
            bne       show_time
            clr       hour

show_time:

            moveq     #70,d6             cursor position
*                                        #144 color version
            move      hour,d0            get hour
            bsr       wrtdec
*           addq      #3,d5              past color info
            bsr       wrtcol
*           addq      #1,d5              past color info

            move      minute,d0          get minute
            bsr       wrtdec
*           addq      #3,d6              past color info
            bsr       wrtcol
*           addq      #1,d6              past color info

            move      second,d0          get second
            bsr       wrtdec

no_show   movem.l    (sp)+,d0-d7/a0-a6
           move.l    hz_save,-(sp)      address of routine
           rts

wrtdec:
            move      #$2f,d1            number 10
wrtdec1   addq       #1,d1
            sub       #10,d0
            bpl       wrtdec1
            add       #$3a,d0            one digit
            move      d0,-(sp)
            move      d1,d0
```

```
            bsr        wrtchar          output
*           btst.l     #0,d6            test cursor position
*           beq        wrtdec2          even add1
*           addq       #3,d6            odd add 3
*           bra        wrtdec3
*wrtdec2 addq          #1,d6
*wrtdec3 move          (sp)+,d0
            move       (sp)+,d0         unit, remove for color
            bra        wrtchar          output


wrtcol   moveq        #$3a,d0                  ':'


*
*       system font ATARI ST
*       LE 9/8/85
*


adelow      equ     36     lowest ascii-code in font
adehigh     equ     38     highest ascii-code in font
cellwd      equ     52     linewidth
fontdat     equ     76     ptr to font data
formwd      equ     80     status of next raster line in
*                          font
formhg      equ     82     number of raster lines / char


linea       equ     $a000


line1       equ     80     bytes per screen line
*                          160 for color
*       write character to graphic ram
*       d0 = character
*       d6 = cursor column
*
wrtchar:
            moveq     #0,d1
            move      d6,d1
            addq      #1,d6            move cursor to next
*                                     column,delete for color
            move.l    fontptr(pc),a3  get font pointer
            add.l     _v_bas_ad,d1    plus screen address
            move.l    d1,a4
            move.l    fontdat(a3),a0  font data pointer
```

```
*          move     formwd(a3),d2     offset of next
*                                     raster line in font
*          move     formhg(a3),d7     form height (number
*                                     of scan lines)
           subq     #1,d7

loop       move.b   (a0,d0),(a4)      onscreen raster
*                                     line
*          add      #line1,a4         pointer to next
*                                     screen line
*          add      d2,a0             pointer to next
*                                     raster line in font
           dbra     d7,loop
           rts


fontptr  ds.l     1
hz_save  ds.l     1
second   ds.w     1
minute   ds.w     1
hour     ds.w     1
time     ds.l     1
```

BASIC loader for Monochrome display time

```
100    open "R",1,"b:time.prg",16: rem disk b
110    field#1,16 as bin$
120    a$="": for i=1 to 16: read x$: if x$="*"then 150
130    a=val("&H"+x$): s=s+a:a$=a$+chr$(a): next
140    lset bin$=a$: rec=rec+1: put 1,rec: goto 120
150    data 60,1A,00,00,01,82,00,00,00,00,00,00,00,00,00,00
160    data 00,00,00,00,00,00,00,00,00,00,00,00,20,6F,00,04
170    data 2C,3C,00,00,01,00,DC,A8,00,0C,DC,A8,00,14,DC,A8
180    data 00,1C,61,0A,42,67,2F,06,3F,3C,00,31,4E,41,A0,00
190    data 70,08,47,FA,01,48,26,B1,00,00,3F,3C,00,17,4E,4E
200    data 54,8F,3E,00,48,7A,00,0C,3F,3C,00,26,4E,4E,5C,8F
210    data 4E,75,30,07,C0,7C,00,1F,E3,48,33,C0,00,00,01,78
220    data 30,07,EA,48,C0,7C,00,3F,33,C0,00,00,01,7A,30,07
230    data 72,0B,E2,68,33,C0,00,00,01,7C,46,FC,27,00,23,F9
240    data 00,00,04,BA,00,00,01,7E,06,B9,00,00,00,C8,00,00
250    data 01,7E,48,7A,00,16,3F,3C,00,45,3F,3C,00,05,4E,4D
260    data 50,8F,23,C0,00,00,01,74,4E,75,48,E7,FF,FE,20,39
270    data 00,00,01,7E,B0,B9,00,00,04,BA,66,6A,06,B9,00,00
280    data 00,C8,00,00,01,7E,52,79,00,00,01,78,0C,79,00,3C
290    data 00,00,01,78,66,32,42,79,00,00,01,78,52,79,00,00
300    data 01,7A,0C,79,00,3C,00,00,01,7A,66,1C,42,79,00,00
310    data 01,7A,52,79,00,00,01,7C,0C,79,00,18,00,00,01,7C
320    data 66,06,42,79,00,00,01,7C,7C,46,30,39,00,00,01,7C
330    data 61,20,61,36,30,39,00,00,01,7A,61,16,61,2C,30,39
340    data 00,00,01,78,61,0C,4C,DF,7F,FF,2F,39,00,00,01,74
350    data 4E,75,72,2F,52,41,90,7C,00,0A,6A,F8,D0,7C,00,3A
360    data 3F,00,30,01,61,06,30,1F,60,02,70,3A,72,00,32,06
370    data 52,46,26,7A,00,28,D2,B9,00,00,04,4E,28,41,20,6B
380    data 00,4C,34,2B,00,50,3E,2B,00,52,53,47,18,B0,00,00
390    data D8,FC,00,50,D0,C2,51,CF,FF,F4,4E,75,00,00,00,00
400    data 00,00,00,00,00,00,00,00,00,00,00,00,00,00,00,00
410    data 00,50,0E,0C,0E,0A,16,0C,12,06,08,08,06,08,08,06
420    data 08,08,08,0a,0a,0c,00,00,00,00,00,00,00,00,00,00
430    data *
440    close 1:if s<> 25074 then ? "ERROR in DATA !!": end
450    print "Ok."
```

BASIC loader for Color display time

```
1000    open"R",1,"A:\CLKCOLOR.PRG",16
1010    field#1,16 as bin$
1020    a$="":for i=1 TO 16:read d$:if d$="*"then 1050
1030    a=val("&H"+d$):s=s+a:a$=a$+chr$(a):next
1040    lset bin$=a$:rec=rec+1:put 1,rec:goto 1020
1050    data 60,1A,00,00,01,98,00,00,00,00,00,00,00,00,00,00
1060    data 00,00,00,00,00,00,00,00,00,00,00,00,20,6F,00,04
1070    data 2C,3C,00,00,01,00,DC,A8,00,0C,DC,A8,00,14,DC,A8
1080    data 00,1C,61,0A,42,67,2F,06,3F,3C,00,31,4E,41,A0,00
1090    data 70,04,47,FA,01,5E,26,B1,00,00,3F,3C,00,17,4E,4E
1100    data 54,8F,3E,00,48,7A,00,0C,3F,3C,00,26,4E,4E,5C,8F
1110    data 4E,75,3E,00,C0,7C,00,1F,E3,48,33,C0,00,00,01,8E
1120    data 3E,00,EA,48,C0,7C,00,3F,33,C0,00,00,01,90,30,07
1130    data 72,0B,E2,68,33,C0,00,00,01,92,46,FC,27,00,23,F9
1140    data 00,00,04,BA,00,00,01,94,06,B9,00,00,00,C8,00,00
1150    data 01,94,48,7A,00,16,3F,3C,00,45,3F,3C,00,05,4E,4D
1160    data 50,8F,23,C0,00,00,01,8A,4E,75,48,E7,FF,FE,20,39
1170    data 00,00,01,94,B0,B9,00,00,04,BA,66,00,00,76,06,B9
1180    data 00,00,00,C8,00,00,01,94,52,79,00,00,01,8E,0C,79
1190    data 00,3C,00,00,01,8E,66,32,42,79,00,00,01,8E,52,79
1200    data 00,00,01,90,0C,79,00,3C,00,00,01,90,66,1C,42,79
1210    data 00,00,01,90,52,79,00,00,01,92,0C,79,00,18,00,00
1220    data 01,92,66,06,42,79,00,00,01,92,3C,3C,00,90,30,39
1230    data 00,00,01,92,61,28,56,46,61,48,52,46,30,39,00,00
1240    data 01,90,61,1A,52,46,61,3A,56,46,30,39,00,00,01,8E
1250    data 61,0C,4C,DF,7F,FF,2F,39,00,00,01,8A,4E,75,72,2F
1260    data 52,41,90,7C,00,0A,6A,F8,D0,7C,00,3A,3F,00,30,01
1270    data 61,12,08,06,00,00,67,04,56,46,60,02,52,46,30,1F
1280    data 60,02,70,3A,72,00,32,06,26,7A,00,28,D2,B9,00,00
1290    data 04,4E,28,41,20,6B,00,4C,34,2B,00,50,3E,2B,00,52
1300    data 53,47,18,B0,00,00,D8,FC,00,A0,D0,C2,51,CF,FF,F4
1310    data 4E,75,00,00,00,00,00,00,00,00,00,00,00,00,00,00
1320    data 00,00,00,00,00,00,00,50,0E,0C,0E,0A,16,0C,14,06
1330    data 08,08,06,08,08,06,08,08,0A,0E,0E,0C,00,00,00,00
1340    data *
1350    close 1:if s<> 26811 then print"ERROR IN DATA!":end
1370    print "Ok."
```

2.2 Print spooler for the ST

Have you ever sat in front of your computer and waited for a 10-page listing to print? While waiting, you could be doing other work on the computer. Here's a very useful utility to cut the time spent waiting for lengthy printouts.

The speed of a printer depends on the printer mechanism, which is usually much slower that the rate at which the computer sends data to the printer. Because of this speed discrepancy, some printers contain a buffer that holds data temporarily as it arrives from the computer. The data is retrieved from the buffer as the print mechanism is ready to print it.

A typical size for a buffer is 2K—roughly one page of text. If the document to be printed is larger than 2K, the buffer fills up and the computer stops sending data to the printer until the buffer can accept more data. One way to avoid this computer-waiting-for-data problem is to install a larger print buffer. Unfortunately, these are rather expensive. But we have a computer with 512K or 1024K of memory. Why not put the print buffer in the ST itself?

Enter the print spooler. To better understand this utility program, we'll briefly describe how data is transferred from the computer to the printer.

Data is transferred one byte at a time over a Centronics interface. So that the computer and the printer can agree on the time of the transfer, two *handshake lines* are used. If the printer is ready to accept data, it signals the computer by setting the BUSY handshake line low. The computer then sends the data to the printer. When the data is sent, the computer sets the STROBE handshake line low.

To set up an intermediate buffer for the data, two routines are needed to coordinate the data flow. One routine writes the data that is normally sent to the printer to the buffer. Another routine sends the data from the buffer to the printer when the printer is ready to accept data.

This program is set to manage a buffer of up to 63K. By clicking the mouse, the program reserves a 32K buffer. This is enough for about 15 pages of text. By running the program as a TTP (TOS Takes Parameters) file, you can specify the buffer size—any value between 1 and 63 sets the size in kilobytes.

If you anticipate using the print spooler often, you can have have it installed each time you boot the operating system. Place a folder called AUTO on the operating system diskette and copy the program to this folder. When the system is booted, all the programs in the AUTO folder are executed alphabetically.

Here's a short description of the print spooler:

So that the print spooler reserves enough space for both itself and the buffer, the size of the memory area is determined. This is found in the *base page*, which is 256 bytes long. It immediately precedes the program. The address of the base page is found on the stack. The lengths of text, data, and block storage segments are added to the length of the base page.

The base page also contains the *command line*. The command line is the text that we entered as parameters of the program to start the program. The parameter represents the buffer size (in kilobytes). The parameter in the command line is converted to a binary number. If a parameter is omitted, a 32K buffer is the default. By shifting the number in a register, the value is converted to the exact buffer size.

Next we change the system for the TRAP #13 instruction to point to our print spooler program. In this program we'll test the parameter on the stack, to determine if either the printer output or the printer status is being requested. If a service other than these two is requested, then the original TRAP #13 routine is performed.

There are several situations that our print spooler must consider:

- If the buffer is empty, we try to output the character directly to the printer.

- If the printer is not ready to accept a character, or the buffer is not empty, then we write the character to the buffer.

- If the buffer is full, then we wait 30 seconds. If the buffer does not have space after 30 seconds we inform the requester that the character cannot be output. This occurs when the buffer is full and the printer is not accepting any more data.

How do we get data from the buffer to the printer?

The BUSY line of the printer generates an interrupt when it is ready to receive the next character. By vectoring this interrupt to our routine labeled `busyint`, we can transfer data from the buffer to the printer. In this interrupt routine, we check to see if there is data remaining in the buffer. If so, one character is removed and sent to the printer. This ends the interrupt routine; control is returned to the interrupted program. The advantage of this method is that the computer doesn't spend time waiting for the printer.

If you install this print spooler and send a 10-page document to the printer, the computer will be ready for further processing in a very short time—even though the printer continues to work for several minutes afterwards.

Following is the assembly language listing for the print spooler program. There is also a BASIC loader program to create an equivalent machine language program on diskette.

```
*
*          print spooler for atari st
*
*          LE/RB, 5/11/85
*

bios      equ      13
keep      equ      $31              hold resident prg
gemdos    equ      1
setexec   equ      5                set xception vector
conout    equ      3                output character
constat   equ      8                output status
prn       equ      0                device # of printer
savptr    equ      $4a2             save area/ register
hz_200    equ      $4ba             200 hz system count

xbios     equ      14
mfpint    equ      13               mfp interrupt
*                                   installed

mfp       equ      $fffa01          mfp 68901
psg       equ      $ff8800          psg ym 2149
isrb      equ      $10              interrupt service
*                                   register b

default   equ      32               standard buffer
*                                   size in kb
timeout   equ      30               30 seconds timeout


*                                   compute program size

          move.l   4(sp),a0         base page address
          move.l   #$100,d6         size of base page
          add.l    12(a0),d6        plus text length
          add.l    20(a0),d6        plus data length
          add.l    28(a0),d6        plus bss length

*                          buffer size from command line
          moveq    #0,d7
          moveq    #0,d0
          lea      129(a0),a0       command line pntr
nextchr   move.b   (a0)+,d0         get character
          sub.b    #'0',d0
```

```
          bmi      exit              no number
          cmp.b    #9,d0
          bgt      exit              no number
          mulu     #10,d7            next place
          add      d0,d7
          bra      nextchr

exit      tst      d7                has no. been input?
          bne      ok                yes
          move     #default,d7       otherwise take
*                                    default number
ok        ext.l    d7
          moveq    #10,d0
          lsl.l    d0,d7             convrt valu to bytes
          add.l    d7,d6             add to place needs
          move     d7,length         and enter in iorec

*                                    initialize vectors

          move.l   #trap13,-(sp)     new vector
          move     #45,-(sp)         vector number
          move     #setexec,-(sp)
          trap     #bios             set vector
          addq.l   #8,sp
          move.l   d0,trapsve        note old vector

          move.l   #busyint,-(sp)
          move     #0,-(sp)          int number
          move     #mfpint,-(sp)
          trap     #xbios            centronics interrupt
*                                    enabled
          addq.l   #8,sp

          clr      -(sp)
          move.l   d6,-(sp)          number of bytes
          move     #keep,-(sp)       hold resident program
          trap     #gemdos           back to desktop

*                                    new trap#13 routine
trap13    move.l   sp,a2             mark ssp
          btst     #5,(sp)           call from supervisor?
          bne      super             yes
          move.l   usp,a2            otherwise use usp
```

```
              subq     #6,a2
super         cmp      #concut,6(a2)  conout-call ?
              bne      normal
              cmp      #prn,8(a2)     printer ?
              bne      normal

              move.l   savptr,a1      pointer to save area
              move     (sp)+,-(a1)    retain status
              move.l   (sp)+,-(a1)    return address
              move.l   a1,savptr      save ptr updates

              move     10(a2),d1      character
              bsr      print

              move.l   savptr,a1
              move.l   (a1)+,-(sp)    return address
              move     (a1)-,-(sp)    status
              move.l   a1,savptr
              rte

normal:
              cmp      #constat,6(a2) printer status ?
              bne      norml
              cmp      #prn,8(a2)
              bne      norml          over old trap#13
*                                     vector

              moveq    #-1,d0         status ok taken
              bsr      getptr         get pointer
              move     tail(a0),d2
              bsr      wrap
              cmp      head(a0),d2    room in buffer?
              bne      room           yes
              moveq    #0,d0          busy, no room
room          rte

norm1         move.l   trapsve,a0     to old trap #13
              jmp      (a0)

print         move     #$2700,sr      interrupt block
              bsr      getptr         pntr to iorec & mfp
              move     head(a0),d2
              cmp      tail(a0),d2    buffer empty?
```

```
              bne       inbuff         no char in buffer

loop          btst      #0,(a1)        printer busy ?
              bne       inbuff         yes,in buffer

notbusy lea             psg,a2         psg address
              move.b    #15,(a2)       reg. number port b
              move.b    d1,2(a2)       output databyte

              move.b    #14,(a2)       reg number port a
              move.b    (a2),d0
              and.b     #$df,d0        strobe low
              move.b    d0,2(a2)

              or.b      #$20,d0        strobe high
              move.b    d0,2(a2)

              moveq     #-1,d0         ok
              rts


inbuff        move      tail(a0),d2    increment
              bsr       wrap           write pointer
              cmp       head(a0),d2    buffer full?
              beq       buffull        yes
inbuff1       move.l    (a0),a1        buffer address
              move.b    d1,(a1,d2)     write char to buffer
              move      d2,tail(a0)    mark new tail index
              moveq     #-1,d0         character disposed of
              rts

buffull       move.l    hz_200,d0
              add.l     #timeout*200,d0 num seconds to wait
              move      #$2300,sr      interrupts freed up
wait          cmp       head(a0),d2    more room in buffer?
              bne       inbuff1        yes-char into buffer
              cmp.l     hz_200,d0      time up yet?
              bhi       wait           no-keep waiting

              moveq     #0,d0          char not disposed of
              rts
*             interrupt routine for sending a character
*             to the printer
```

```
busyint movem.l d0-d2/a0-a2,-(sp)   retain
*                                    register
        bsr      getptr             get pointer
        move     head(a0),d2
        cmp      tail(a0),d2        send buffer empty?
        beq      empty              yes- ready
        bsr      wrap               incremnt read pointer
        move.l   (a0),a2            buffer address
        move.b   (a2,d2),d1         send char from
        bsr      notbusy            buffer to printer
        move     d2,head(a0)        mark new head index
empty   bclr     #0,isrb(a1)        clr  service bit
        movem.l  (sp)+,d0-d2/a0-a2 restore registers
        rte

getptr  lea      iorec,a0           pointer to
*                                   buffer file record
        lea      mfp,a1
        rts

wrap    addq     #1,d2              pointer to next pos.
        cmp      len(a0),d2         reachd end-of-buffer?
        bcs      nowrap             no
        moveq    #0,d2              otherwise start
*                                   at the beginning
nowrap  rts

        .data
iorec   dc.l     buf                buffer address
length  ds.w     1                  buffer size
        dc.w     0                  write index
        dc.w     0                  read index

buffer  equ      0                  offset in iorec
len     equ      4
head    equ      6
tail    equ      8

        .bss
trapsve ds.l     1                  alter trap#13 vector
buf     equ      *        start of buffer memory
```

BASIC loader for print spooler

```
100 open "R",1,"b:spool.prg",16: rem drive b
110 field#1,16 as bin$
120 a$="": for i=1 to 16: read x$: if x$="*"then 150
130 a=val("&H"+x$): s=s+a:a$=a$+chr$(a): next
140 lset bin$=a$: rec=rec+1: put 1,rec: goto 120
150 data 60,1A,00,00,01,B0,00,00,00,0A,00,00,00,04,00,00
160 data 00,00,00,00,00,00,00,00,00,00,00,00,20,6F,00,04
170 data 2C,3C,00,00,01,00,DC,A8,00,0C,DC,A8,00,14,DC,A8
180 data 00,1C,7E,00,70,00,41,E8,00,81,10,18,90,3C,00,30
190 data 6B,0E,B0,3C,00,09,6E,08,CE,FC,00,0A,DE,40,60,EA
200 data 4A,47,66,02,7E,20,48,C7,70,0A,E1,AF,DC,87,33,C7
210 data 00,00,01,B4,2F,3C,00,00,00,7C,3F,3C,00,2D,3F,3C
220 data 00,05,4E,4D,50,8F,23,C0,00,00,01,BA,2F,3C,00,00
230 data 01,6C,3F,3C,00,00,3F,3C,00,0D,4E,4E,50,8F,42,67
240 data 2F,06,3F,3C,00,31,4E,41,24,4F,08,17,00,05,66,04
250 data 4E,6A,5D,4A,0C,6A,00,03,00,06,66,30,0C,6A,00,00
260 data 00,08,66,28,22,79,00,00,04,A2,33,1F,23,1F,23,C9
270 data 00,00,04,A2,32,2A,00,0A,61,42,22,79,00,00,04,A2
280 data 2F,19,3F,19,23,C9,00,00,04,A2,4E,73,0C,6A,00,08
290 data 00,06,66,20,0C,6A,00,00,00,08,66,18,70,FF,61,00
300 data 00,C2,34,28,00,08,61,00,00,C8,B4,68,00,06,66,02
310 data 70,00,4E,73,20,79,00,00,01,BA,4E,D0,46,FC,27,00
320 data 61,00,00,A0,34,28,00,06,B4,68,00,08,66,2E,08,11
330 data 00,00,66,28,45,F9,00,FF,88,00,14,BC,00,0F,15,41
340 data 00,02,14,BC,00,0E,10,12,C0,3C,00,DF,15,40,00,02
350 data 80,3C,00,20,15,40,00,02,70,FF,4E,75,34,28,00,08
360 data 61,6E,B4,68,00,06,67,0E,22,50,13,81,20,00,31,42
370 data 00,08,70,FF,4E,75,20,39,00,00,04,BA,D0,BC,00,00
380 data 17,70,46,FC,23,00,B4,68,00,06,66,DC,B0,B9,00,00
390 data 04,BA,62,F2,70,00,4E,75,48,E7,E0,E0,61,24,34,28
400 data 00,06,B4,68,00,08,67,0E,61,26,24,50,12,32,20,00
410 data 61,82,31,42,00,06,08,A9,00,00,00,10,4C,DF,07,07
420 data 4E,73,41,F9,00,00,01,B0,43,F9,00,FF,FA,01,4E,75
430 data 52,42,B4,68,00,04,65,02,74,00,4E,75,00,00,01,BE
440 data 00,00,00,00,00,00,00,00,00,44,06,12,06,88,AE,18
450 data 00,00,00,00,00,00,00,00,00,00,00,00,00,00,00,00
460 data *
470 close 1:if s<> 29742 then print "Error in DATA!!": end
480 print "Ok."
```

2.3 RAM-disk for the ST

If you've done any program development on the ST, then you're familar
with the number of steps required to create an executable PRG file from the
source. You need the editor, source file, compiler or assembler, linker, etc.
In addition, several temporary files are created and deleted. These
activities—editing, compiling and linking—are disk-intensive activities.
Longer programs may take 15 minutes or more to compile. In our opinion,
too much of the time is spent loading and saving data in disk files.

One way to speed up the process is to use a hard drive. This speeds up disk
access by about 30 times. Another alternative, which is faster and much less
expensive, is the *RAM disk*.

What is a RAM disk? Quite simply, a RAM disk is a disk drive facsimile
that's located in memory. By setting aside an area of memory in the ST and
treating it like a peripheral device—a disk drive—you can get a super fast
and super cheap disk drive.

When data from the computer is sent to a RAM disk, it is not sent to the
disk controller, but to the reserved memory. And it's done at the lightning
speed of the 68000 processor—not at the plodding mechanical speed of a
real disk drive.

Reading and writing to and from the RAM disk is equivalent to copying data
from one area of memory to another.

To simulate the RAM disk, several routines are required. One routine is tied
to the operating system. Three vectors are *patched*. These vectors are
designed to be used by the hard disk, but can be used for our purposes
here. They involve calls to the BIOS for reading/writing sectors, getting the
BIOS parameter block (contains information about the physical organization
of a disk) and determining if the diskette is changed.

The RAM disk here will have the designation C. This corresponds to a
value of 2 in the BIOS (0=drive A, 1=drive B, etc.). In the program, the
normal vectors are altered to point to our routines. We determine if the RAM
disk (drive C) is the intended destination by checking the drive number on
the stack. If drive C is not the destination, we return control to the normal
vector for drives A and B.

When starting the RAM disk program, the size of the RAM disk is passed as a parameter. You specify the capacity of the RAM disk in kilobytes (same as for the print spooler). You are not limited to the preset disk sizes (180, 360, and 720K)—any size from 80K to 640K (on a 1040 ST) can be specified.

On a 520 ST, values from 100 to 220K are possible. If you don't specify a parameter, the default is 100K. Using the assembler, you can change the default RAM disk capacity by changing the appropriate source code.

Using the BASIC loader, you must change the underlined values with your new default value (high byte, low byte; example, for 300K: 01 2C). Remember if you change these values the checksum will no longer work, so first run the BASIC loader 'as is' to verify it is correct. The RAM disk program automatically configures the BIOS parameter block for the specified parameter, creates a boot sector in RAM, and initializes the directory.

To install the RAM disk, execute the RAMDISK.PRG program, with or without parameters. The capacity of the RAM disk is specified by installing this application from the OPTIONS menu as a TTP (TOS Takes Parameters) file. When the RAMDISK.PRG application is started, simply enter the desired capacity in the dialog box and press <RETURN>. Next click the icon for drive A and choose the selection INSTALL DISK DRIVE from the OPTIONS menu. Enter C for the disk drive identifier, and RAM_DISK for the icon label. Then click the INSTALL box. A new disk icon appears on the screen with the label RAM_DISK.

You can now open the RAM disk by double-clicking this icon. A window with the identification C then appears, containing 0 objects with 0 bytes. You can copy programs or files from drive A or B to the RAM disk. This is done exactly as if we were using actual disk drives.

Try loading a program from the RAM disk. Programs up to 100K will load in less than one second!

How can we best use the RAM disk? If you write a lot of programs and documents you should put the editor and source program on the RAM disk. If you have enough room, put the compiler, assembler and linker on the RAM disk also. A complete assembler pass may take up to ten minutes with a regular disk drive. The same pass will take less than a minute with the RAM disk.

Warning: Remember that your data on the RAM disk is only in RAM—it will be lost forever when you turn the power off! Copy the results of your work from the RAM disk to a real disk drive before turning the computer off! You should also do the same before you start untested programs that might cause the system to crash.

Here are a few hints for working with the RAM disk:

- It's not possible to back up an entire floppy disk to the RAM disk, or vice versa. Instead, try the following method. Open a window of the drive *to* which you want to copy. Then drag the icon of the diskette *from* which you want to copy into the window.

- You should also not try to format the RAM disk. Doing so may damage the diskettes in drives A and B. Instead, draw a box around all the file icons on the RAM disk, and drag them to the trash. This is done very quickly with the RAM disk.

- You can also automatically install the RAM disk after power-up. To do this, place a folder titled AUTO on your system disk and copy the installation program RAMDISK.PRG to it. When you select SAVE DESKTOP from the OPTIONS menu, your configuration with the installed RAM disk is stored in the file DESKTOP.INF. Make sure this file is saved on drive A and not drive C. If it is saved on drive C copy it to drive A. From then on, every time the system is booted, the RAM disk is automatically installed as drive C.

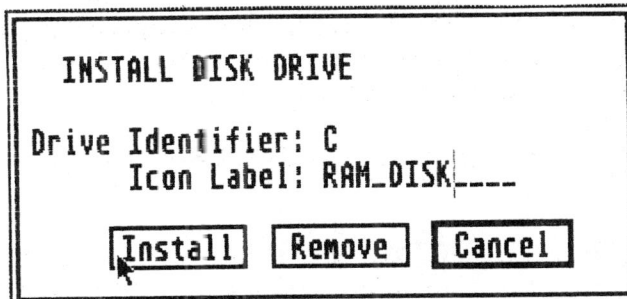

```
INSTALL DISK DRIVE

Drive Identifier: C
     Icon Label: RAM_DISK____

  [Install]   [Remove]   [Cancel]
```

```
*
*           RAM disk for ATARI ST
*           LE/RB, 6/11/85
*

hdv_bpb  equ      $472              bios parameter block
hdv_rw   equ      $476              read/write sectors
hdv_mediach   equ      $47e

drvbits  equ      $4c2              bit vectors of
*                                   active drives

gemdos   equ      1
keep     equ      $31

xbios    equ      14
super    equ      38

default  equ      100               standard capacity
*                                   in kb

init     move.l   4(sp),a0          base page address
         move.l   #$100,d6          size of base page
         add.l    12(a0),d6         text length
         add.l    20(a0),d6         data length
         add.l    28(a0),d6         bss length

         moveq    #0,d7
         moveq    #0,d0
         lea      129(a0),a0        pointer to
*                                   command line
nextchr  move.b   (a0)+,d0          first character
*                                   from command line
         sub.b    #'0',d0
         bmi      exit
         cmp.b    #9,d0             number?
         bgt      exit
         mulu     #10,d7
         add      d0,d7             next digit
         bra      nextchr

exit     tst      d7                input done there?
         bne      ok
```

```
          move.w   #default,d7        default value

ok        moveq    #0,d1
          move     d7,d1              capacity in k
          add      #9,d1              plus 9 k
          lsl.l    #8,d1
          lsl.l    #2,d1              * 1024
          add.l    d1,d6              add to memory
*                                     requirements


          move.l   #init1,-(sp)
          move     #super,-(sp)       initialization in
*                                     supervisor mode
          trap     #xbios
          addq.l   #6,sp

          clr      -(sp)
          move.l   d6,-(sp)           number of bytes
          move     #keep,-(sp)        leave resident prg
          trap     #gemdos            return to desktop


init1     move.l   hdv_bpb,bpbsave
          move.l   #bpb,hdv_bpb

          move.l   hdv_rw,rwsave      set vectors to
*                                     new routines
          move.l   #rw,hdv_rw

          move.l   hdv_mediach,mediasave
          move.l   #media,hdv_mediach


install   moveq    #0,d1
          lea      ramdisk,a0
          move     #2*9*512/4-1,d0
*                                     clear tracks 0 and 1
iloop1    move.l   d1,(a0)+           of ram disk
          dbra     d0,iloop1

*                                     generate boot sector
          lea      ramdisk+11,a0
```

```
              lea       boottab,a1
              moveq     #tabend-boottab-1,d0
bloop         move.b    (a1)+,(a0)+        copy data in
*                                          boot sector
              dbra      d0,bloop

              move      d7,numcl           capacity in kb
*                                          in bpb

              lsl       #1,d7              sector capacity
              add       #18,d7             plus 18 sectors
              lea       ramdisk+19,a0
              move.b    d7,(a0)+           low-byte
              lsr       #8,d7
              move.b    d7,(a0)            high-byte

              or.l      #%100,drvbits      inform drive c
              rts

bpb:          cmp       #2,4(sp)           drive c ?
              beq       bpb1               yes

              move.l    bpbsave,a0         old routine
              jmp       (a0)

bpb1          move.l    #bpbtab,d0         pointer to bios
*                                          parameter block
              rts

rw            cmp       #2,14(sp)          drive c ?
              beq       rw1                yes

              move.l    rwsave,a0          old routine
              jmp       (a0)

rw1           move      12(sp),d0          recno, logical
*                                          sector number
              ext.l     d0
              lsl.l     #8,d0
              lsl.l     #1,d0              times 512

              move.l    6(sp),a0           buffer address
```

```
        move      10(sp),d1        number of sectors
        subq      #1,d1
        lea       ramdisk,a1       basis address
        add.l     d0,a1            plus relative
*                                  address in ram disk

        move      4(sp),d0         rwflag
        btst      #0,d0            read?
        beq       rloop0           yes
        exg       a0,a1            exchange destination
*                                  and source

rloop0  move      #511,d0          copy a sector
rloop   move.b    (a1)+,(a0)+      to buffer
        dbra      d0,rloop
        dbra      d1,rloop0        next sector
        moveq     #0,d0            ok
        rts


media   cmp       #2,4(sp)         drive c ?
        beq       media1           yes

        move.l    mediasave,a0     old routine
        jmp       (a0)

media1  moveq     #0,d0            diskete not changed
        rts

        .data
bpbtab:
recsiz: dc.w      $200             sector size
clsiz   dc.w      2                cluster size
*                                  in sectors
clsizb  dc.w      $400             cluster size
*                                  in bytes
rdlen   dc.w      7                directory length
*                                  in sectors
fsiz    dc.w      5                fat size
fatrec  dc.w      6                fat sectors
datrec  dc.w      18               sectors for
*                                  data management
numcl   ds.w      1                capacity in kb
```

```
flags     ds.w    8

boottab:          *                    data in 8086 format
          dc.b    0,2                  bytes per sector
          dc.b    2                    sectors per cluster
          dc.b    1,0                  reserved sectors
          dc.b    2                    fats
          dc.b    112,0                directory entries
          ds.b    2                    sectors on media
          dc.b    0                    media descriptor
          dc.b    5,0                  sectors per fat
          dc.b    9,0                  sectors per track
          dc.b    1,0                  sides
          dc.b    0                    hidden
tabend    equ     *

          .bss

bpbsave ds.l      1                    room for old
*                                      floppy vectors
rwsave    ds.l    1
mediasave         ds.l    1

ramdisk equ       *                    ram disk starts here
```

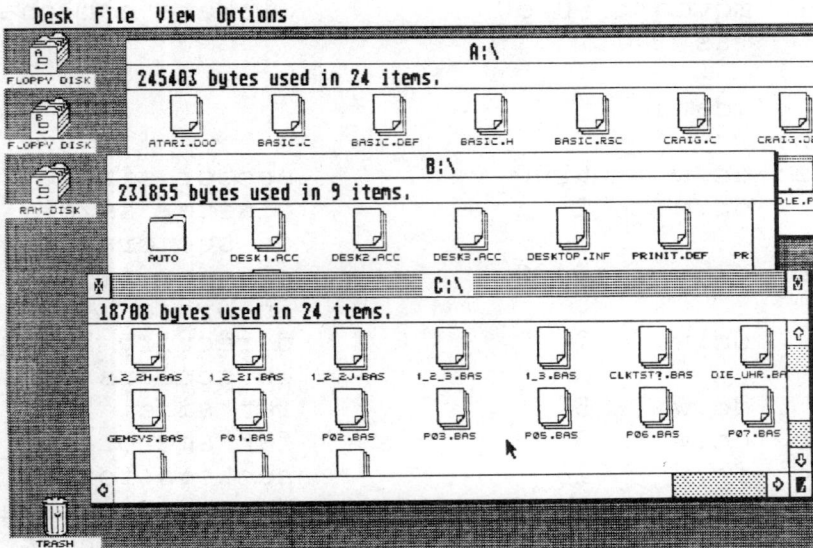

```
100  open "R",1,"b:ramdisk.prg",16: rem drive b
110  field#1,16 as bin$
120  a$="": for i=1 to 16: read x$: if x$="*"then 150
130  a=val("&H"+x$): s=s+a:a$=a$+chr$(a): next
140  lset bin$=a$: rec=rec+1: put 1,rec: goto 120
150  data 60,1A,00,00,01,5E,00,00,00,32,00,00,00,0C,00,00
160  data 00,00,00,00,00,00,00,00,00,00,00,00,20,6F,00,04
170  data 2C,3C,00,00,01,00,DC,A8,00,0C,DC,A8,00,14,DC,A8
180  data 00,1C,7E,00,70,00,41,E8,00,81,10,18,90,3C,00,30
190  data 6B,0E,B0,3C,00,09,6E,08,CE,FC,00,0A,DE,40,60,EA
200  data 4A,47,66,04,3E,3C,00,64,72,00,32,07,D2,7C,00,09
210  data E1,89,E5,89,DC,81,2F,3C,00,00,00,62,3F,3C,00,26
220  data 4E,4E,5C,8F,42,67,2F,06,3F,3C,00,31,4E,41,23,F9
230  data 00,00,04,72,00,00,01,90,23,FC,00,00,00,E8,00,00
240  data 04,72,23,F9,00,00,04,76,00,00,01,94,23,FC,00,00
250  data 01,00,00,00,04,76,23,F9,00,00,04,7E,00,00,01,98
260  data 23,FC,00,00,01,4A,00,00,04,7E,72,00,41,F9,00,00
270  data 01,9C,30,3C,0E,FF,20,C1,51,C8,FF,FC,41,F9,00,00
280  data 01,A7,43,F9,00,00,01,7E,70,11,10,D9,51,C8,FF,FC
290  data 33,C7,00,00,01,6C,E3,4F,DE,7C,00,12,41,F9,00,00
300  data 01,AF,10,C7,E1,4F,10,87,00,B9,00,00,00,04,00,00
310  data 04,C2,4E,75,0C,6F,00,02,00,04,67,08,20,79,00,00
320  data 01,90,4E,D0,2C,3C,00,00,01,5E,4E,75,0C,6F,00,02
330  data 00,0E,67,08,23,79,00,00,01,94,4E,D0,30,2F,00,0C
340  data 48,C0,E1,88,E3,88,20,6F,00,06,32,2F,00,0A,53,41
350  data 43,F9,00,00,01,9C,D3,C0,30,2F,00,04,08,00,00,00
360  data 67,02,C1,49,30,3C,01,FF,10,D9,51,C8,FF,FC,51,C9
370  data FF,F4,70,00,4E,75,0C,6F,00,02,00,04,67,08,20,79
380  data 00,00,01,98,4E,D0,70,00,4E,75,02,00,00,02,04,00
390  data 00,07,00,05,00,06,00,12,00,00,00,00,00,00,00,00
400  data 00,00,00,00,00,00,00,00,00,00,00,02,02,01,00,02
410  data 70,00,00,00,00,05,00,09,00,01,00,C0,00,00,00,4C
420  data 1C,06,0E,06,0E,06,0C,10,06,0E,0C,20,08,10,1C,2E
430  data *
440  close 1:if s<> 26687 then ? "Error in DATA!!": end
450  print "Ok."
1000 rem change 00,64 in line 200 to alter default size
1010 rem 100K = 00,64 : 200K = 00,C8 : 400K = 01,90
1020 rem if altered checksum in line 440 will not work
```

2.4 Auto-starting TOS applications

On early versions of ST, the operating system is loaded from disk to memory and started. To initiate this procedure, the ST has a boot ROM which automatically executes when the computer is turned on. The boot ROM loads a special boot sector from the system diskette, which in turn loads the rest of the operating system.

The boot sector occupies the first sector on the system disk (track zero, sector one) and contains data about the disk format, capacity, number of tracks and sectors, and size and organization of the directory. The boot program is contained only on a systems disk. So that the ST can recognize a system disk, the checksum of this sector is $1234.

Normally, after the operating system is loaded, the GEM desktop is started. But the operating system can start a program called COMMAND.PRG instead. This may be a user program which runs under TOS, for example. How do we get the operating system to do this?

Within the boot sector is a flag which determines whether the desktop or COMMAND.PRG is started. If the flag is zero, the desktop is started. If the value at the address is not zero, COMMAND.PRG is started. The value of the flag is copied to the system variable cmdload which is found at $482. After the operating system is loaded, it uses cmdload to decide which program to start.

To be able to start an application on boot-up, we must modify the boot sector. Following is a small utility program to do this.

The program performs several functions:

First the boot sector from drive A is read and the flag for cmdload is set in the boot sector.

Now we can rewrite the boot sector to drive B. But, recall that there is a checksum to identify the boot sector. Changing a value within the sector changes the checksum. The operating system will no longer recognize the disk as a systems disk. Instead of determining the new checksum, we can let the operating system do it for us. Function protobt creates a boot sector or changes one already existing.

We specify that the boot sector is to be executable and all other parameters are to remain unchanged. This routine recalculates the checksum and rewrites the boot sector.

Finally we can copy the application to be automatically started after booting to the modified disk. The program must have the name COMMAND . PRG.

If we reboot with this disk in drive A, this program is automatically started!

This program requires a disk with a boot sector to be in drive A, such as the system disk. This program will read the boot sector and then write the modified boot sector to drive B.

```
*
*          modification of boot sectors for cmdload
*          LE 11/11/85
*

gemdos    equ      1

xbios     equ      14

floprd    equ      8              read sector
flopwr    equ      9              write sector
protobt   equ      18             genrate boot sector

cmdload   equ      $1e            offset in boot sector

*                   load boot sector

          move     #1,-(sp)            one sector
          move     #0,-(sp)            side zero
          move     #0,-(sp)            track zero
          move     #1,-(sp)            sector zero
          move     #0,-(sp)            drive a
          clr.l    -(sp)
          move.l   #buffer,-(sp)  buffer address
          move     #floprd,-(sp)  boot read sector
          trap     #xbios
          add.l    #20,sp

          tst      d0                  error occurred?
          bne      exit                yes- break

*                   boot sector modified

          lea      buffer,a0      buffer address
          move.b   #1,cmdload(a0) set cmdload flag

*                   make boot sector operational again

          move     #1,-(sp)            make boot sector
*                                      operational
          move     #-1,-(sp)           disk type stays same
          move.l   #-1,-(sp)           serial number
*                                      stays the same
```

```
          move.l    #buffer,-(sp) boot sector address
          move      #protobt,-(sp)call function
          trap      #xbios
          add.l     #14,sp

*                   write altered boot sector back in

          move      #1,-(sp)         one sector
          move      #0,-(sp)         side zero
          move      #0,-(sp)         track zero
          move      #1,-(sp)         sector zero
          move      #1,-(sp)         drive b
          clr.l     -(sp)
          move.l    #buffer,-(sp) buffer address
          move      #flopwr,-(sp) boot zero
          trap      #xbios
          add.l     #20,sp

exit      clr       -(sp)
          trap      #gemdos          return to desktop

          .bss
buffer    ds.b      512              room for a sector
```

```
100 open "R",1,"b:cmdload.prg",16 : rem drive b
110 field#1,16 as bin$
120 a$="": for i=1 to 16: read x$: if x$="*"then 150
130 a=val("&H"+x$): s=s+a:a$=a$+chr$(a): next
140 lset bin$=a$: rec=rec+1: put 1,rec: goto 120
150 data 60,1A,00,00,00,84,00,00,00,00,00,00,02,00,00,00
160 data 00,00,00,00,00,00,00,00,00,00,00,00,3F,3C,00,01
170 data 3F,3C,00,00,3F,3C,00,00,3F,3C,00,01,3F,3C,00,00
180 data 42,A7,2F,3C,00,00,00,84,3F,3C,00,08,4E,4E,DF,FC
190 data 00,00,00,14,4A,40,66,54,41,F9,00,00,00,84,11,7C
200 data 00,01,00,1E,3F,3C,00,01,3F,3C,FF,FF,2F,3C,FF,FF
210 data FF,FF,2F,3C,00,00,00,84,3F,3C,00,12,4E,4E,DF,FC
220 data 00,00,00,0E,3F,3C,00,01,3F,3C,00,00,3F,3C,00,00
230 data 3F,3C,00,01,3F,3C,00,01,42,A7,2F,3C,00,00,00,84
240 data 3F,3C,00,09,4E,4E,DF,FC,00,00,00,14,42,67,4E,41
250 data 00,00,00,18,16,1A,28,00,00,00,00,00,00,00,00,00
260 data *
270 close 1:if s<> 8275 then print "Error in DATA !!": end
280 print "Ok."
```

2.5 Using machine language and C

In this section we'll demonstrate how to use machine language subroutines from C programs.

Writing a program in C is usually much easier and faster than writing it in machine language. But when it comes to optimizing time-critical parts of a program, you must often rewrite these sections in machine language. Since the C compiler creates an assembly language program as an intermediate step, you might be tempted to optimize these parts by hand—changing the assembly language program.

How can you pass parameters between the C program and assembly language subroutine and get a result back? Parameters are usually passed on the stack:

```
int parameter1, parameter2;
long parameter3;
function(parameter1,parameter2,parameter3);
```

The C compiler generates the following assembler language statements from the above call:

```
move.l    parameter3,-(sp)
move.w    parameter2,-(sp)
move.w    parameter1,-(sp)
jsr       _function
addq.l    #8,sp
```

Note that the parameter list is processed from the back to the front, and also that the function is called with the JSR instruction. The C compiler places an underline character in front of the subroutine name. So that the linker can find the name in the assembly language program, it is declared as global.

For the assembly language program, the parameters are found on the stack as follows:

```
8(sp)      long, parameter3
6(sp)      word, parameter2
4(sp)      word, parameter1
0(sp)      long, return address from jsr call
```

You must ensure that the types of the parameters in the call match those in the subroutine; the compiler and linker cannot check types.

You must also pay attention to the register usage. An assembly language subroutine may change the contents of registers D0-D2 and A0-A2. No other register contents may be changed. If a function returns a result, it is expected in register D0. In this case, the compiler assumes that the function value is of type int or word, as with the following call:

```
a=function(parameter);
```

If the function returns a long result, it must be explicitly declared before the function is called, like this:

```
long function();
long a;

a=function(parameter);
```

Armed with this knowledge, you should be able to use assembly language subroutines. Following is an example of such a subroutine; it displays the directory. You'll see several GEMDOS calls. Toward the end of the listing is the short program main.

The function expects two parameters: The first determines the drive (0=A, 1=B); the second is a selection string that you can specify to select subdirectories, for example. If the second parameter is a null string, then all files are displayed. Twenty files are displayed per screen. Pressing a key displays the next twenty files.

```
*
*          Display directory
*
*          LE 11/11/85
*

*          BIOS-functions
bios     equ    13        TRAP#
conin    equ    2         console input
conout   equ    3         console output
con      equ    2         console device#

*          GEMDOS-functicns
gemdos   equ    1         TRAP#
wrtstr   equ    9         string output
setdrv   equ    $e        drive selection
setdma   equ    $1a       declare dma-address
getspc   equ    $36       free bytes
sfirst   equ    $4e       search first
snext    equ    $4f       search next

cr       equ    13        carriage return
lf       equ    10        line feed

filetyp equ     %11001    file attribute

wrtchar  move   d0,-(sp)          output char in d0
         move   #con,-(sp)
         move   #conout,-(sp)
         trap   #bios
         addq.l #6,sp
         rts

blank    move.b #' ',d0            output blanks

         bra    wrtchar

newline lea     crlf(pc),a0       new line

wrttxt   move.l a0,-(sp)          text address
         move   #wrtstr,-(sp)     string output
         trap   #gemdos
         addq.l #6,sp
```

```
        rts

        .globl  _directory      open access for C

*       6(sp)   filename pointer
*       4(sp)   drive number
*       0(sp)   return address

_directory:

        move    4(sp),curdrv    drive number
        move.l  6(sp),a0        filenames
        movem.l d3-d7/a3-a6,-(sp)        retain
*                                        C-register
        move.l  a0,a3
        move.l  #dmabuf,-(sp)
        move    #setdma,-(sp)   dma buffer address
        trap    #gemdos
        addq.l  #6,sp
        move    curdrv,-(sp)
        move    #setdrv,-(sp)   select drive
        trap    #gemdos
        addq.l  #4,sp
        tst.b   (a3)            filename onhand?
        bne     dir1            yes
        lea     allfile(pc),a3  '*.*' as name
dir1    move    #filetyp,-(sp)
        move.l  a3,-(sp)        filename pointer
        move    #sfirst,-(sp)
        trap    #gemdos
        addq.l  #8,sp
        tst     d0              file onhand?
        bne     enddir
dircont moveq   #20-1,d7        number of lines
nxtfile bsr     wrtname         output filename
        move.l  size,d0         size in bytes
        bsr     wrtlng          output as dec num.
        bsr     blank
        move    date,d3         date
        bsr     wrtdate         output
        bsr     blank           blank line
        move    time,d3         time
        bsr     wrttime         output
```

94

```
          bsr       newline                new line
          move      #snext,-(sp)
          trap      #gemdos                look for next file
          addq.l    #2,sp
          tst       d0                     onhand?
          dbne      d7,nxtfile
          bne       enddir                 no
          move      #con,-(sp)             wait for keypress
          move      #conin,-(sp)
          trap      #bios
          addq.l    #4,sp
          bra       dircont                and continue

enddir    move      curdrv,-(sp)           drive
          addq      #1,(sp)                1=a,  2=b
          move.l    #buffer,-(sp)
          move      #getspc,-(sp)          free space on disk
          trap      #gemdos
          addq.l    #8,sp
          move      buffer+2,d0            size
          bsr       wrt3dec                show as 3-digit
*                                          dec. number
          lea       kfree(pc),a0
          bsr       wrttxt
          movem.l   (sp)+,d3-d7/a3-a6           C-register
*                                              return
return    rts

wrtname   lea       filenam,a6             filename formatted
*                                          output
          clr       d6
namloop   move.b    (a6)+,d0               get character
          beq       endnam1                name to end?
          cmp.b     #'.',d0
          beq       extens                 continue via
*                                          extension
          addq      #1,d6
          bsr       wrtchar                output character
          bra       namloop
extens    cmp       #9,d6                  fill name to 8
*                                          places
          beq       contue
          addq      #1,d6
```

```
           bsr      blank               fill with blanks
           bra      extens
contue     move.b   (a6)+,d0            extension output
           beq      endnam1
           addq     #1,d6
           bsr      wrtchar
           bra      contue
endnam1    cmp      #14,d6              end of name?
           beq      return
           bsr      blank               fill with blanks
           addq     #1,d6
           bra      endnam1

wrtdate    bsr      blank               date display
           move     d3,d0
           and      #%11111,d0          isolate day
           bsr      wrt2dec             and display
           bsr      wrtpkt              '.' as separator
           move     d3,d0
           lsr      #5,d0
           and      #%1111,d0           isolate month and
           bsr      wrt2dec             display
           bsr      wrtpkt                 '.' as separator

           move     d3,d0
           lsr      #8,d0
           lsr      #1,d0               isolate year
           add      #80,d0              add offset
           bra      wrt2dec             and output

wrtpkt     move.b   #'.',d0             output period
           bra      wrtchar

wrttime    bsr      blank               output time
           move     d3,d0
           lsr      #8,d0
           lsr      #3,d0               isolate hour
           bsr      wrt2dec             and output
           bsr      wrtcol                 ':' as separator

           move     d3,d0
           lsr      #5,d0
           and      #%111111,d0         isolate minutes
```

96

```
          bsr       wrt2dec              and output
          bsr       wrtcol               ':' as separator
          move      d3,d0
          and       #%11111,d0
          lsl       #1,d0                isolate seconds
          bra       wrt2dec              and output

wrtcol    move.b    #':',d0              output colon
          bra       wrtchar

wrt3dec   moveq.l   #3,d6                display d0 as
*                                        3-digit no.
          clr       d4                   suppress leading
*                                        zeroes
          ext.l     d0
          bra       wrtlng1

wrt2dec   moveq     #2,d6
          ext.l     d0                   d0 as 2-digit
*                                        decimal number
          st        d4                   leading zeroes not
*                                        suppressed
          bra       wrtlng1

*              hex number in d0.1 to decimal

wrtlng    clr       d4                   suppress leading
*                                        zeroes flag
          moveq     #10,d6

wrtlng1   movem.l   d1-d3/d6-d7,-(sp)
          move.l    d0,d7
wrtdec5   moveq     #1,d2
          move.l    d5,d1
          subq.l    #1,d1
          beq       wrtdec1
wrtdec0   move      d2,d3                10*d3.1 to d3
          mulu      #10,d3
          swap      d2
          mulu      #10,d2
          swap      d3
          add       d3,d2
          swap      d2
```

```
            swap      d3
            move      d3,d2
            subq.l    #1,d1
            bne       wrtdec0
wrtdec1     clr.l     d0
wrtdec3     cmp.l     d2,d7
            blt       wrtdec2
            addq.l    #1,d0
            sub.l     d2,d7
            bra       wrtdec3
wrtdec2     tst.b     d0              zero?
            bne       wrtdec4         no-- output
            tst       d4
            bne       wrtdec4         suppress leading
*                                     zeroes
            cmp       #1,d6           last place?
            beq       wrtdec4         yes-- display zero

            bsr       blank           leading zeroes
*                                     displayed as blanks
            bra       wrtdec6
wrtdec4     add.b     #'0',d0
            bsr       wrtchar         display number
            st        d4              set flag
wrtdec6     subq.l    #1,d6
            bne       wrtdec5
            movem.l   (sp)+,d1-d3/d6-d7
            rts

allfile     dc.b      "*.*",0         all files
kfree       dc.b      " K free."
crlf        dc.b      cr,lf,0


            .bss
dmabuf      ds.b      22              dma buffer for gemdos
time        ds.w      1               time
date        ds.w      1               date
size        ds.l      1               file size
filenam     ds.b      14              file name
curdrv      ds.w      1               current drive number
buffer      ds.b      16              file size buffer
```

98

The following short program in C can serve as a test for the directory subroutine.

```
/*
 *       test program for directory display
 *       LE 11/11/85
 */

main ()

{
        directory (0, '");
                      /* drive a, all files       */

        directory (1, '*.PRG");
                      /* drive b, prg-files only  */

}
```

If you call the C source program dir ec.c and the assembly language program dir.s, then you would use the following command line after compilation and assembly for linking:

```
dir.68k=apstart,direc,dir
```

BASIC loader for directory display

```
1000    open"R",1,"b:dir.prg",16
1010    field#1,16 as bin$
1020    a$="":for i=1 TO 16:read d$:if d$="*"then 1050
1030    a=val("&H"+d$):s=s+a:a$=a$+chr$(a):next
1040    lset bin$=a$:rec=rec+1:put 1,rec:goto 1020
1050    data 60,1A,00,00,02,72,00,00,01,64,00,00,04,42,00,00
1060    data 00,00,00,00,00,00,00,00,00,00,00,00,2A,4F,2E,7C
1070    data 00,00,07,D6,2A,6D,00,04,20,2D,00,0C,D0,AD,00,14
1080    data D0,AD,00,1C,D0,BC,00,00,01,00,2F,00,2F,0D,3F,00
1090    data 3F,3C,00,4A,4E,41,DF,FC,00,00,00,0C,4E,B9,00,00
1100    data 00,4A,2F,3C,00,00,00,00,4E,41,22,2F,00,04,30,3C
1110    data 00,C8,4E,42,4E,75,4E,56,FF,FC,2E,BC,00,00,03,CE
1120    data 42,67,4E,B9,00,00,00,9A,54,8F,2E,BC,00,00,03,CF
1130    data 3F,3C,00,01,4E,B9,00,00,00,9A,54,8F,4E,5E,4E,75
1140    data 3F,00,3F,3C,00,02,3F,3C,00,03,4E,4D,5C,8F,4E,75
1150    data 10,3C,00,20,60,EA,41,FA,01,E2,2F,08,3F,3C,00,09
1160    data 4E,41,5C,8F,4E,75,33,EF,00,04,00,00,08,06,20,6F
1170    data 00,06,48,E7,1F,1E,26,48,2F,3C,00,00,07,DA,3F,3C
1180    data 00,1A,4E,41,5C,8F,3F,39,00,00,08,06,3F,3C,00,0E
1190    data 4E,41,58,8F,4A,13,66,04,47,FA,01,94,3F,3C,00,19
1200    data 2F,0B,3F,3C,00,4E,4E,41,50,8F,4A,40,66,46,7E,13
1210    data 61,70,20,39,00,00,07,F4,61,00,01,14,61,92,36,39
1220    data 00,00,07,F2,61,00,00,9E,61,86,36,39,00,00,07,F0
1230    data 61,00,00,C0,61,80,3F,3C,00,4F,4E,41,54,8F,4A,40
1240    data 56,CF,FF,CE,66,0E,3F,3C,00,02,3F,3C,00,02,4E,4D
1250    data 58,8F,60,BA,3F,39,00,00,08,06,52,57,2F,3C,00,00
1260    data 08,08,3F,3C,00,36,4E,41,50,8F,30,39,00,00,08,0A
1270    data 61,00,00,AC,41,FA,01,1C,61,00,FF,40,4C,DF,78,F8
1280    data 4E,75,4D,F9,00,00,07,F8,42,46,10,1E,67,28,B0,3C
1290    data 00,2E,67,08,52,46,61,00,FF,08,60,EE,BC,7C,00,09
1300    data 67,08,52,46,61,00,FF,0A,60,F2,10,1E,67,08,52,46
1310    data 61,00,FE,EE,60,F4,BC,7C,00,0E,67,C4,61,00,FE,F2
1320    data 52,46,60,F2,61,00,FE,EA,30,03,C0,7C,00,1F,61,56
1330    data 61,18,30,03,EA,48,C0,7C,00,0F,61,4A,61,0C,30,03
1340    data E0,48,E2,48,D0,7C,00,50,60,3C,10,3C,00,2E,60,00
1350    data FE,B0,61,00,FE,BC,30,03,E0,48,E6,48,61,28,61,16
1360    data 30,03,EA,48,C0,7C,00,3F,61,1C,61,0A,30,03,C0,7C
1370    data 00,1F,E3,48,60,10,10,3C,00,3A,60,00,FE,84,7C,03
1380    data 42,44,48,C0,60,0C,7C,02,48,C0,50,C4,60,04,42,44
1390    data 7C,0A,48,E7,73,00,2E,00,74,01,22,06,53,81,67,1A
1400    data 36,02,C6,FC,00,0A,48,42,C4,FC,00,0A,48,43,D4,43
```

```
1410 data 48,42,48,43,34,03,53,81,66,E6,42,80,BE,82,6D,06
1420 data 52,80,9E,82,60,F6,4A,00,66,10,4A,44,66,0C,BC,7C
1430 data 00,01,67,06,61,00,FE,3A,60,0A,D0,3C,00,30,61,00
1440 data FE,20,50,C4,53,86,66,B0,4C,DF,00,CE,4E,75,2A,2E
1450 data 2A,00,20,4B,20,66,72,65,65,2E,0D,0A,00,00,00,01
1460 data 00,02,01,01,02,01,01,00,01,01,02,01,01,01,01,01
1470 data 00,00,00,00,00,00,00,00,00,00,01,00,00,01,00,03
1480 data 05,00,05,05,00,00,01,01,02,01,00,10,07,01,02,01
1490 data 00,00,00,00,00,00,00,00,00,00,01,01,01,02,01,01
1500 data 02,01,01,02,01,01,01,01,02,01,01,01,00,00,00,00
1510 data 00,00,00,00,00,00,00,00,02,01,01,01,01,01,06,01
1520 data 01,04,01,01,01,03,01,02,01,01,04,02,01,08,01,01
1530 data 00,00,00,00,00,00,01,01,01,09,01,01,01,01,01,01
1540 data 01,00,00,05,01,00,00,00,00,00,00,00,00,00,00,00
1550 data 00,00,00,00,00,00,00,00,00,00,00,00,00,00,00,00
1560 data 00,00,00,00,00,00,00,00,00,00,00,00,00,00,00,00
1570 data 00,00,04,03,00,08,03,00,06,01,00,08,01,00,08,01
1580 data 00,04,01,01,03,01,01,00,05,00,01,01,01,00,05,00
1590 data 00,01,01,00,01,01,00,00,00,00,00,00,00,00,00,00
1600 data 00,00,00,00,00,00,00,00,00,00,00,00,00,00,00,02
1610 data 02,00,00,00,00,00,00,00,00,00,00,00,00,00,00,00
1620 data 00,00,00,00,00,00,00,00,00,00,00,00,05,01,00,05
1630 data 01,00,01,01,00,01,01,00,02,05,00,06,01,00,02,01
1640 data 00,01,01,00,06,05,00,00,00,00,00,01,01,00,01,00
1650 data 02,01,00,02,01,01,01,01,01,00,00,00,00,00,00,00
1660 data 00,00,00,00,00,00,00,00,00,01,02,03,01,02,01,01
1670 data 01,01,01,01,00,01,01,00,01,02,00,2A,2E,50,52,47
1680 data 00,00,00,00,00,04,2E,1E,08,08,0A,34,10,0E,2C,0C
1690 data 0C,2A,08,0E,18,00,00,00,00,00,00,00,00,00,00,00
1700 data *
1710 close 1:if s<> 49400 then print"ERROR IN DATA!":end
1730 print "Ok."
```

Sample screen dump of directory display program

```
                                    0    12.00.98    12:36:52
                         .          0    12.00.98    12:36:52
         CMDLOAD    PRG           168    04.01.86    19:19:10
         DIR        0            1004    29.05.85    18:22:34
         DIR        S            7563    04.01.86    19:19:20
         DIR        PRG          1030    04.01.86    19:19:28
         CMDLOAD    BAS           958    04.01.86    19:19:32
         DIREC      0             212    29.05.85    17:34:06
         DISKTIME   BAK          4594    04.01.86    19:19:42
         SPOOL      BAS          2136    04.01.86    19:19:48
         RAMDISK    BAS          1962    04.01.86    19:19:54
         RAMDISK    PRG           449    04.01.86    19:20:02
         SPOOL      PRG           481    04.01.86    19:20:06
         CMDLOAD    S            1918    04.01.86    19:20:10
         DIREC      C             221    29.05.85    17:34:02
         DISKTIME   S            4608    29.05.85    18:10:34
         RAMDISK    S            5363    04.01.86    19:20:28
         SPOOL      S            7890    04.01.86    19:20:34
         DISKTIME   BAS          1998    29.05.85    18:26:18
         DISKTIME   PRG           448    29.05.85    18:26:54
```

Chapter 3

Hardcopy in color

3.1 ST hardcopy

One of the ST's most fascinating features is its great graphic capabilities. We don't have to tell you how crisp the hi-res mode is with the monochrome monitor. You can enjoy its graphics the minute you turn it on.

But there is one problem: how do we put these terrific images on paper? To be sure, there is as hardcopy routine in GEM. But this works only on a "normal" dot matrix printer. The various colors are shown as levels of grey. There is even a routine for a special color printer, but we never found out which one. Consequently, we wrote our own routine—and it's written so that it can be easily adapted to other printer models.

We also tried to get hardcopy on standard (color) plotters with a demo version of the drawing program GEMDRAW. We ran into problems with this, because we didn't know of a suitable hardcopy algorithm. But we solved this problem as well, as you'll see shortly.

We have also included a section on the layout of the graphics RAM. This layout will certainly prove useful when you implement your own graphics ideas.

The programs are all documented, so it won't be hard to modify them to suit your own needs. In addtion, we have listed both programs in BASIC, so even if you don't have an assembler you can still use the programs.

3.2   The screen display

The ST's screen display is memory mapped from video RAM. This is both a strength and weakness. 32K of video RAM is set aside for the screen display.

For graphics, the setup of video RAM is ideal. Points can be easily set and reset, thereby making graphics display extremely fast.

For text, the setup is less than ideal. To display a character, the character's image is copied pixel by pixel from the RAM-based font set directly to video RAM. This method is much slower than other hardware character generators, and the slow speed is especially noticeable during scrolling, when a large amount of memory must be moved. This would be unbearable if the 68000 wasn't so fast.

Obviously the ST is designed to optimize graphics at the expense of text. Let's talk more about the ST's graphics.

In high-resolution mode (640x400), the ST allows two colors: black and white. Figure 3.2-1 illustrates the relationship of video RAM to the screen display. Since there are only two colors in hi-res mode, one bit suffices to determine the color. Thus one bit in video RAM corresponds to one point on the screen. The high-order bit of the first word of video RAM corresponds to the upper left-hand point of the screen. Figure 3.2-2 is a hardcopy of this screen display mode.

In medium-resolution mode (640x200), the ST allows four colors. How is the color represented in video RAM? In this mode, two bits of video RAM correspond to one point on the display. The two bits represent the color of that point. Two bits can contain up to four different values: 0, 1, 2 and 3. As you can see from figure 3.2-3, the two bits are adjacent words in video RAM. So that the display appears full with a reduced number of vertical points, a point in medium resolution mode is stretched, so that a point is really a short vertical line.

Figure 3.2-1

High Resolution Mode (2)

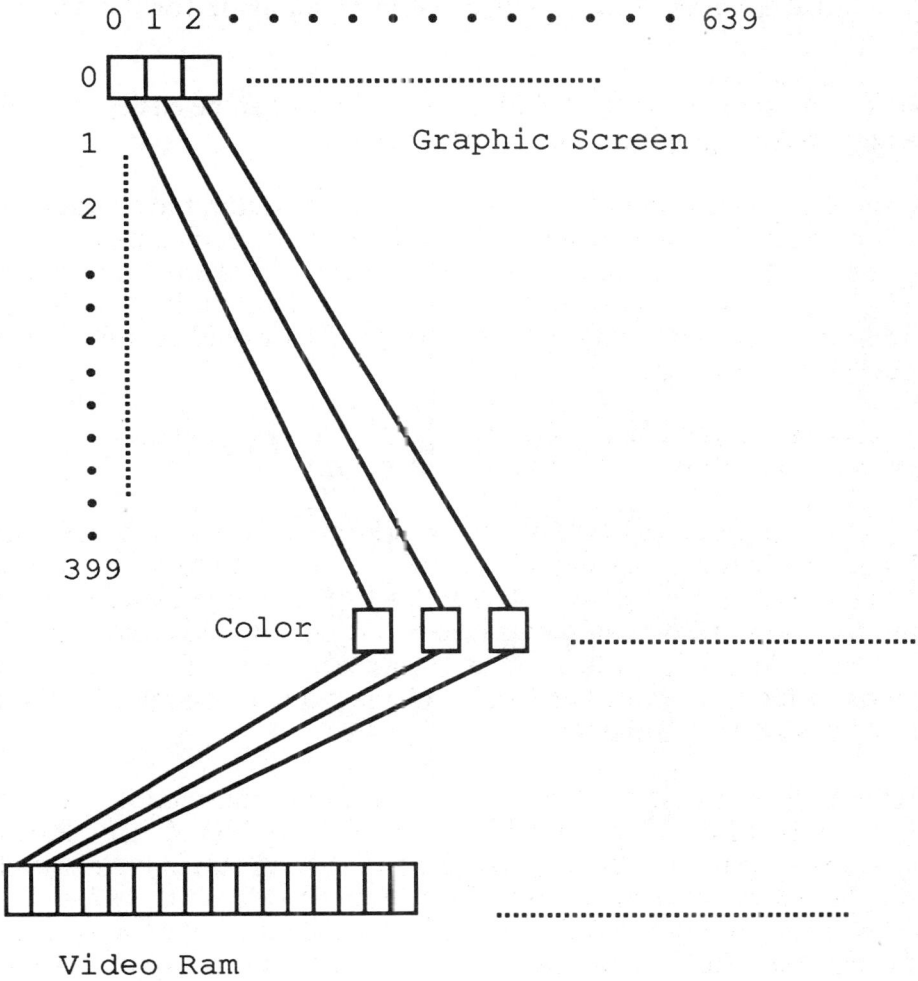

Figure 3.2-2

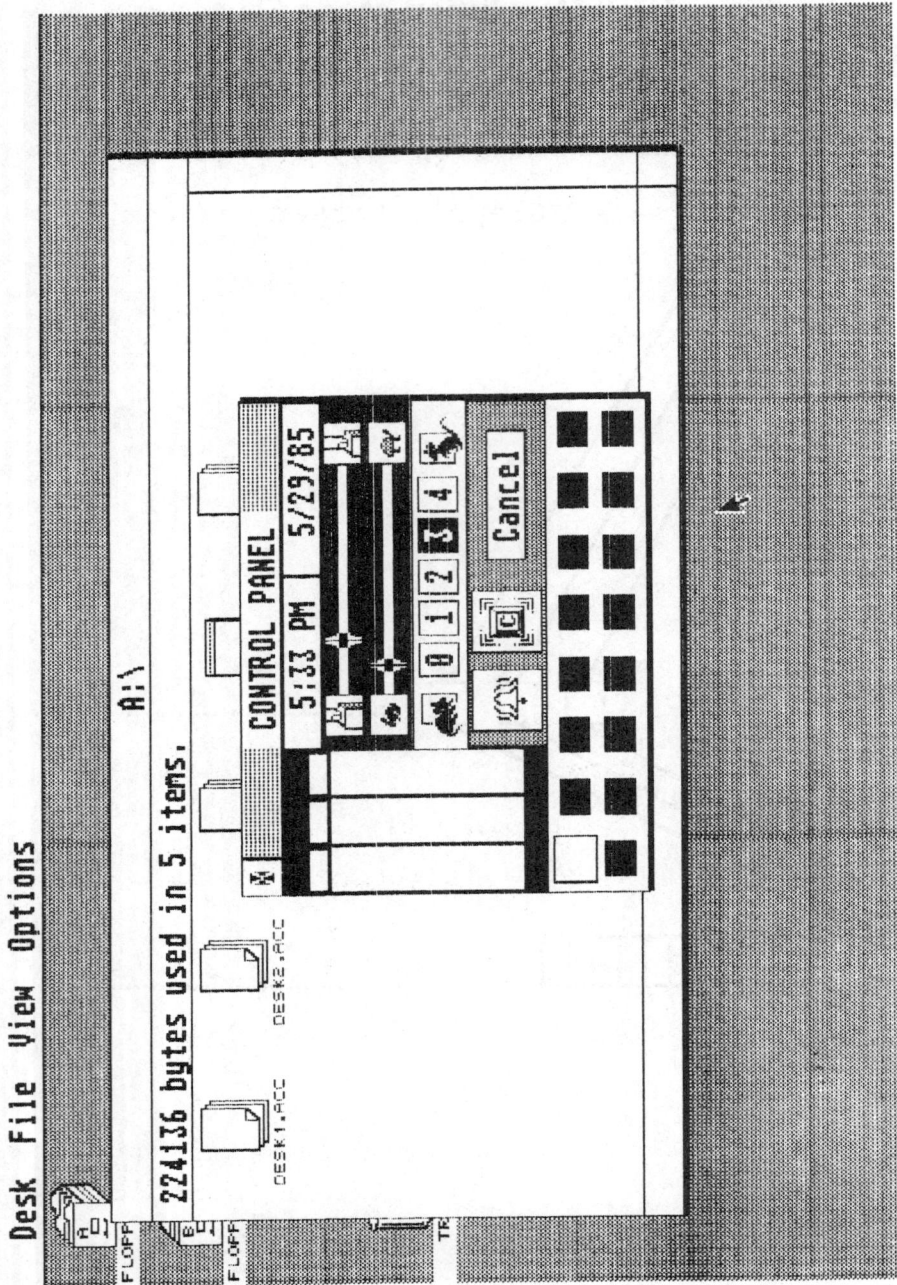

Figure 3.2-3

Medium Resolution Mode (1)

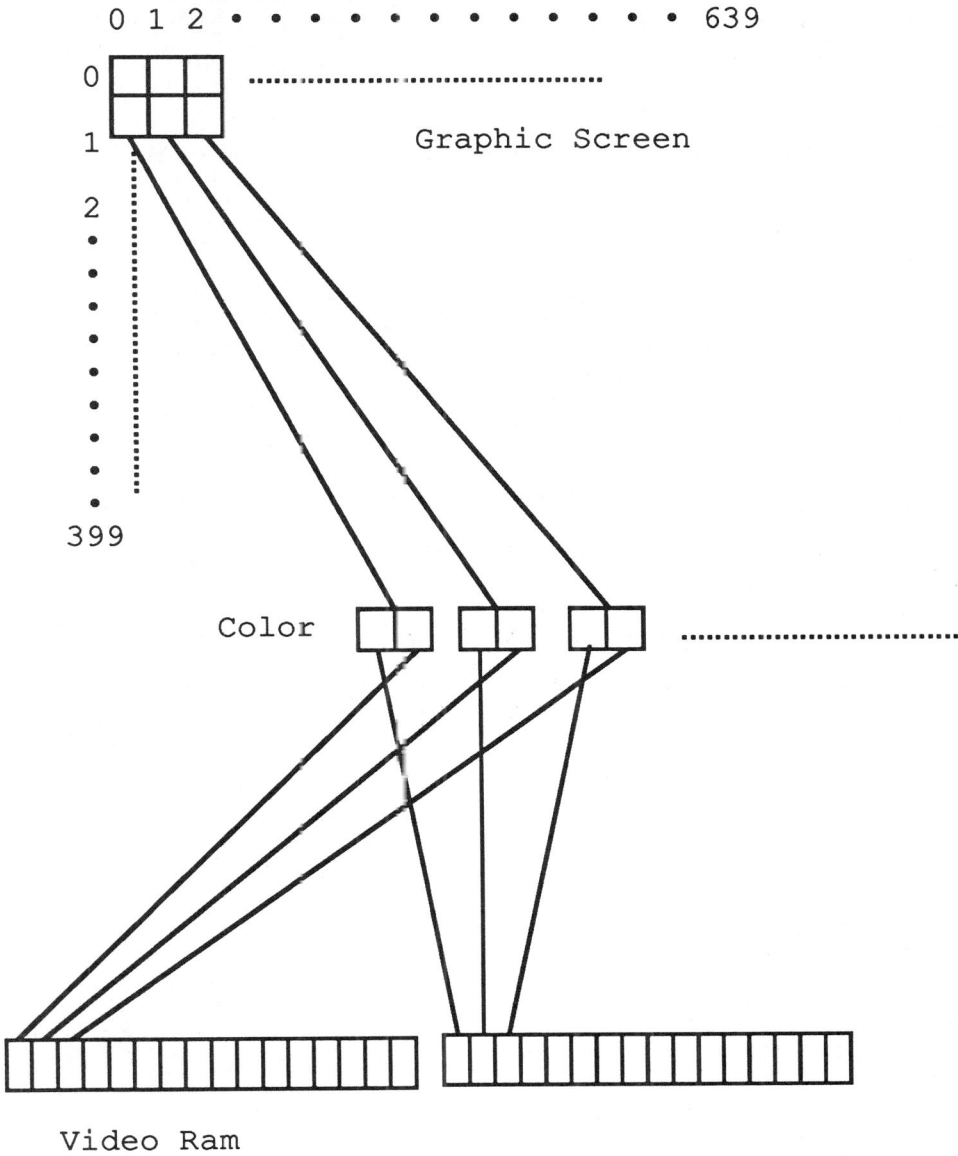

You can see the results of the stretched pixels in figure 3.2-4. The letters appear to be taller than in hi-res mode.

In low-resolution mode (320x200), the ST allows up to 16 colors. This is done similarly to the medium resolution mode, but four bits are are used to represent one "point" on the screen. Four bits can contain up to 16 different values, each one representing a different color. Figure 3.2-5 illustrates how four adjacent words are used to represent one point. A "point" is stretched horizontally and vertically.

You can see the results of the stretched pixels in lo-res mode in figure 3.2-6.

Figure 3.2-4

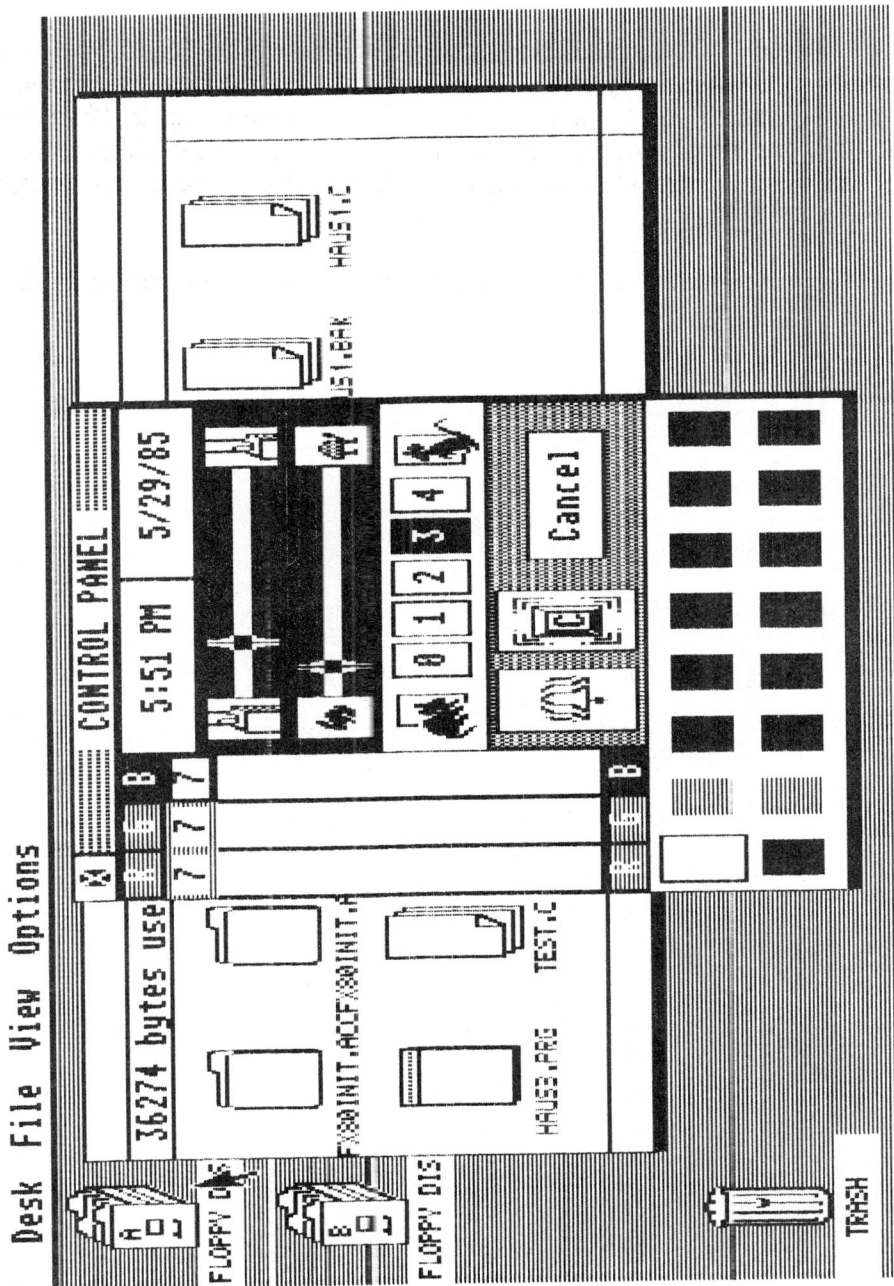

Figure 3.2-5

Low Resolution Mode (0)

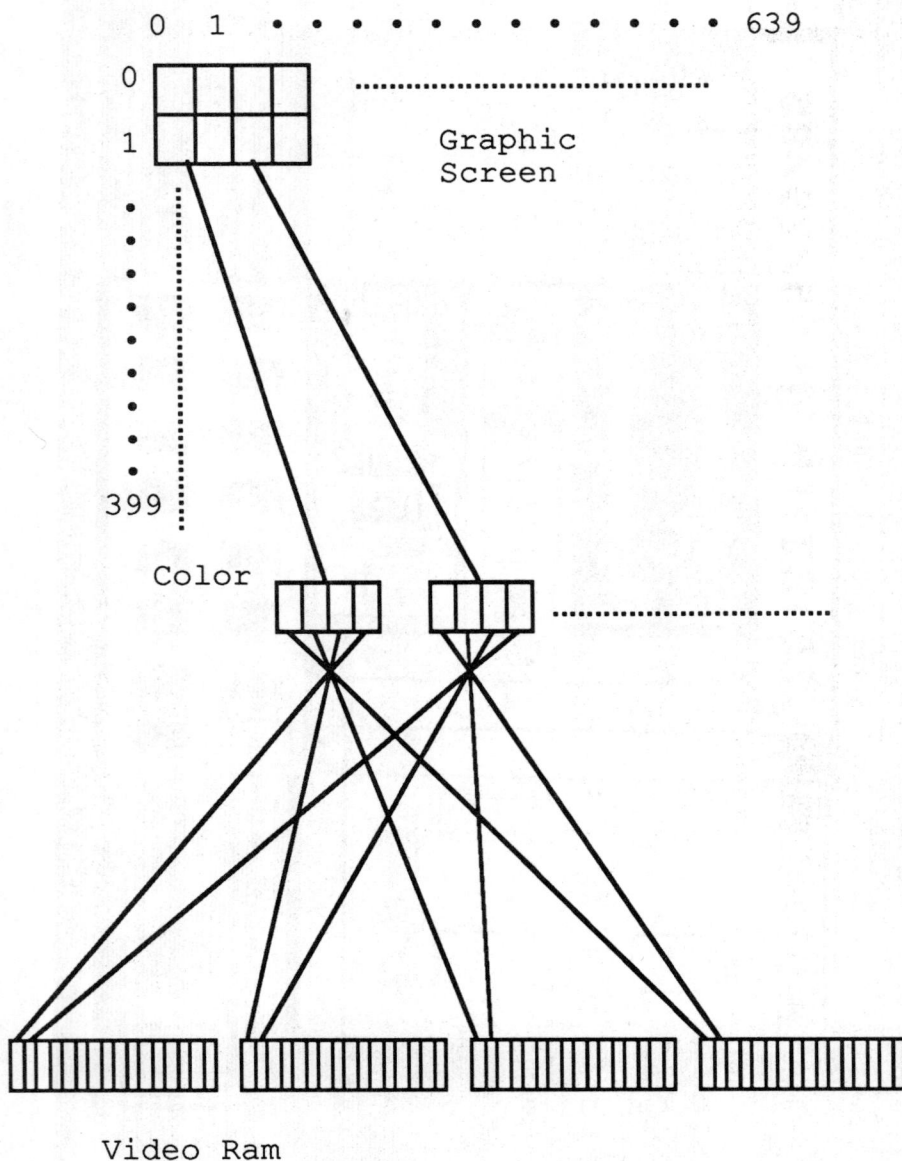

Figure 3.2-6

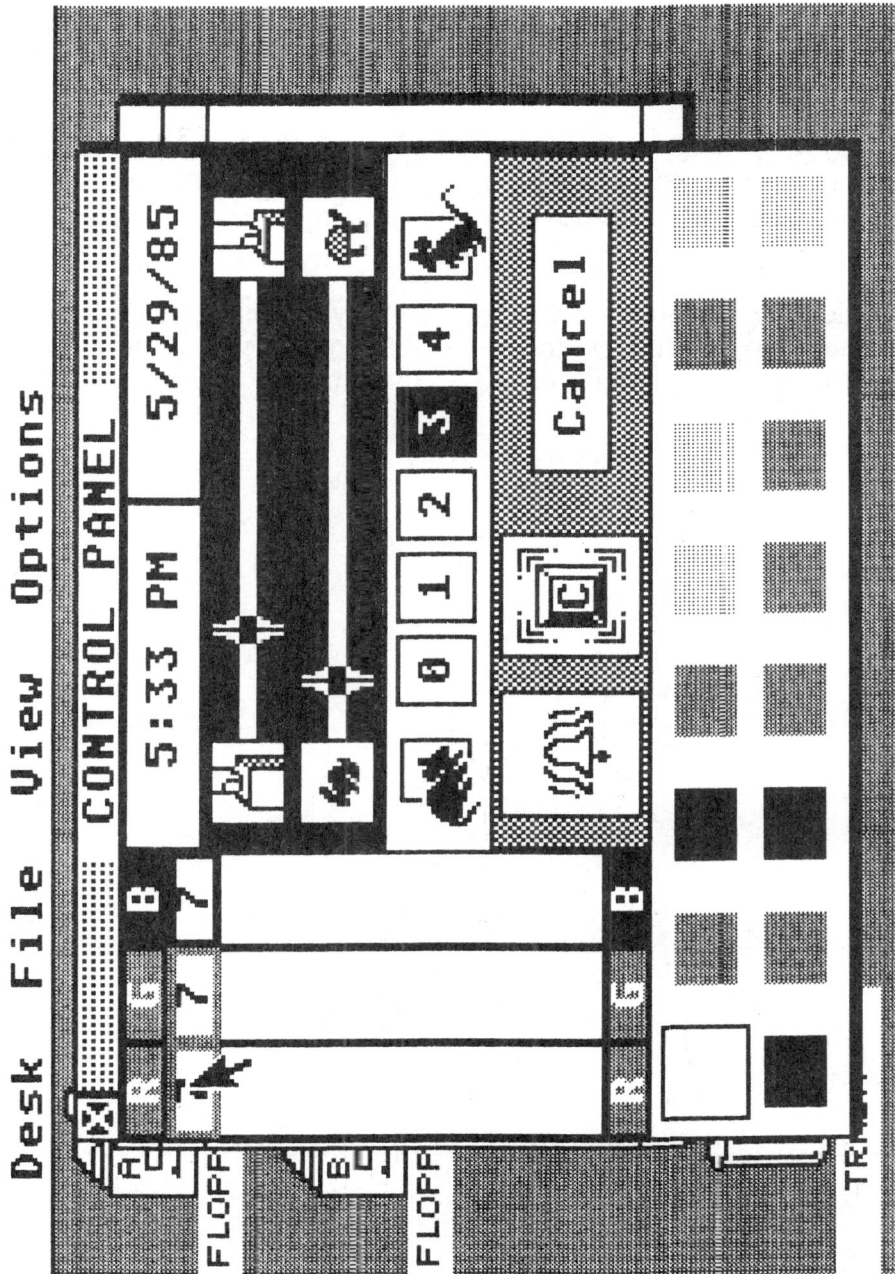

3.3 Color hardcopy programs

Next we have two programs for getting hardcopy. One produces hardcopy to a color dot-matrix printer, and the other to a plotter.

We've chosen to use common peripherals. We've used Epson devices because they are readily available and reasonably priced. These routines may be adapted for other devices by changing a few constants in the program.

Both hardcopy programs are designed so they can be started simply and easily. Each copies itself behind video RAM (where there are 768 bytes free) and remains there while the ST's power is on. Hardcopy is activated by <ALT> <HELP>.

3.3.1   Color dot-matrix printer hardcopy

This program was a difficult one for us to write.

First we had to decide how to represent the screen on paper. Without color, the screen appears dark while the paper is white. We decided to make light colors on the screen appear light on the paper as well. This may sometimes result in unsatisfactory pictures, as in Plate 4.

This version of the hardcopy works with an Epson JX-80, which is a color version of the popular FX-80. The JX-80 has a wide color ribbon. The three basic colors and black are organized in narrow bands on the ribbon. This yields seven colors that the printer can produce automatically. This program is limited to these seven colors.

To change the color, a motor moves the ribbon color in front of the printhead. Each screen line is scanned for a specific color and the appropriate pixels on the line are printed in this color.

Following is the assembly language listing for the color printer hardcopy:

```
*          Epson jx-80 hardcopy
*          org     $cba
gemdos   equ     1
xbios    equ     14
prchar   equ     5
sbase    equ     2
getres   equ     4
aff      equ     -2        no. colors
afc      equ     -4        color counter
pwf      equ     -6        words/pixel
hmf      equ     -8        hor multipl
vmf      equ     -10       vert multipl
zbl      equ     -14       base line
zwf      equ     -16       no. words/line
zwc      equ     -18       no. words counter
znf      equ     -20       no. points/line
znc      equ     -22       no. points counter
baf      equ     -24       vert status
zzc      equ     -26       line counter
zol      equ     -30       line offset
ab       equ     -31       even bits found
fl       equ     -32       div flags
*          bit     0         bit of corresponding color found
*          bit     1         0=test / 1=print
ctf      equ     -48       color table
maf      equ     -64       mask  no.
pflag    equ     $4ee      flag alt/help
super    equ     32        supervisor mode
stcol    equ     7         setcolor


dummy    lea     dummy,a0          dummy for dumb loader
         clr.l   -(a7)
         move.w  #super,-(a7)
         trap    #gemdos
         addq.l  #6,a7
         move.l  d0,d6
         move.w  #sbase,-(a7)
         trap    #xbios
         addq.l  #2,a7
         movea.l d0,a0
         adda.w  #$7d00,a0
         lea     (a0),a2
         lea     start(pc),a1
```

```
            move.l   #fin-start-1,d0
reloc       move.b   (a1)+,(a0)+
            dbra     d0,reloc

            movea.l  $456,a0
            adda     #28,a0
            move.l   a2,(a0)
            move.l   d6,-(a7)
            move.w   #super,-(a7)
            trap     #gemdos
            addq.l   #6,a7
*           rts                      in case basic is called
            clr.l    -(a7)
            trap     #gemdos
start:
            tst      pflag           want hardcopy?
            beq      st0             yes--
            rts
```

```
*****************************************************************
*                                                               *
*       parameter initialization                                *
*                                                               *
*****************************************************************
```

```
st0         link     a6,#-66         ceate room for working space

            move.w   #sbase,-(a7)    get physical
            trap     #xbios          screen base
            addq.l   #2,a7
            move.l   d0,zbl(a6)
            move.w   #getres,-(a7)
            trap     #xbios
            addq.l   #2,a7
            lsl.w    #1,d0
            move.w   d0,(a6)
            lea      aft(pc),a1
            move.w   0(a1,d0.w),aff(a6)
            moveq    #1,d7           if high-res, prepare color no.
```

```
              moveq    #8,d0              and mask no.
              move.b   #7,ctf(a6)
              clr.b    ctf+1(a6)
              cmpi.w   #1,aff(a6)         hi-res ?
              beq      st52               yes
              move.w   aff(a6),d7
st1           move.w   #-1,-(a7)
              move.w   d7,-(a7)
              move.w   #stcol,-(a7)
              trap     #xbios             color to d0
              addq.l   #6,a7
              clr.w    d4
              clr.b    maf(a6,d7.w)
              move.w   d0,d1
              moveq    #2,d5
              lsl.w    #4,d1
st10          lsr.b    #4,d1
              or.b     d1,d4              hue > d4
              lsr.w    #4,d1
              dbra     d5,st10

              move.b   d4,maf(a6,d7.w)
              cmpi.b   #1,d4              black intensity under
*                                        stepped?
              bls      st22               yes--
              moveq    #2,d6
              move     #$444,d5           load mask
st11          move     d5,d3
              and      d0,d3              look for highest bit
              bne      st12               found >
              lsr      #1,d5              mask set below
              dbra     d6,st11

st12          moveq    #2,d4
              clr.w    d5
st2           andi     #$7ff,d3           determine color (to d5)
              cmpi.w   #$ff,d3
              bls      st21
              bset.l   d4,d5
st21          lsl.w    #4,d3
              dbra     d4,st2

              cmpi.b   #7,d5              white?
```

```
          bne      st5              no--
          cmpi.b   #5,maf(a5,d7)    pure white?
          bhi      st5              yes--
          addq.b   #2,maf(a5,d7)    thin out mask and
st22      clr      d5               set black
st5       move.b   d5,ctf(a5,d7.w)
          cmpi.b   #6,d5            yellow?
          bne      st50             no--
          subq.b   #2,maf(a5,d7)    widen mask
st50      dbra     d7,st1

          moveq    #15,d7
st51      moveq    #8,d0
          cmpi.b   #3,maf(a6,d7)    brightness > lowest
*                                   intensity?
          bls      st52             no--
          lsr      #1,d0
          cmpi.b   #6,maf(a6,d7.w)  brightness > highest
*                                   intensity?
          bls      st52             no--
          clr      d0
st52      move.b   d0,maf(a6,d7.w)
          dbra     d7,st51

          move.w   (a6),d0
          lea      pwt(pc),a1
          move.w   0(a1,d0.w),pwf(a6)
          lea      hmt(pc),a1
          move.w   0(a1,d0.w),hmf(a6)
          lea      vmt(pc),a1
          move.w   0(a1,d0.w),vmf(a6)
          lea      zwt(pc),a1
          move.w   0(a1,d0.w),zwf(a6)
          lea      znt(pc),a1
          move.w   0(a1,d0.w),znf(a6)
          lea      bat(pc),a1
          move.w   0(a1,d0.w),baf(a6)
          move.w   #50,zzc(a6)
          clr.b    fl(a6)
          bra      nl0
```

```
***************************************************************
*                                                             *
*       next line                                             *
*                                                             *
***************************************************************


nl:
        subq.w  #1,zzc(a6)          line counter run through?
        beq     exit                yes--
        move.l  zbl(a6),d7          line basis
        addi.l  #640,d7             to increment
        move.l  d7,zbl(a6)          a line
nl0     lea     lftab(pc),a5        linefeed
        moveq   #4,d7               on
        bsr     lf                  printer
        move.w  aff(a6),afc(a6)     color counter
        movea.l zbl(a6),a3          line basis
        bra     sl0


***************************************************************
*                                                             *
*       next color                                            *
*                                                             *
***************************************************************


sl:
        tst.w   pflag               hardcopy break?
        bne     exit                yes--
        subq.w  #1,afc(a6)          color counter done running?
        bmi     nl                  yes-- new line
        bra     sl0
sl100   bchg.b  #1,fl(a6)           last run just a test ?
        bne     sl                  no-- it was printed
        btst.b  #0,fl(a6)           point in the line  found?
        beq     sl100               no--
        lea     ctf(a6),a1
        adda.w  afc(a6),a1
        clr.w   d6
        move.b  (a1),d6
        cmpi.b  #7,d6               white?
        beq     sl100               yes-- don't print it
```

```
           lea      pre1(pc),a5        color change
           moveq    #3,d7              on
           bsr      1f                 printer
           lea      ct(pc),a1
           move.b   0(a1,d6.w),d0
           bsr      chout
           lea      pre2(pc),a5
           moveq    #5,d7
           bsr      1f
sl0        move.w   zwf(a6),zwc(a6)    no. of words/line
           bclr.b   #0,fl(a6)
           lea      0,a4
           move.w   afc(a6),d7         color number sought
           clr.w    d0
           move.b   maf(a6,d7.w),d0    load mask
           lea      mask(pc),a0
           move.l   0(a0,d0.w),d2
           bra      sw0
```

```
*****************************************************************
*                                                             *
*       next word                                             *
*                                                             *
*****************************************************************
```

```
sw:
           subq.w   #1,zwc(a6)         word counter run?
           beq      sl00               yes--
           movea.l  zol(a6),a4         line offset
           adda.w   pwf(a6),a4         words/pixel
           adda.w   pwf(a6),a4         *2
sw0        move.w   #$8000,d5          bitmask for test
           move.l   a4,zol(a6)         save line offset
           bra      sb0
```

```
*****************************************************************
*                                                             *
*       next bit                                              *
*                                                             *
*****************************************************************
```

```
sb:
           lsr.w    #1,d5              all bits in word ready?
```

```
          beq      sw                    yes--
sb0       move.w   znf(a6),znc(a6)      no. of pins/line
          clr.b    d4
          movea.l  zol(a6),a4
          bra      tb
```

```
***************************************************************
*                                                             *
*          next pin                                           *
*                                                             *
***************************************************************
```

```
bs:
          clr.l    d7
          move.w   vmf(a6),d7           vertical multiplier
          subq     #1,d7
bs0       lsl.b    #1,d4
          or.b     ab(a6),d4
          dbra     d7,bs0
          adda.w   baf(a6),a4           vertical condition of points
          subq.w   #1,znc(a6)           pin counter run?
          bne      tb                   no-- test points
          tst.b    d4                   a point given?
          beq      bs00                 no--
          bset.b   #0,fl(a6)
bs00      btst.b   #1,fl(a6)            should it be printed?
          beq      sb                   no--
          clr.l    d7
          move.w   hmf(a6),d7           horizontal multiplier
          subq     #1,d7
bs1       move.b   d4,d0
          and.b    d2,d0                byte masked
          bsr      chout                and output
          ror.l    #8,d2                rotate raster mask
          dbra     d7,bs1
          bra      sb
```

```
***************************************************************
*                                                             *
*          test bit                                           *
*                                                             *
***************************************************************
```

```
tb:
          clr.w    d3
          clr.l    d6
          move.w   pwf(a6),d6        words/pixel
          move.w   d6,d0
          lsl.w    #1,d0             next word
          subq.b   #1,d6
          lea      0(a3,a4),a0
          lea      0(a0,d0.w),a5
tb1       lsl.b    #1,d3             bits collected for color
*                                    number
          subq.l   #2,a5
          move.w   (a5),d7
          and.w    d5,d7             bit set?
          beq      tb2              no--
          bset.l   #0,d3
tb2       dbra     d6,tb1
          clr.b    ab(a6)
          cmp.w    afc(a6),d3       color number being sought?
          bne      tb3              no--
          bset.b   #0,ab(a6)        point marked as found
tb3       bra      bs


****************************************************************
*                                                              *
*         output                                               *
*                                                              *
****************************************************************


exit:
          unlk     a6               free up workspace

          move.w   #-1,pflag        hardcopy ready
          rts


****************************************************************
*                                                              *
*         string on (a5) output with counter in d7            *
*                                                              *
****************************************************************


lf:
          andi.l   #$ffff,d7
```

123

```
        subq    #1,d7
lf0     move.b  0(a5,d7),d0
        bsr     chout
        dbra    d7,lf0
        rts
```

```
****************************************************************
*                                                              *
*       character in d0 to printer                             *
*                                                              *
****************************************************************
```

```
chout:
        move.w  d0,-(a7)
        move.w  #prchar,-(a7)
        trap    #gemdos
        addq.l  #4,a7
        rts
```

```
****************************************************************
*                                                              *
*       constants                                              *
*                                                              *
****************************************************************
```

```
aft     dc.w    15,3,1              no. of colors
pwt     dc.w    4,2,1               words belonging to a pixel
hmt     dc.w    2,1,1               horizontal doubling
vmt     dc.w    2,2,1               vertical doubling
zwt     dc.w    20,40,40            words/line
znt     dc.w    4,4,8               pins/line
bat     dc.w    160,160,80          vertical state of lines
mask    dc.l    $44001100           color dimming
        dc.l    $aa55aa55           averaging out from
        dc.l    -1                  full
ct      dc.b    0,2,6,2,1,3,4,0     printer color
lftab   dc.b    24,"J",27,13        linefeed 8 pins
pre1    dc.b    "r",27,13           color choice
pre2    dc.b    2,128,4,"*",27      graphic mode & point counter
fin     equ     *
        .end
```

The data in the last 6 lines can be changed to adapt the program to other printers. Here you can enter the printer-specific control codes. Note that the control sequences are arranged in reverse order.

If you do not have an assembler but still want to make changes "by hand" in the BASIC program, make sure that the length and position of the strings don't change. If this happens, you'll have to change the reference addresses.

The machine language program for loading from BASIC differs slightly from the assembler version. Since the program is called with CALL, it must be terminated with RTS and not with TERM via GEMDOS.

```
5       rem BASIC loader for Epson JX-80 hardcopy
10      dim a%(415)
20      for i=0 to 415
30      read a%(i)
40      next i
50      b=varptr(a%(0))
60      call b
70      end
950     data &H42A7,&H3F3C,&H0020
960     data &H4E41,&H5C8F,&H2C00,&H3F3C,&H0002,&H4E4E,&H548F,&H2040
970     data &HD0FC,&H7D00,&H45D0,&H43FA,&H0028,&H203C,&H0000,&H02F9
980     data &H10D9,&H51C8,&HFFFC,&H2079,&H0000,&H0456,&HD0FC,&H001C
990     data &H208A,&H2F06,&H3F3C,&H0020,&H4E41,&H5C8F,&H4E75,&H4E41
1000    data &H4A79,&H0000,&H04EE,&H6702,&H4E75,&H4E56,&HFFBE,&H3F3C
1010    data &H0002,&H4E4E,&H548F,&H2D40,&HFFF2,&H3F3C,&H0004,&H4E4E
1020    data &H548F,&HE348,&H3C80,&H43FA,&H0288,&H3D71,&H0000,&HFFFE
1030    data &H7E01,&H7008,&H1D7C,&H0007,&HFFD0,&H422E,&HFFD1,&H0C6E
1040    data &H0001,&HFFFE,&H6700,&H009A,&H3E2E,&HFFFE,&H3F3C,&HFFFF
1050    data &H3F07,&H3F3C,&H0007,&H4E4E,&H5C8F,&H4244,&H4236,&H70C0
1060    data &H3200,&H7A02,&HE949,&HE809,&H8801,&HE849,&H51CD,&HFFF8
1070    data &H1D84,&H70C0,&H0C04,&H0001,&H633A,&H7C02,&H3A3C,&H0444
1080    data &H3605,&HC640,&H6606,&HE24D,&H51CE,&HFFF6,&H7802,&H4245
1090    data &H0243,&H07FF,&H0C43,&H00FF,&H6302,&H09C5,&HE94B,&H51CC
1100    data &HFFF0,&H0C05,&H0007,&H660E,&H0C36,&H0005,&H70C0,&H6206
1110    data &H5436,&H70C0,&H4245,&H1D85,&H70D0,&H0C05,&H0006,&H6604
1120    data &H5536,&H70C0,&H510F,&HFF86,&H7E0F,&H7008,&H0C36,&H0003
1130    data &H70C0,&H630C,&HE248,&H0C36,&H0006,&H70C0,&H6302,&H4240
1140    data &H1D80,&H70C0,&H510F,&HFFE4,&H3016,&H43FA,&H01CA,&H3D71
1150    data &H0000,&HFFFA,&H43FA,&H01C6,&H3D71,&H0000,&HFFF8,&H43FA
1160    data &H01C2,&H3D71,&H0000,&HFFF6,&H43FA,&H01BE,&H3D71,&H0000
1170    data &HFFF0,&H43FA,&H01BA,&H3D71,&H0000,&HFFEC,&H43FA,&H01B6
1180    data &H3D71,&H0000,&HFFE8,&H3D7C,&H0032,&HFFE6,&H422E,&HFFE0
1190    data &H6016,&H536E,&HFFE6,&H6700,&H014C,&H2E2E,&HFFF2,&H0687
```

125

```
1200    data &H0000,&H0280,&H2D47,&HFFF2,&H4BFA,&H01A4,&H7E04,&H6100
1210    data &H0140,&H3D6E,&HFFFE,&HFFFC,&H266E,&HFFF2,&H6054,&H4A79
1220    data &H0000,&H04EE,&H6600,&H011E,&H536E,&HFFFC,&H6BC4,&H6042
1230    data &H086E,&H0001,&HFFE0,&H66E6,&H082E,&H0000,&HFFE0,&H67F0
1240    data &H43EE,&HFFD0,&HD2EE,&HFFFC,&H4246,&H1C11,&H0C06,&H0007
1250    data &H67DE,&H4BFA,&H015E,&H7E03,&H6100,&H00F6,&H43FA,&H0148
1260    data &H1031,&H6000,&H6100,&H00FE,&H4BFA,&H014B,&H7E05,&H6100
1270    data &H00E0,&H3D6E,&HFFF0,&HFFEE,&H08AE,&H0000,&HFFE0,&H49F9
1280    data &H0000,&H0000,&H3E2E,&HFFFC,&H4240,&H1036,&H70C0,&H41FA
1290    data &H010A,&H2430,&H0000,&H6012,&H536E,&HFFEE,&H6792,&H286E
1300    data &HFFE2,&HD8EE,&HFFFA,&HD8EE,&HFFFA,&H3A3C,&H8000,&H2D4C
1310    data &HFFE2,&H6004,&HE24D,&H67E0,&H3D6E,&HFFEC,&HFFEA,&H4204
1320    data &H286E,&HFFE2,&H6044,&H4287,&H3E2E,&HFFF6,&H5347,&HE30C
1330    data &H882E,&HFFE1,&H51CF,&HFFF8,&HD8EE,&HFFE8,&H536E,&HFFEA
1340    data &H6628,&H4A04,&H6706,&H08EE,&H0000,&HFFE0,&H082E,&H0001
1350    data &HFFE0,&H67C0,&H4287,&H3E2E,&HFFF8,&H5347,&H1004,&HC002
1360    data &H6162,&HE09A,&H51CF,&HFFF6,&H60AA,&H4243,&H4286,&H3C2E
1370    data &HFFFA,&H3006,&HE348,&H5306,&H41F3,&HC000,&H4BF0,&H0000
1380    data &HE30B,&H558D,&H3E15,&HCE45,&H6704,&H08C3,&H0000,&H51CE
1390    data &HFFF0,&H422E,&HFFE1,&HB66E,&HFFFC,&H6606,&H08EE,&H0000
1400    data &HFFE1,&H6082,&H4E5E,&H33FC,&HFFFF,&H0000,&H04EE,&H4E75
1410    data &H0287,&H0000,&HFFFF,&H5347,&H1035,&H7000,&H6106,&H51CF
1420    data &HFFF8,&H4E75,&H3F00,&H3F3C,&H0005,&H4E41,&H588F,&H4E75
1430    data &H000F,&H0003,&H0001,&H0004,&H0002,&H0001,&H0002,&H0001
1440    data &H0001,&H0002,&H0002,&H0001,&H0014,&H0028,&H0028,&H0004
1450    data &H0004,&H0008,&H00A0,&H00A0,&H0050,&H4400,&H1100,&HAA55
1460    data &HAA55,&HFFFF,&HFFFF,&H0002,&H0602,&H0103,&H0400,&H184A
1470    data &H1B0D,&H721B,&H0D02,&H8004,&H2A1B
```

3.3.2 Color plotter hardcopy

Hardcopy to a plotter is quite different than hardcopy to a dot-matrix printer.

While it's possible to draw point by point with the dot-matrix printer, the method is really not practical with a plotter. By nature of its construction, a plotter is suited to drawing lines. How do we write a program to make the plotter draw actual lines, rather than a series of points?

We can distinguish a line on the screen because of our familiarity with them as geometric forms. But a program recognizes a line only as a set of points. The programming objective is to make the computer recognize points that belong together, and then draw them as a curve or line.

Our program uses the following method to accomplish this "point-to-line" conversion:

When a point is found, we lower the pen and then turn a quarter of a rotation to the left (in screen memory) to see if a point is set there. If not, we rotate right (in screen memory) in eigths of a step to search for points in these directions. If we find a point, we move the pen to it, and start the procedure all over again. This continues until there is no bordering point is found at the current location.

This complex-sounding procedure has the effect that all the contours of larger objects are traced. This is important for the appearance of the finished picture. You can clearly see this effect in the unfinished picture of figure 3.3.2-2.

This procedure has a disadvantage. After a point is found, it is removed from the screen, so that in later searches it is no longer recognized. Consequently, this procedure destroys the screen image. But it allows you to follow the program's progress on the screen.

Figure 3.3.2-1

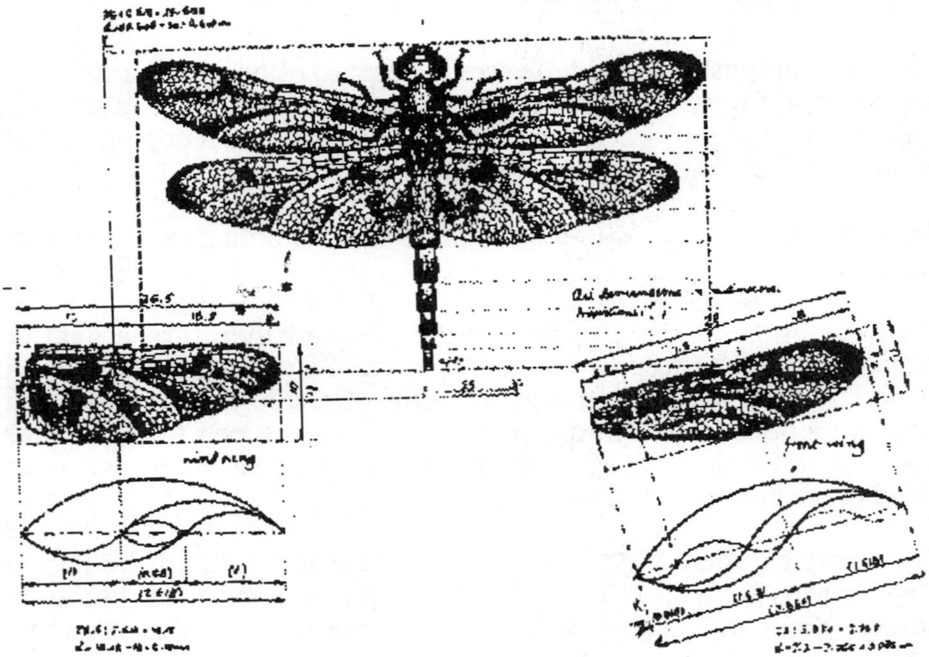

Figure 3.3.2-2

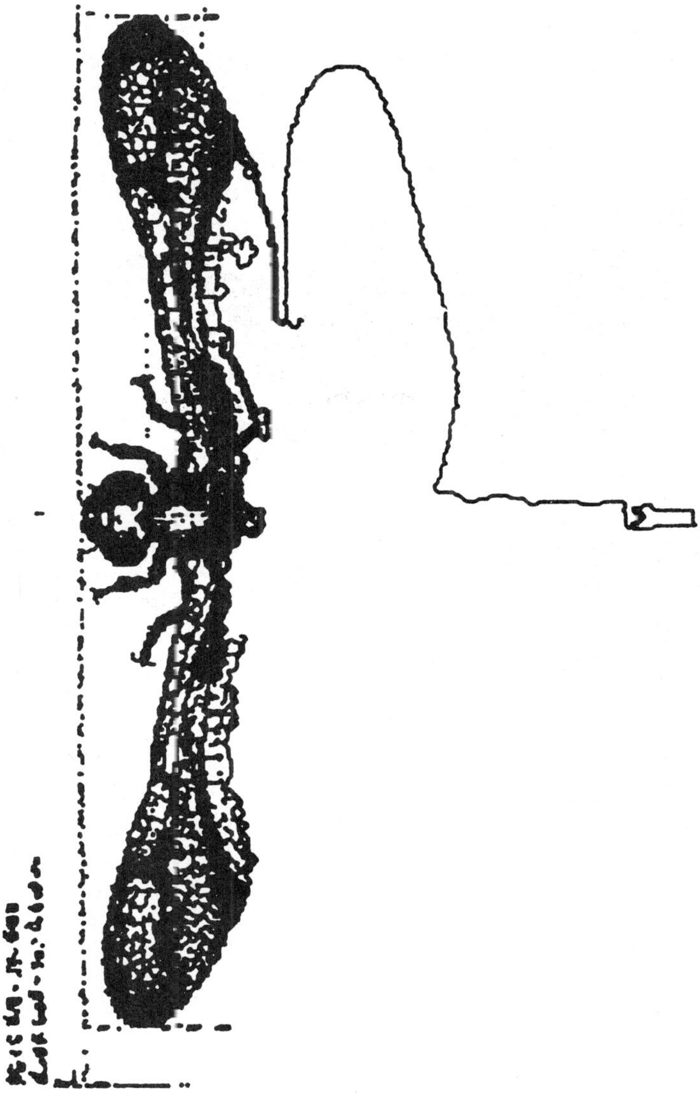

When the hardcopy is completed, the screen is completely white. Therefore, make sure that your picture is saved, otherwise it will be destroyed.

The program is designed for the Epson HI-80 plotter. You can easily adapt it for other plotters, since the command language is completely parameterized.

The operation of the program takes longer than for the dot-matrix printer hardcopy. To allow for change of pens, for more than four colors, the plotter stops at the next color change after you press <ALT> <HELP> keys. Once you've changed the pens, press <ALT> <HELP> again to continue.

You can stop the current color output by pressing <ALT> <HELP> three times.

Figure 3.3.2-3, dot-matrix hardcopy, and figure 3.3.2-4, plotter hardcopy, show the difference in results. Notice that diagonal lines are smoother on the plotter hardcopy.

The assembly language listing follows.

Figures 3.3.2-3

Figures 3.3.2-4

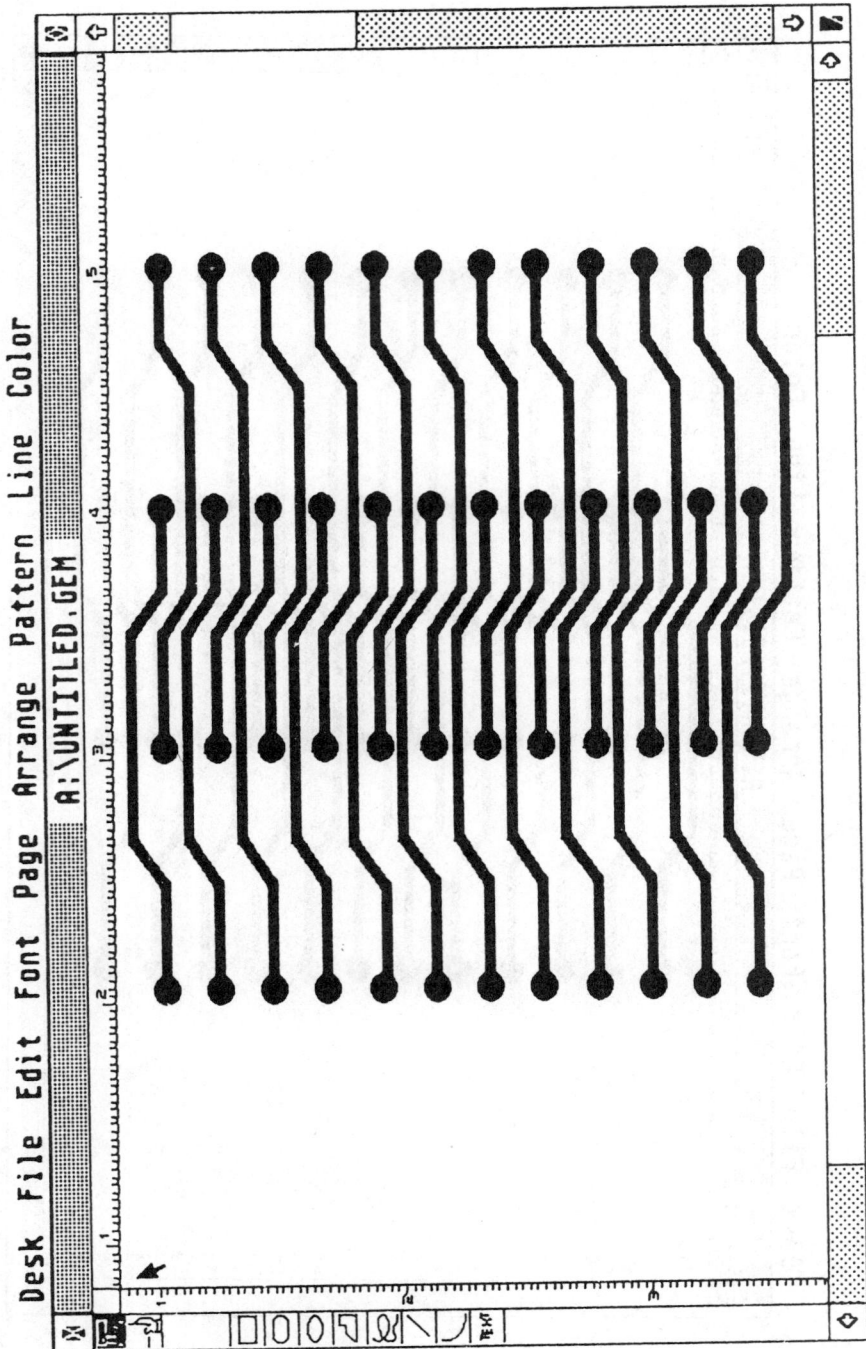

```
*          Epson HI-80 plotter hardcopy
*          org       $cba
gemdos    equ       1
bios      equ       13
xbios     equ       14
bconout   equ       3
prt       equ       0
phybas    equ       2
setscr    equ       5
super     equ       32
intin     equ       8
ptsin     equ       12
wrmod     equ       36
init      equ       $a000
setpix    equ       $a001
getpix    equ       $a002
yko       equ       2
pflag     equ       $4ee           flag alt/help
apix      equ       -4             total no. of pixels
pscalx    equ       -6             factor x
pscaly    equ       -8             factor y
adir      equ       -10            precise direction
pdir      equ       -12            orig. direction
maxx      equ       -14            number of x pixels
maxy      equ       -16            number of y pixels
ccol      equ       -18            precise color number
acol      equ       -20            number of colors
comma     equ       -22            comma w/ draw



****************************************************************
*                                                              *
*          program moves behind video ram                      *
*                                                              *
****************************************************************


dummy     lea       dummy,a0       dummy for dumb loader
          clr.l     -(a7)          set up
          move.w    #super,-(a7)   a privileged
          trap      #gemdos        regis-
          addq.l    #6,a7          ter
          move.l    d0,d6
          move.w    #phybas,-(a7)  program start
```

133

```
                trap      #xbios          is                    ⸮
                addq.l    #2,a7           video-basis
                movea.l   d0,a0           +
                adda.w    #$7d00,a0       length of
                lea       (a0),a2         video-ram
                lea       start(pc),a1
                move.l    #fin-start-1,d0 load counter
reloc           move.b    (a1)+,(a0)+     move
                dbra      d0,reloc        program

                movea.l   $456,a0         program hooks up
                adda      #28,a0          to the
                move.l    a2,(a0)         vblank-queue
                move.l    d6,-(a7)        priv.-
                move      #super,-(a7)    status
                trap      #gemdos         re-
                addq.l    #6,a7           turns
*               rts                       if called from basic
                clr       -(a7)
                trap      #gemdos         terminate
start:
                tst       pflag           hardcopy desired?
                beq       param           yes--
                rts



****************************************************************
*                                                              *
*          parameter initialization                           *
*                                                              *
****************************************************************


param           move      #phybas,-(a7)   get physical
                trap      #xbios          screen
                addq.l    #2,a7           basis
                move      #-1,-(a7)       and
                move.l    d0,-(a7)        match
                move.l    d0,-(a7)        with
                move      #setscr,-(a7)   logical
                trap      #xbios          basis
                adda.l    #12,a7
                dc.w      init            get screen parameters
                link      a6,#-24         make room for work register
```

```
          movea.l  intin(a0),a3
          movea.l  ptsin(a0),a4
          clr      wrmod(a0)        set write mode
          move     (a0),d7          no. of planes
          andi     #6,d7
          lea      scalx(pc),a0
          move     0(a0,d7),pscalx(a6)
          lea      scaly(pc),a0
          move     0(a0,d7),pscaly(a6)
          lea      max(pc),a0
          move     0(a0,d7),maxx(a6)
          lea      may(pc),a0
          move     0(a0,d7),maxy(a6)
          lea      colc(pc),a0
          move     0(a0,d7),acol(a6)
          move     maxx(a6),d6
          mulu     maxy(a6),d6
          move.l   d6,apix(a6)
          move     #1,ccol(a6)      color no. 1
init1     cmpi     #1,pflag         stop for color choice?
          bne      init3            no--
          bsr      caps
init2     cmpi     #2,pflag         go on?
          bne      init2            no--
          clr      pflag
init3     bsr      setcol           color choice
          bsr      home             plotter in output state
          pea      -1               search begins at upper left


*******************************************************
*                                                     *
*      look for first pixel in a line                 *
*                                                     *
*******************************************************

srch  move.l   (a7)+,d7
      addq.l   #1,d7
      cmp.l    apix(a6),d7      all pixels viewed?
      beq      exit             yes--
      move.l   d7,-(a7)         save current position
      bsr      chkpix           look for next point
```

```
            cmp     ccol(a6),d0      looked for color?
            bne     srch             no--
            move    #3,adir(a6)      search direction is right


*****************************************************************
*                                                               *
*           draw connected points                               *
*                                                               *
*****************************************************************

plot        bsr     mov              plotter to new position
            bsr     pendwn           pen down
            bsr     erase            clear point found
plot1       clr     d0
            bsr     nexpix           look for a connected point

            tst     d0               past color found?
            bne     plot2            yes--
            bsr     outcr            delimiter output
            bsr     penup            pen up
            bra     srch
plot2       bsr     draw             lines to next point
            bsr     erase            clear point drawn
            bra     plot1            look for next point


*****************************************************************
*                                                               *
*           look for next connected point                       *
*                                                               *
*****************************************************************

nexpix      subq    #2,adir(a6)      1/4-turn left
            andi    #7,adir(a6)      0-7 only allowed
            move    adir(a6),pdir(a6) mark output direction
            bra     nex3
nex1        movem   (a7)+,d3-d4      get old coordinates
            addq    #1,adir(a6)      1/8-turn right
            andi    #7,adir(a6)      only 0-7 allowed
            move    pdir(a6),d7
            cmp     adir(a6),d7      output point again?
            bne     nex3             no--
```

```
          clr      d0
          rts
nex3      move     adir(a6),d7         jump
          lsl      #1,d7               dependent upon
          lea      j(pc),a0            direction
          adda     0(a0,d7),a0         save previous
          movem    d3-d4,-(a7)         coordinates
          jsr      (a0)                jump
          cmp      ccol(a6),d0         past colors found?
          bne      nex1                no-look in another direction

          addq.l   #4,a7               correct stack
          rts                          connect the dots



**************************************************************
*                                                            *
*          direction-dependent jumps                         *
*                                                            *
**************************************************************


j         dc.w     re-j,ru-j,un-j,lu-j,li-j,lo-j,ob-j,ro-j

re        addq     #1,d3               right
          cmp      maxx(a6),d3         reached end-of-line?
          bcs      askpix              no--
          rts

ru        addq     #1,d3               lower right
          cmp      maxx(a6),d3         end-of-line?
          bcs      un                  no--
          rts

un        addq     #1,d4               bottom
          cmp      maxy(a6),d4         end-of-screen?
          bcs      askpix              no--
          rts

lu        addq     #1,d4               lower left
          cmp      maxy(a6),d4         end-of-screen?
          bcs      li                  no--
          rts
```

137

```
li        subq     #1,d3              left
          bpl      askpix             still no end
          rts

lo        subq     #1,d3              upper left
          bpl      ob                 still no end
          rts

ob        subq     #1,d4              top
          bpl      askpix             still no end
          rts

ro        subq     #1,d4              upper right
          bpl      re                 still no end
          rts
```

```
****************************************************************
*                                                              *
*         test for set pixels                                  *
*                                                              *
****************************************************************
```

```
chkpix    divu     maxx(a6),d7        convert
          move     d7,d4              d7 to
          swap     d7                 y
          move     d7,d3              and x
askpix    cmpi     #3,pflag           ruin the color?
          bcs      ask1               no--
          move     #1,pflag           eventual pen change enabled
          bra      exit               color ready   >
ask1      move     d3,(a4)            coordinates
          move     d4,yko(a4)         loaded
          dc.w     getpix             line a   reads point
          rts
```

```
****************************************************************
*                                                              *
*         pixel cleared                                        *
*                                                              *
****************************************************************
```

```
erase     move      d3,(a4)              load coordinates
          move      d4,yko(a4)
          clr       (a3)                 colro 0
          dc.w      setpix               line a sets point
          rts
```

```
*******************************************************
*                                                     *
*         diverse output-routines                     *
*                                                     *
*******************************************************
```

```
home      lea       hm(pc),a2            plotter in home position

          bra       outstrx

setcol    lea       sccls(pc),a2         color put in from ccol
          bsr       outstrx
          lea       sccln(pc),a2
          move      cccl(a6),d7
          move.b    -1(a2,d7),d0
          bsr       outchr
          bra       outcr

penup     lea       pup(pc),a2           pen up
          bra       outstrx

pendwn    clr       comma(a6)            pen down
          lea       pdw(pc),a2
          bra       outstrx

mov       lea       mv(pc),a2            positioning w/o pen
          bsr       outstrx
          bsr       outcor
          bra       outcr

draw      tst       comma(a6)            positioning w/ pen
          bne       draw1
          st        comma(a6)
          lea       dr(pc),a2
          bsr       outstrx
          bra       outcor
```

```
drawl    bsr      outcom

outcor   move     d3,d6              coord pair output as ascii

         mulu     pscalx(a6),d6
         bsr      outw
         bsr      outcom            output comma
         move     maxy(a6),d7       reversal of
         sub      d4,d7             y-coordinate
         move     d7,d6
         mulu     pscaly(a6),d6

outw     move.l   #1000,d7           hex no. in d6 output as ascii

outw1    andi.l   #$3fff,d6
         divu     d7,d6
outw3    move     d6,d0
         ori      #48,d0
         bsr      outchr
         swap     d6
outw4    divu     #10,d7
         bne      outw1
         rts

outstrx  clr      d2           string output (counter-1 on (a2))
         move.b   (a2)+,d2
outstr   move.b   (a2)+,d0          string in (a2) output
*                                   (counter in d2)
         bsr      outchr
         dbra     d2,outstr
         rts

caps     lea      cap(pc),a2
         bsr      outstrx

outcr    move     #13,d0            c/r
         bra      outchr

outcom   move     #44,d0            comma

outchr   movem.l  d0-d2/a0-a2,-(a7)
         andi     #255,d0
         move     d0,-(a7)          character in d0
```

```
        move     #prt,-(a7)        output to
        move     #bconout,-(a7)    printer
        trap     #bios
        addq.l   #6,a7
        movem.l  (a7)+,d0-d2/a0-a2
        rts
```

```
**********************************************************
*                                                        *
*        output                                          *
*                                                        *
**********************************************************
```

```
exit    addq     #1,ccol(a6)       color sought +1
        move     accl(a6),d7
        cmp      cccl(a6),d7       all colors utilized?
        bpl      init1             no--
exitx   unlk     a6                free up reserved space
        move     #-1,pflag         hardcopy-flag cleared
        bsr      home              plotter in home position
        bra      caps              pen tip
```

```
**********************************************************
*                                                        *
*        constants                                       *
*                                                        *
**********************************************************
```

```
scalx   dc.w     4,4,4             x factors
scaly   dc.w     4,4,4             y factors
max     dc.w     640,640,320       number of x pixels
may     dc.w     400,200,200       number of y pixels
colc    dc.w     1,3,15            number of colors
mv      dc.b     1,"MA"            move absolute
cap     dc.b     3,"SP-1"          pen change
pup     dc.b     5,"MR0,0",13      move relative(pen up)
pdw     dc.b     5,"DR0,0",13      draw relative(pen down)
dr      dc.b     1,"DA"            draw absolute
hm      dc.b     3,13,"HO",13      home position state
scols   dc.b     1,"SP"            color change
scoln   dc.b     "123412341234123"
fin     equ      *
        .end
```

You can adapt the program to a different plotter. The commands for the HI-80 plotter are defined in the last section under `constants`, and can be easily adapted for another plotter.

`scalx` and `scaly` specify the number of steps the plotter will make for a point on the screen. The number of steps depends on the thickness of the pen. In this example, the pen thickness is 0.4 mm.

Here's the equivalent BASIC loader:

```
5       rem BASIC loader for plotter hardcopy
10      dim a%(411)
20      for i=0 to 411
30      read a%(i)
40      next i
50      b=varptr(a%(0))
60      call b
70      end
950     data &H42A7,&H3F3C,&H0020
960     data &H4E41,&H5C8F,&H2C00,&H3F3C,&H0002,&H4E4E,&H548F,&H2040
970     data &HD0FC,&H7D00,&H45D0,&H43FA,&H0028,&H203C,&H0000,&H02F1
980     data &H10D9,&H51C8,&HFFFC,&H2079,&H0000,&H0456,&HD0FC,&H001C
990     data &H208A,&H2F06,&H3F3C,&H0020,&H4E41,&H5C8F,&H4E75,&H4E41
1000    data &H4A79,&H0000,&H04EE,&H6702,&H4E75,&H3F3C,&H0002,&H4E4E
1010    data &H548F,&H3F3C,&HFFFF,&H2F00,&H2F00,&H3F3C,&H0005,&H4E4E
1020    data &HDFFC,&H0000,&H000C,&HA000,&H4E56,&HFFE8,&H2668,&H0008
1030    data &H2868,&H000C,&H4268,&H0024,&H3E10,&H0247,&H0006,&H41FA
1040    data &H0264,&H3D70,&H7000,&HFFFA,&H41FA,&H0260,&H3D70,&H7000
1050    data &HFFF8,&H41FA,&H025C,&H3D70,&H7000,&HFFF2,&H41FA,&H0258
1060    data &H3D70,&H7000,&HFFF0,&H41FA,&H0254,&H3D70,&H7000,&HFFEC
1070    data &H3C2E,&HFFF2,&HCCEE,&HFFF0,&H2D46,&HFFFC,&H3D7C,&H0001
1080    data &HFFEE,&H0C79,&H0001,&H0000,&H04EE,&H6614,&H6100,&H01CE
1090    data &H0C79,&H0002,&H0000,&H04EE,&H66F6,&H4279,&H0000,&H04EE
1100    data &H6100,&H012C,&H6100,&H0120,&H4879,&HFFFF,&HFFFF,&H2E1F
1110    data &H5287,&HBEAE,&HFFFC,&H6700,&H01CC,&H2F07,&H6100,&H00D2
1120    data &HB06E,&HFFEE,&H66E8,&H3D7C,&H0003,&HFFF6,&H6100,&H012C
1130    data &H6100,&H011E,&H6100,&H00E4,&H4240,&H6118,&H4A40,&H660A
1140    data &H6100,&H0180,&H6100,&H0104,&H60C4,&H6100,&H0118,&H6100
1150    data &H00CA,&H60E4,&H556E,&HFFF6,&H026E,&H0007,&HFFF6,&H3D6E
1160    data &HFFF6,&HFFF4,&H601C,&H4C9F,&H0018,&H526E,&HFFF6,&H026E
1170    data &H0007,&HFFF6,&H3E2E,&HFFF4,&HBE6E,&HFFF6,&H6604,&H4240
1180    data &H4E75,&H3E2E,&HFFF6,&HE34F,&H41FA,&H0016,&HD0F0,&H7000
1190    data &H48A7,&H1800,&H4E90,&HB06E,&HFFEE,&H66CA,&H588F,&H4E75
1200    data &H0010,&H001A,&H0024,&H002E,&H0038,&H003E,&H0044,&H004A
1210    data &H5243,&HB66E,&HFFF2,&H6542,&H4E75,&H5243,&HB66E,&HFFF2
1220    data &H6502,&H4E75,&H5244,&HB86E,&HFFF0,&H652E,&H4E75,&H5244
```

```
1230    data &HB86E,&HFFF0,&H65C2,&H4E75,&H5343,&H6A1E,&H4E75,&H5343
1240    data &H6A02,&H4E75,&H5344,&H6A12,&H4E75,&H5344,&H6AC2,&H4E75
1250    data &H8EEE,&HFFF2,&H38C7,&H4847,&H3607,&H0C79,&H0003,&H0000
1260    data &H04EE,&H650C,&H33FC,&H0001,&H0000,&H04EE,&H6000,&H00D6
1270    data &H3883,&H3944,&H00C2,&HA002,&H4E75,&H3883,&H3944,&H0002
1280    data &H4253,&HA001,&H4E75,&H45FA,&H0113,&H6000,&H0082,&H45FA
1290    data &H0110,&H6100,&H007A,&H45FA,&H010B,&H3E2E,&HFFEE,&H1032
1300    data &H70FF,&H6100,&H0084,&H6000,&H007A,&H45FA,&H00DE,&H605E
1310    data &H426E,&HFFEA,&H45FA,&H00DB,&H6054,&H45FA,&H00C6,&H614E
1320    data &H6116,&H605E,&H4A6E,&HFFEA,&H660C,&H50EE,&HFFEA,&H45FA
1330    data &H00C8,&H613A,&H60C2,&H614E,&H3C03,&HCCEE,&HFFFA,&H610E
1340    data &H6144,&H3E2E,&HFFF0,&H9E44,&H3C07,&HCCEE,&HFFF8,&H2E3C
1350    data &H0000,&H03E8,&H02E5,&H0000,&H3FFF,&H8CC7,&H3006,&H0040
1360    data &H0030,&H6124,&H4845,&H8EFC,&H000A,&H66E8,&H4E75,&H4242
1370    data &H141A,&H101A,&H6112,&H51CA,&HFFFA,&H4E75,&H45FA,&H0067
1380    data &H61EC,&H700D,&H60C2,&H702C,&H48E7,&HE0E0,&H0240,&H00FF
1390    data &H3F00,&H3F3C,&H0000,&H3F3C,&H0003,&H4E4D,&H5C8F,&H4CDF
1400    data &H0707,&H4E75,&H526E,&HFFEE,&H3E2E,&HFFEC,&HBE6E,&HFFEE
1410    data &H6A00,&HFDF0,&H4E5E,&H33FC,&HFFFF,&H0000,&H04EE,&H6100
1420    data &HFF26,&H60B8,&H0004,&H0004,&H0004,&H0004,&H0004,&H0004
1430    data &H0280,&H0280,&H0140,&H0190,&H00C8,&H00C8,&H0001,&H0003
1440    data &H000F,&H014D,&H4103,&H5350,&H2D31,&H054D,&H5230,&H2C30
1450    data &H0D05,&H4452,&H302C,&H300D,&H0144,&H4103,&H0D48,&H4F0D
1460    data &H0153,&H5031,&H3233,&H3431,&H3233,&H3431,&H3233,&H3431
1470    data &H3233
```

Chapter 4

The GEM programming environment

The GEM programming environment

GEM is designed to be an easy-to-use interface between the user and the ST. Additionally, GEM is designed to provide a convenient means for the programmer writing applications for the ST itself.

In principle, it is simpler and faster to write a program for the ST than to write a program for a different computer. GEM contains dozens of subroutines which perform a variety of powerful functions. The programmer can use these routines simply by including them in his application.

Designing applications for the ST is quite different than designing them for other computers.The programmer is responsible for maintaining the work station, window management, mouse and keyboard inputs, etc. Most ST programmers build their own collection of subroutines into a library to handle their programming housekeeping chores.

Next we'll introduce you to several GEM routines that each application may use. We'll also describe how accessories and applications may be developed.

4.1 Inside GEM

GEM is the graphics-oriented interface that makes the ST so easy to use . A user takes for granted the enormous complexity of this operating system that isolates him from the details of mouse control, icon structure, drop-down menu construction or window manipulation. He need not be concerned with the technical aspects of the ST.

How long would it take a programmer to produce an application if he had to write his own routines for all these tasks?

GEM's routines relieve the programmer of many of the repetitive details of using the ST. Most of the programming languages available for the ST offer libraries that provide access to GEM. The naming conventions are more or less uniform for the programming languages—allowing a programmer to easily move to a different language if he wants.

GEM has simple routines for performing data input and output, and complex routines for managing dialog boxes.

The two main parts of GEM are the VDI, or Virtual Device Interface, and the AES, or Application Environment Services.

The VDI provides services for the hardware components of the computer. It handles all the device-specific details, such as converting coordinates for screen output or printer output, providing the graphics primitives such as line, circle or fill, or writing text to a disk file.

The AES handles the "larger" tasks such as windows, drop-down menus and icons. It is responsible for controlling the mouse and keyboard input. The AES also handles *multi-tasking* operations. You may recall that the print spooler and clock display run concurrently while another application is active. These are multi-tasking operations.

4.1.1 The Virtual Device Interface

The VDI consists of two parts:

- the GDOS, or Graphics Device Operating System, which contains a number of the device-independent graphics routines

- the GIOS, or Graphics Input/Output System, which contains the device-specific routines and fonts for performing input and output.

The VDI recognizes two coordinate systems:

- NDC — or normalized device coordinates
- RC   — or raster coordinates

Raster coordinates correspond to the physical points on a device. On the ST screen, these range from 320x200 through 640x400. On a plotter, they measure the x and y steps.

Normalized device coordinates refer to an idealized screen surface.The NDC orientation corresponds to our usual Cartesian system: point 0,0 lies at the lower left corner, and the largest values for x and y lie at the upper right corner of the drawing surface. The range of values for the NDC is from 0, 0 to 32767, 32767, and corresponds to a geometrically correct screen with very high resolution.

The programmer can select the coordinate system he wants to use. If you use the NDC, the GDOS converts the coordinates to the appropriate raster coordinates. Thus, if you ask to draw a square of 100 units, it appears square on the display. If you use RC, the coordinates are not converted. You yourself are responsible for making the object appear square.

The major advantage of using the NDC is that graphics can be exchanged between different peripheral devices. For example, the display screen has an aspect ratio of 1: 1.8. A square on the display screen is actually 1" x 1.8". If this picture is sent to a printer using raster coordinates, the square will no longer appear square on the hardcopy. Using the NDC, the square will appear correctly on the hardcopy.

The VDI makes the necessary conversions. Graphics of any type appear on any peripheral device in the proper ratio. The disadvantage of NDC is that it takes much longer to convert a graphic point to the coordinate system, compared to the speed of raster coordinates. For this reason it is advisable to work with the RC. However, the RC requires you to be more meticulous when writing programs to ensure they remain portable.

4.1.2 The Application Environment Services

The AES is composed of several parts:

- the subroutine libraries
- the dispatcher
- the shell
- the desk accessory buffer
- the menu/alarm buffer

The menu/alarm buffer makes possible the fast operation of GEM. For example, the menu data buffer stores the part of the screen that is overlaid by a drop-down menu. After using the drop-down menu, a subroutine of the AES restores the desktop at lightning speed. Neither the application nor the programmer need be concerned with these details. As long as there is enough memory to save one-fourth of the screen contents, the AES can perform its tasks.

The desk accessory buffer is used similarly. In addition to data, utility programs such as PRINIT (the Print Initialize utility in this section) can be stored in the desk accessory buffer.

The dispatcher makes it possible for the ST to process several tasks simultaneously. "Simultaneous" is a relative term—for us it means at apparently the same time.

To conserve valuable processing time, the dispatcher has two lists. The first is the *ready list*, in which all the currently-running programs are listed and are waiting for a CPU assignment. The other is the *not ready list*, in which all processes which are waiting for a certain event to occur are listed.

Such an event could be:

- a keypress
- pressing a mouse button
- a mouse movement
- a report
- the elapse of a time interval

Thus our printer initialization utility is first put on the *not ready list* and waits until the desk accessory FXINIT (FX-80 Initialize) is called to install the utility.

After FXINIT is installed, the printer initialization utility is removed from the *not ready list* and placed in the *ready list*. The dispatcher then "rotates" the tasks on the ready list. The first task from the ready list is processed for a predetermined amount of time, after which it is placed at the end of the ready list. Then the next task on the ready list is briefly processed, put at the end of the ready list, and so on. Using this method, the dispatcher evenly divides the CPU's time between the currently running program, a background program such as a print spooler, and the operating system. The dispatcher can manage up to six tasks.

The AES is a library containing subroutines to manipulate windows, read and handle the mouse, display system messages, interact with dialog boxes, and display drop-down menus.

The screen manager assumes control of the mouse when the cursor is positioned outside the work surface of the currently active window. The contents of the window are defined as the work surface. The title and information line are not part of the work surface. The screen manager becomes active when the user exits the bordered area of the topmost window—such as when he uses the drop-down menus of the menu bar. It supervises the actions of the user and lets him know if the current window needs to be redrawn.

The *shell* is also part of the AES. After the desktop is accessed, the shell is placed at the top of the ready list. It is responsible for calling an application. The desktop passes information to the shell indicating whether it is a TOS or GEM application, and gives the pathname to the application's subdirectory (folder). The desktop then terminates and the shell is responsible for loading and starting the application. When the application ends, the shell is called again to reactivate the desktop or start another application.

Figure 4-1

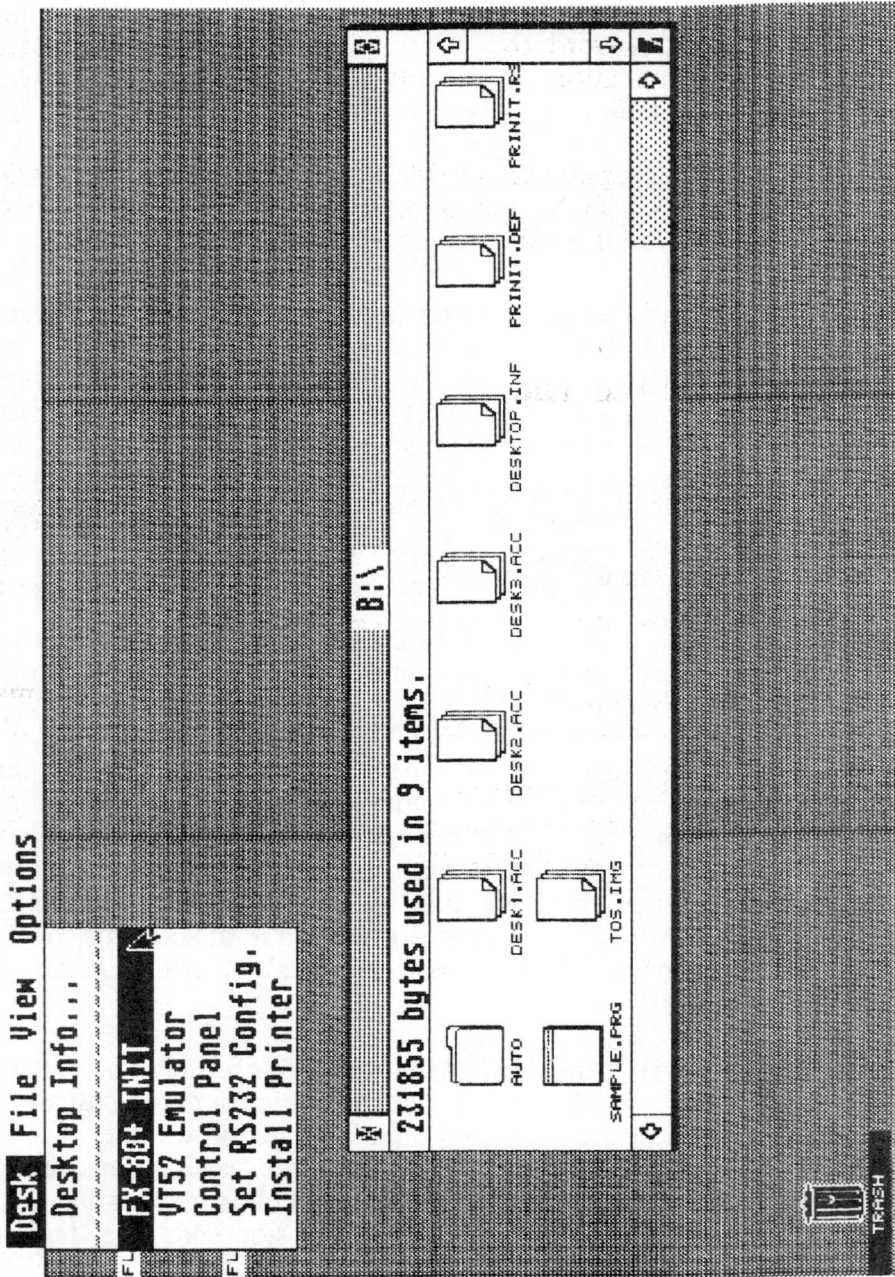

Before writing a program for the ST, we must first distinguish between an application and an accessory.

An application is what we normally think of as a program on a conventional non-GEM computer. A wordprocessor or database management system is an example of an application. Applications are normally loaded into main memory and then started.

An accessory is a mini-application loaded into the accessory buffer during the boot procedure of TOS, and concurrently started. The role of an accessory is to wait until it is called into action by a main application.

4.1.3 The resource file

GEM uses a concept called a *resource file* to make applications flexible and easy to change. The resource file contains the structure of the pull-down menus, and the text of dialog boxes and alert messages. If the text of a menu or message needs to be altered, the program does not have to be changed. Instead, only the resource file need be changed.

The resource file for an application has the extension .RSC. It may be edited using the Resource Construction Set, which we'll discuss shortly.

Separating the text from the program makes it is easy to adapt an application to different countries. A developer need only edit the resource file to "move" an application, for example, from German to English.

4.1.4 Working with TOS

Adapting an application to use the features of GEM is quite complicated. For this reason, many applications have been "ported" to the ST and do not use any of the GEM features such as pull-down menus or icons.

By sidestepping GEM, applications that were developed for other computers (in C, for example) can be easily adapted to the ST. By ignoring the special AES and VDI calls, the C programmer can be as comfortable with the ST as with a non-GEM computer.

The next example is a C program that does not use GEM. Instead, it is a pure TOS application.

4.2 Twenty-one

We'll explore TOS programming by writing a simple game. The name of the game's *Twenty-one*. Its not the same game as the card game Blackjack, but a simple strategy game of the Nim variety.

Twenty-one is a two-player game. A counter is initially set to zero. Each player takes alternate turns, adding one or two to the counter. The winner is the player who reaches exactly twenty-one points on his turn. Naturally, one player is represented by the computer.

Here's one possible winning strategy in Twenty-one. Our goal, reaching a count of twenty-one, may be split into several subgoals. One strategy is to avoid reaching a count of 19 on our turn, or else our opponent will be able to reach 21. Instead, we want our opponent to reach 19—that is one of our subgoals. By the same token, another of our subgoals is to reach 16, since then our opponent cannot prevent us from reaching 19. If our opponent adds 1 to 16, then we add 1—thereby forcing him to reach 19 or 20.

By following a similar strategy we find these subgoals: 1, 4, 7, 10, 13, 16, and 19. Our strategy is to perform a corresponding move (+1 or +2) that will reach the next winning number.

Let's give a little thought to the structure of the program. It is a linear program, with parts for game initialization (init), game state output (output), player move (computer), evaluation and termination.

In the first section, the game instructions are displayed on the screen, the counter is set to zero, and the player is given a choice as to who will make the first move.

The player move section is made up of a simple function followed by a multiple choice (getchr, switch case). Getchar is a standard C library function to read a single digit. For this game, a single call is sufficient, since we'll only need to read a single digit. This value is then added to the counter using the increment operator ++. The C statement state++ is similar to the BASIC statement. state=state+1.

Before the next player's turn, we check to see if the winning score has been reached within the main loop of the program— while (state<goal).

This is done using:

```
if (state==goal) break;
```

With the routine `computer()`, the computer will always try to reach the
next winning subgoal. If this isn't possible because the opponent has
reached the same subgoal, then it doesn't matter if the move is +1 or +2 (+1
is the default).

If you're a beginning user of the C language, these explanations may
interest you:

A C program is made up of a sequence of functions. When the program is
started, the function `main()` is called. Every C program must contain a
`main()` function.

You may use the `#include` and `#define` statements.

The `#include` statement instructs the compiler to insert the file `stdio.h`
at this point in the source file. `stdio.h` contains the standard input/output
functions commonly used by C programs. Providing these functions as a
standard library ensures that this source program can run on other
computers after compilation.

The `#define` statement lets you define symbolic constants. For example,
you can define the symbol `YES` with the value of 1 (for true) or the symbol
`NO` with a value of 0 (for false). For each subsequent occurence of a symbol
within the source file, the compiler substitutes the corresponding value.
This makes it easier to read and write programs, since the symbolic
constants are more understandable than pure numeric or alpha values.

```
/* 21 - JW 16.08.1985   21 game*/

#include "stdio.h"

#define YES 1
#define NO 0

int objt,stand,sp,game;


main()
{
      hello();
start:init();
      if (sp == YES)
      {
                output();
                player();
      }

      while(stand<objt)
                {
                output();
                computer();
                if (stand == objt)
                        break;
                output();
                player();
                }
      end();
      printf("Another game ?\n");

      game=getchar();
      if (game == 'y')
          {
          goto start;
          }
}
```

```
hello()
{
   printf("******* T W E N T Y - O N E *****\n");
    printf("Object of the game is to get the \n");
   printf(" number 21 by adding by 1 or 2.   \n");
}


init()
{
      objt=21;
      stand=0;
      printf("\n\nWant to start?");

      game=getchar();
          if (game == 'y')
                sp = YES;
          else sp = NO;
      printf("\n");
}


output()
{
      printf("Game standing: %d\n",stand);
}


player()
{
   sp = YES;
      game=0;
      printf("\nWant to raise by 1 or 2 ?\n");

      game = (getchar() - '0');
      switch(game)
      {
          case 1 :
          {
              printf("\nOkay !\n");
              stand++;
              break;
          }
```

```
            case 2 :
            {
                printf("\nThat's fine, too!\n");
                stand++;
                stand++;
                break;
            }
            default :
            {
                printf("\nNot so many!!\n");
                player();
            }
        }
}


computer()
{
    sp = NO;
        switch(stand)
        {
            case 2:
            case 5:
            case 8:
            case 11:
            case 14:
            case 17:
            case 20:
            {
                plusone();
                break;
            }
            case 1:
            case 4:
            case 7:
            case 10:
            case 13:
            case 16:
            case 19:
            {
                printf("\nI raise by 2.\n");
                stand++;
                stand++;
```

```
                break;
            }
        default:
            {
                plusone();
            }
        }
    }
}


plusone()
{
      printf("\nI raise by 1.\n");
      stand++;
}


end()
{
   if (sp == YES)
        printf("\n\nYou win!.\n\n");
   else
        printf("\n\nI was very lucky. \n\n");
}
```

Since a basic loader for this program would be quite large and really serve
no useful purpose, we have not included one. For the BASIC programmers
we have included the same program written in BASIC. You can compare
the BASIC version with the C source code.

```
10        rem 21 program in basic
20        rem
30        YES = 1
40        NO = 0
50        rem main program
60        rem
70        gosub hello
80        start: gosub init
90        if sp = YES then gosub output: gosub player
100       while stand < obj
120       gosub output
130       gosub computer
140       if stand =obj then goto 150
145       gosub output: gosub player
150       wend
160       gosub ende
170       print"Another Game?";
180       game$ = input$(1)
190       if game$ = "y" then goto start
200       end
210       rem
220       rem
500       hello: fullw 2: clearw 2
510       print"****** T W E N T Y - O N E *****"
520       print"Object of the game is to get the"
530       print"number 21 by adding 1 or 2         "
540       return
550       rem
600       init: obj=21
610       stand = 0
620       print: print" Want to start" ;
630       game$ = input$(1)
640       if game$ = "y" then sp= YES else sp = NO
645       print
650       return
660       rem
700       output :print"Game standing:";stand
705       print
```

```
710     return
720     rem
800     player: sp = YES
810     game = 0
820     print "Want to raise by 1 or 2 ";
830     input game
850     if game = 1 then print"OK" : stand=stand+1 :
        return
860     if game = 2 then print"OK" : stand=stand+2 :
        return
870     print"Not so many": goto 810: rem call player
880     return
890     rem
900     computer: sp = NO
910     if stand = 1 goto plustwo
911     if stand = 4 goto plustwo
912     if stand = 7 goto plustwo
913     if stand = 10 goto plustwo
914     if stand = 13 goto plustwo
915     if stand = 16 goto plustwo
916     if stand = 19 goto plustwo
920     if stand = 2 goto plusone
921     if stand = 5 goto plusone
922     if stand = 8 goto plusone
923     if stand = 11 goto plusone
924     if stand = 14 goto plusone
925     if stand = 17 goto plusone
926     if stand = 20 goto plusone
930     goto plusone        : rem default
950     plusone: print"I raise by one"
955     stand= stand +1
958     return
960     plustwo: print "I raise by two"
965     stand = stand + 2
968     return
980     rem
1000    ende: if sp = YES then print "You win" else
        print"I was very lucky"
1010    return
```

4.3 The next step: A GEM application

Now that you've become acquainted with the C language and understand terms like include resource files and symbolic constants, we want to introduce you to a GEM application.

As previously illustrated, GEM, and especially the Virtual Device Interface, provides a very convenient user interface for a variety of graphic devices. The VDI can convert the output of any device—a raster screen, a dot-matrix printer, or a pen plotter—to the proper device-specific codes. The programmer need not concern himself with these codes.

To make use of any VDI services, the programmer must pass a request through a series of parameters. These parameters are five arrays:

- the control array (`contrl`)
- the input array (`intin`)
- the input array for point coordinates (`ptsin`)
- the output array (`intout`)
- the output array for point coordinates (`ptsout`)

All array elements are two bytes long, so corresponding variables are defined as integers in C. In the following example, the definitions appear at the beginning of the global variables.

The first step in a GEM program is to initialize these arrays. Next the workstation parameters are set, in order to open the workstation. The VDI function OPEN WORKSTATION loads the corresponding driver (not yet implemented on the ST), sets the output device for graphics operation, and prepares it for subsequent use.

At this time, certain workstation characteristics may be specified. For example, we may request that lines appear as black and dotted, rather than as solid lines. A variety of characteristics may be specified and passed on as parameters, shown as follows:

- Line type (dashed, shaded,...)
- Color of lines
- Marker type
- Color of the poly marker
- Type style
- Type color
- Fill pattern for drawing polygons
- Fill pattern
- Fill color

Most of these parameters have defaults with a value of 1.

One parameter is particularly important to us. Within the input array (int_in), the value of one element (10) determines the coordinate system. A value of zero selects normalized device coordinates (NDC) and a value of two selects raster coordinates (RC). Since we place a priority on speed, we select RC.

```
open_vwork()
{
int i;
    for (i = 1; i <10; i++) {
        int_in[i] = 1;
    }
    int_in[10] = 2;
    v_opnvwk(int_in, &handle, int_out);
}
```

To initialize the workstation we call v_opnvwk(int_in, &handle, int_out) Using the value passed by handle, we can address the work area created for our application.

If you look at main(), you will notice two other GEM calls.

Appl_init prepares a similar control array to use the AES. An identification code (ap_id) is returned to the application. The code is used to distinguished between multiple applications using the same resources (multi-tasking).

Draw() is our actual main program—in this example, where we draw the outline of a house.

Each GEM application must be properly terminated. Memory and other resources must be released so that other applications may make use of them.

Here are a few notes concerning the following listing:

All source statements preceding draw() may be placed in a separate file. In other programs these statements may be #included. To ensure the orderly termination of your application, the last lines of the program should be:

```
desktop();
```

At the end of the listing you'll find the click() function. This allows you to view the screen until the left mouse button is pressed.

(

```
/**********************************************************/
/*****            program: HOUSE1.C              ****/
/***** draw a house -- wait for the left mouse key   ****/
/*****             JW October 1985               ****/
/**********************************************************/
                        /* include files            */
#include "obdefs.h"     /* first time all are brought in  */
#include "define.h"
#include "gemdefs.h"
#include "osbind.h"
#include "gembind.h"


                    /*global variables                */
int contrl[12];
int intin[128];
int ptsin[128];
int intout[128];
int ptsout[128];    /* enough space for all purposes    */

int handle,i;       /* virtual workstation handle     */
int phys_handle;    /* physical workstation handle    */
int pxyarray[12];   /* Array for x,y coordinates      */
int int_in[11];     /* input in GSX array             */
int int_out[57];    /* output from GSX array          */

int ap_id;          /* i.d. of application            */

int dummy;

main()
{
    ap_id=appl_init();
                /* initialize    GEMAES array-structures */
    handle=graf_handle(&dummy,&dummy,&dummy,&dummy);
                /* Desktop maintenance                */
    open_vwork();
                /* Set up workspace                   */
    graf_mouse(256,&dummy);
                /* Mouse stuck                        */
    draw();
                /* produce artwork                    */
    v_gtext(handle,1,350,"Please click LEFT button..");
```

166

```
        click();    /* wait for left mouse key    ...        */
        desktop(); /* End-cf-program                         */
}


open_vwork()
{
int i;
        for (i = 1; i <10; i++){
          int_in[i] = 1;
                /* init int_in array: linetype, color,    */
          }      /* fillstyles etc.                        */
        int_in[10] = 2;
                /* used RC - coordinates                  */
        v_opnvwk(int_in, &handle, int_out);
                /* now it can go ....              */
}


desktop()
{
        v_clsvwk(handle);      /* workstation assigned        */
        appl_exit();           /* no more GEM calls           */
}


click()                        /* wait for mouse click (left)  */
{
        evnt_button(1,1,1,&dummy,&dummy,&dummy,&dummy);
}


/*--here follows the program section --*/


draw()
        {
        int style;  /* Variable for fill pattern          */
        style = 3;  /* Choose fill pattern                 */
        pxyarray[0] = 100;   /* x-coordinate Point 1        */
        pxyarray[1] = 100;   /* y-coordinate point 1        */
        pxyarray[2] = 100;  /* Point 2                      */
```

```
        pxyarray[3] = 300;
        pxyarray[4] = 500;      /* Point 3                    */
        pxyarray[5] = 300;
        pxyarray[6] = 500;
        pxyarray[7] = 100;
        pxyarray[8] = 300;
        pxyarray[9] = 50;
        pxyarray[10] = 100;
        pxyarray[11] = 100;

        v_pline(handle, 6, pxyarray);
                    /* Polygon in workspace    :        */
                /* 6 points with coordinates fr.pxyarray  */

        vsf_interior(handle, style);
                    /* set fill interior style: solid/hollow*/
        v_fillarea(handle, 6, pxyarray);
                    /* fill from polygon-generated      */
                    /* surface                          */
}
```

HOUSE1.PRG

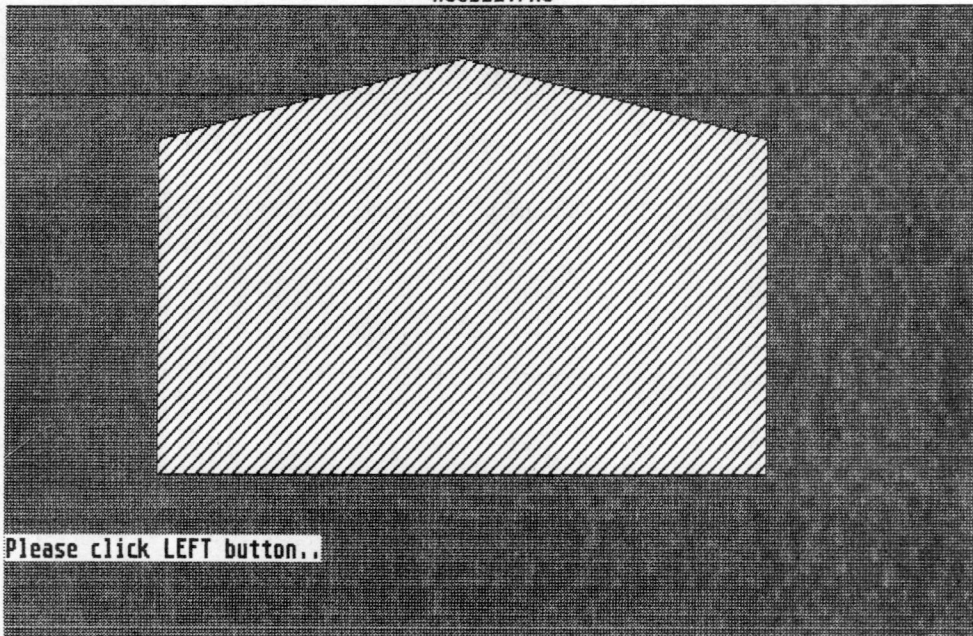

Please click LEFT button..

Hopefully we've succeeded in running an application on the desktop. The next step is the creation of a routine `open_window()`, which prepares a window as a work area for us.

Let's first give some thought to the size that our window should have. In GEM, the convention is to specify the upper left corner of an object as the reference point in pixel coordinates, and then specify the width and height, also in pixel units, relative to this point.

But few of us want to count out pixels or do conversions. The desktop is actually a window of maximum size. The VDI function `wind_get` returns these measurements to us.

Let's build upon the previous program HOUSE1 with the call:

```
wind_get(0,WF_WORKXYWH,&xdesk,&ydesk,&wdesk,&hdesk);
```

Remember to enter the new variables in the declaration list:

```
int xdesk, ydesk, wdesk, hdesk;
```

The `wind_create()` function is used to create a window. It returns a window number (`wi_handle`) for identification. To create a window several parameters are specified. Each characteristic of a window is assigned one bit in an integer, as follows:

0x0001	NAME	title line with name
0x0002	CLOSER	close field
0x0004	FULLER	field for full size (top right)
0x0008	MOVER	window can be moved
0x0010	INFO	info line (such as 123456 bytes used)
0x0020	SIZER	enlargement field (lower left)
0x0040	UPARROW	arrow up
0x0080	DNARROW	arrow down
0x0100	VSLIDE	vertical slider
0x0200	LFARROW	arrow left
0x0400	RTARROW	arrow right
0x0800	HSLIDE	horizontal slider

If your window is just a border around the work area with a title line, the first parameter when calling `wind_create` must have a value of 1. To close the window during termination, the first parameter is set to three (bit 00000011). Using bits can become complicated. One alternative is to use symbolic constants, which are defined within an `#include` file for this purpose.

The above symbols are standardized. In the case of C language, they are found in the file `GEMBIND.H`. The programmer can then use just the symbolic constants within his program:

```
#define WI_KIND (SIZER MOVER FULLER CLOSER NAME)
```

Once the window format is set, the title is set using the function `wind_set()`, and the window is finally opened.

We recommend that you place this sequence of instructions in a separate file to be `#included` in programs (thanks to the symbolic constants they can be easily used for any window):

```
open_window()
{
    wi_handle=wind_create(WI_KIND,xdesk,ydesk,wdesk,hdesk);
    wind_set(wi_handle, WF_NAME, " Tips & Tricks ",0,0);
    wind_open(wi_handle,xdesk,ydesk,wdesk,hdesk);
}
```

This creates a window on the screen. But many of the window features are inoperative. The event library, a part of the AES, tests for the special features. To determine if a mouse button is pressed, for example, we use the function in `click()` and test for the state `evnt_button`.

Messages between the user and GEM are communicated through an array called the message buffer (`msgbuff`). The message is placed in the first element `msgbuff(1)`. An indentifcation code for which this message applies is placed in `msgbuff(2)`. Information about required parameters are placed in the remaining entries.

If a menu entry is selected with the mouse—for example, the code 10 for MN_SELECTED—it is placed in `msgbuff(0)`. The pointer to the menu (e.g. DESK or FILE) is placed in `msgbuff(3)`, and the pointer of the selected object is placed in `msgbuff(4)`. This lets you determine the desired action.

The name MN_SELECTED is the designation for the symbolic constant defined in the #include file. The following symbolic constants are also used:

MN_SELECTED	Menu entry selected
WM_REDRAW	The window must be redrawn
WM_TOPPED	This window should be activated
WM_CLOSED	The close field was activiated
WM_FULLED	The maximum size was set
WM_ARROWED	A arrow was clicked
WM_HSLID	The horizontal slider was used
WM_VSLID	The vertical slider was used
WM_MOVED	The window was moved
WM_NEWTOP	The window was activiated
AC_OPEN	Sent to the accessory selected in the desk menu
AC_CLOSE	Sent to the accessory to be closed

To use all of the GEM window features, an application must handle all of the above conditions.

Using the evnt_multi() call, an application can be made to wait for a message, a mouse event, or a keypress, for example.

If you've written an application that seems to "hang up", but the pointer can still be moved with the mouse, then the ST probably hasn't crashed. Instead, you have not requested it to wait for an external event. Your application should probably be designed as a large loop that can't be exited until a specific termination condition is fulfilled. This can be a mouse click or the activation of the close field.

An example of this:

```
do (
    evnt_multi(....);
    window_control;

    your program follows here;

    ) while close field is not activated
```

The outline above is typical for an application. An accessory requires a somewhat different structure. For the time being, the following example demonstrates how to shrink, enlarge and move the window.

```
/***************************************************************/
/*******            Program: HOUSE3.C            ******/
/*******          complete window control        ******/
/*******              JW October 1985            ******/
/***************************************************************/

                    /* include files                    */
#include "obdefs.h" /* first time around, so it gets all */
#include "define.h" /* data necessary ...                */
#include "gemdefs.h"
#include "osbind.h"
#include "gembind.h"

                    /* Definition for later reference  */

#define WI_KIND    (SIZER|MOVER|FULLER|CLOSER|NAME)
                   /* work window: Title, border......  */
#define MIN_WIDTH  (2*gl_wbox)
#define MIN_HEIGHT (2*gl_hbox)

extern int gl_apid;
                   /*global variables                     */
int contrl[12];
int intin[128];
int ptsin[128];
int intout[128];
int ptsout[128];   /* enough space for all cases         */

int handle,i;      /* virtual workstation handle         */
int phys_handle;   /* physical workstation handle        */
int pxyarray[12];  /* Array for  x,y coordinates         */
int int_in[11];    /* Input in GSX array                 */
int int_out[57];   /* Output from GSX array              */

int wi_handle;     /* Handling the applicable window     */
int top_window;    /* Open window                        */
int xdesk, ydesk, wdesk, hdesk;
                   /* Parameters for window size         */
int xold, yold, hold, wold;
int xwork, ywork, hwork, wwork;

int mx, my;    /* x and y coordinates of mouse           */
int butdown;
```

```
int ap_id;          /* Application id                          */
int menu_id;        /* Working window id                       */
int fulled;
int hidden;

int msgbuff[8];     /* event message buffer                    */
int keycode;        /* contains char. codes from evnt_keybrd */

int gl_wchar, gl_hchar; /* Char. height                        */
int gl_wbox, gl_hbox;

int dummy;


/**************************************************************/
/* Necessary initialization                                 */
/**************************************************************/

open_vwork()
{
int i;
      for (i = 0; i <10; i++){
         int_in[i] = 1;
                   /* init int_in array: linetype, color,   */
         }         /* fillstyles etc.                       */
      int_in[10] = 2;     /* RC - coordinates used           */
      handle=phys_handle;
      v_opnvwk(int_in, &handle, int_out); /* off we go... */
}

/**************************************************************/
/* open window                                              */
/**************************************************************/

open_window()
{
   wi_handle=wind_create(WI_KIND,xdesk,ydesk,wdesk,hdesk);
   wind_set(wi_handle, WF_NAME," The T&T House",0,0);

graf_growbox(xdesk+wdesk/2,ydesk+hdesk/2,gl_wbox,gl_hbox,xde
sk,ydesk,wdesk,hdesk);
```

173

```
    wind_open(wi_handle,xdesk,ydesk,wdesk,hdesk);

wind_get(wi_handle,WF_WORKXYWH,&xwork,&ywork,&wwork,&hwork);
}


/*********************************************************/
/* Show mouse / conceal mouse                            */
/*********************************************************/

show_mouse()
{
     graf_mouse(257,&dummy);
}

hide_mouse()
{
     graf_mouse(256,&dummy);
}


/*********************************************************/
/* clipping parameter set                                */
/*********************************************************/

set_clip(x,y,w,h)
int x,y,w,h;
{
int clip[4];
   clip[0]=x;
   clip[1]=y;
   clip[2]=x+w;
   clip[3]=y+h;
   vs_clip(handle,1,clip);
}
```

```
/*********************************************************/
/* Re-appear after windo manipulation                   */
/*********************************************************/

do_redraw(xc,yc,wc,hc)
int xc,yc,wc,hc;
{
GRECT t1,t2;

    hide_mouse();
    wind_update(TRUE);
    t2.g_x=xc;
    t2.g_y=yc;
    t2.g_w=wc;
    t2.g_h=hc;

wind_get(wi_handle,WF_FIRSTXYWH,&t1.g_x,&t1.g_y,&t1.g_w,&t1.
g_h);
    while (t1.g_w && t1.g_h)
        {
        if (rc_intersect(&t2,&t1))
            {
            set_clip(t1.g_x, t1.g_y, t1.g_w, t1.g_h);
            draw_house();
            }

wind_get(wi_handle,WF_NEXTXYWH,&t1.g_x,&t1.g_y,&t1.g_w,&t1.g
_h);
        }
    wind_update(FALSE);
    show_mouse();
}


/*********************************************************/
/*  Read from events: Window, Mouse, Keyboard           */
/*********************************************************/

multi()
{
int event;

        do{
```

```
      event = evnt_multi(MU_MESAG | MU_BUTTON | MU_KEYBD,
         1,1,butdown,
         0,0,0,0,0,
         0,0,0,0,0,
         msgbuff,0,0,&mx,&my,&dummy,&dummy,&keycode,&dummy);


/**********************************************************/
/* WINDOW(): Window management: shifting, sizes. etc.    */
/**********************************************************/

   wind_update(TRUE);

   if (event & MU_MESAG)
     switch (msgbuff[0]) {

     case WM_REDRAW:

do_redraw(msgbuff[4],msgbuff[5],msgbuff[6],msgbuff[7]);
         break;

     case WM_NEWTOP:
     case WM_TOPPED:
       wind_set(wi_handle,WF_TOP,0,0,0,0);
       break;

     case WM_SIZED:
     case WM_MOVED:
       if(msgbuff[6]<MIN_WIDTH)msgbuff[6]=MIN_WIDTH;
       if(msgbuff[7]<MIN_HEIGHT)msgbuff[7]=MIN_HEIGHT;

wind_set(wi_handle,WF_CURRXYWH,msgbuff[4],msgbuff[5],msgbuff
[6],msgbuff[7]);

wind_get(wi_handle,WF_WORKXYWH,&xwork,&ywork,&wwork,&hwork);
         break;

     case WM_FULLED:
       if(fulled){
       wind_calc(WC_WORK,WI_KIND,xold,yold,wold,hold,
           &xwork,&ywork,&wwork,&hwork);
       wind_set(wi_handle,WF_CURRXYWH,xold,yold,wold,hold);}
       else{
```

```
        wind_calc(WC_BORDER,WI_KIND,xwork,ywork,wwork,hwork,
            &xold,&yold,&wold,&hold);
        wind_calc(WC_WORK,WI_KIND,xdesk,ydesk,wdesk,hdesk,
            &xwork,&ywork,&wwork,&hwork);

wind_set(wi_handle,WF_CURRXYWH,xdesk,ydesk,wdesk,hdesk);
        }
        fulled ^= TRUE;
        break;

      } /* switch (msgbuff[0]) */

   if ((event & MU_BUTTON)&&(wi_handle == top_window))
      if(butdown) butdown = FALSE;
      else butdown = TRUE;

      if(event & MU_KEYBD){
         do_redraw(xwork,ywork,wwork,hwork);
      }

   wind_update(FALSE);

         }while(!((event  &  MU_MESAG)  &&  (msgbuff[0]  ==
WM_CLOSED)));
                      /* Enclosure was chosen            */
        wind_close(wi_handle);

graf_shrinkbox(xwork+wwork/2,ywork+hwork/2,gl_wbox,gl_hbox,x
work,ywork,wwork,hwork);
        wind_delete(wi_handle);     /* Free up memory      */
        v_clsvwk(handle);           /* assign workstation  */
        appl_exit();                /* and goto Desktop     */

}


main()
{
        appl_init(); /* initialize GEM AES array-structures */

        phys_handle=graf_handle(&gl_wchar, &gl_hchar,
                        &gl_wbox, &gl_hbox);
```

```
                                    /* Handling the  Desktop  */
    wind_get(0,WF_WORKXYWH, &xdesk, &ydesk, &wdesk, &hdesk);

    open_vwork();                 /* Open workspace            */
    open_window();                /* Open application window   */
    graf_mouse(ARROW,&dummy);      /* Mouse form               */


    hidden=FALSE;
    fulled=FALSE;
    butdown=TRUE;
    multi();                      /* What does the user do?  */

}



/*-- Program follows from here to end of source--*/


draw_house()
    {
    int style;                    /* Fill-pattern variable  */
    int temp[4];

    vsf_interior(handle,2);        /* blank screen fill    */
    vsf_style(handle,8);           /* set fill  solid      */
    vsf_color(handle,0);           /* set color to white   */
    temp[0]=xwork;                 /* set coordinates      */
    temp[1]=ywork;
    temp[2]=xwork+wwork-1;
    temp[3]=ywork+hwork-1;
    v_bar(handle,temp);             /* draw large bar       */

    style = 3;                      /* Choose fill-pattern  */
    pxyarray[0] = 100;              /* x-coordinate point 1 */
    pxyarray[1] = 100;              /* y-coordinate point 1 */
    pxyarray[2] = 100;              /* Point 2              */
    pxyarray[3] = 300;
    pxyarray[4] = 500;              /* Point 3              */
    pxyarray[5] = 300;
    pxyarray[6] = 500;
```

```
        pxyarray[7] = 100;
        pxyarray[8] = 300;
        pxyarray[9] = 50;
        pxyarray[10] = 100;
        pxyarray[11] = 100;

        vsf_color(handle,1);            /* set color to  black */

        v_pline(handle, 6, pxyarray);/*Polygon in workspace */

                /* 6 points w/ coordinates in    pxyarray*/

        vsf_interior(handle, style);
                    /* set fill interior style: solid/hollow*/

        v_fillarea(handle, 6, pxyarray);
                    /* fill Polygon-enclosed surface      */

        v_gtext(handle,10,gl_hchar*3,"This   is   the   T&T
House.");
}
```

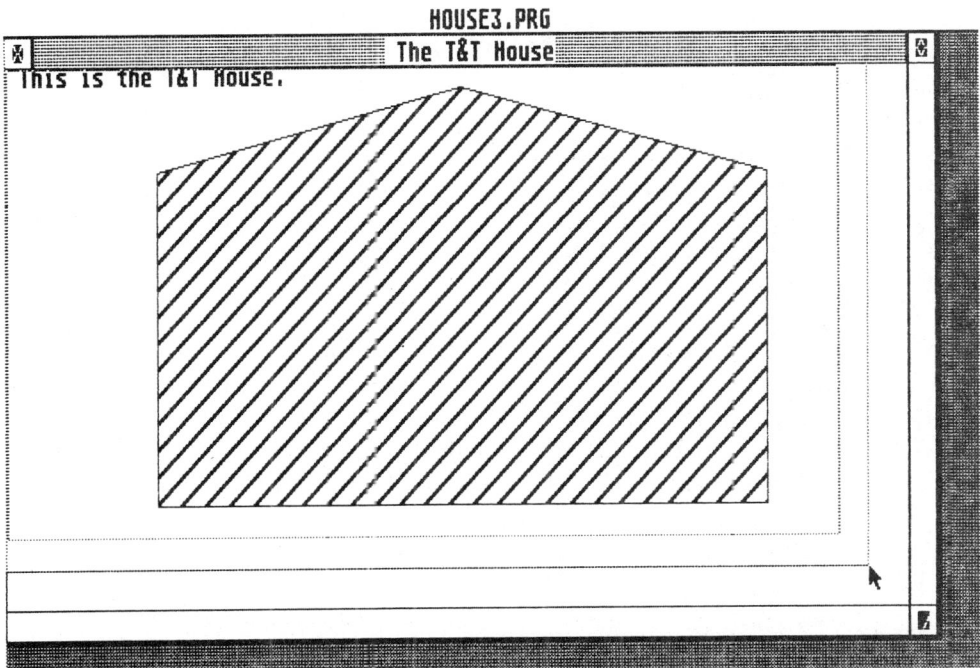

HOUSE3.PRG

The T&T House

This is the T&T House.

Since a basic loader for this program would serve no useful purpose, we have not included one. For the BASIC programmers we have included the HOUSE3 program written in BASIC. You can compare the BASIC version with the C source code. You will notice that the BASIC version is much shorter since BASIC takes care of the necessay GEM initializations. Parts of the program should look familiar. They are from Chapter 1 and merged into this program.

```
10      rem house3 in basic
20      gosub gem.arrays
30      x1=0:a$="This is the T&T house"
40      poke int.in  ,3
50      poke int.in+2,2
60      x1=varptr(a$)
70      poke int.in+4,x1 / 2^16
80      poke int.in+6,x1 and &hffff
90      poke int.in+8,0
100     poke int.in+10,0
110     gemsys 105
120     '
130     rem main
140     '
150     fullw 2:clearw 2
160     gosub house : rem draw
170     '
180     mouse:rem read right mouse button
190     poke contrl,124
200     poke contrl+2,0
210     poke contrl+4,0
220     vdisys
230     button = peek(intout)
240     if button <>2 then goto mouse
250     end
260     house: style = 2 : index = 3 : colour = 1
270     linef 100,100,100,300
280     linef 100,300,500,300
290     linef 500,300,500,100
300     linef 500,100,300,50
310     linef 300,50 ,100,100
320     color colour,colour,colour,style,index
330     fill 150,150
```

```
340     gotoxy 0,0: print"This is the T&T house,
        right mouse button to exit";
350     return
360     gem.arrays:
370     a# = gb:int.in = peek(a#+8):
        rem old basic int.in   = peek(gb+8) *2^16 +
        peek(gb+10)
380     return
```

Desk File Run Edit Debug

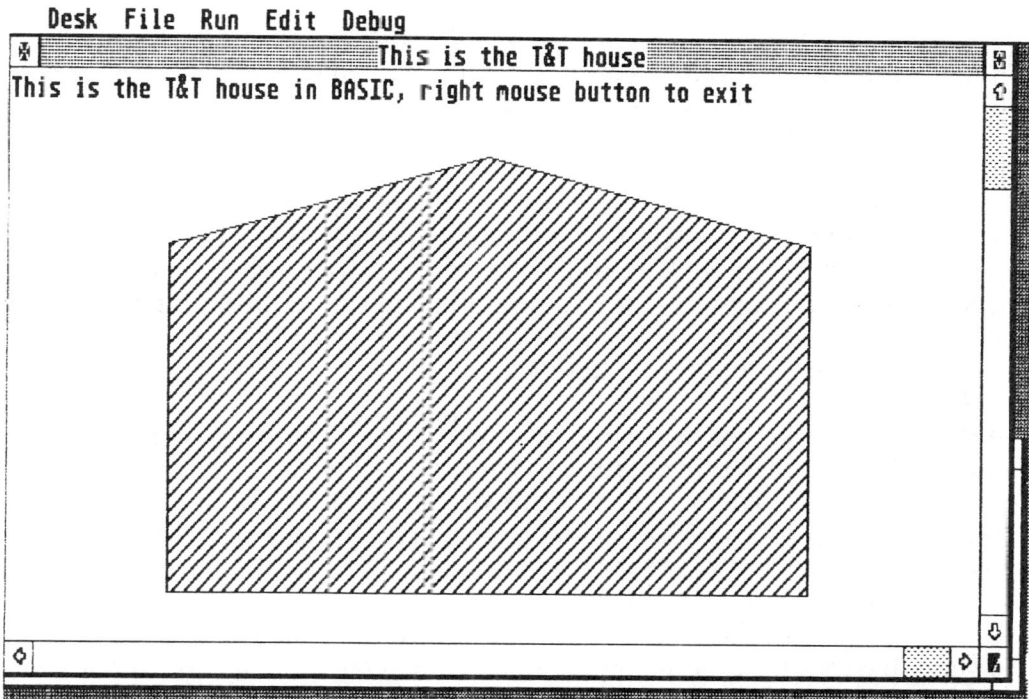

4.3.1 PRINIT - An example application

Now that we've used some pratical GEM techniques, let's create our first real application. Then we'll show you how to create an accessory, for use within DESK on the menu bar.

The application is a short program to set a printer to different type fonts, margins, etc. This is a good candidate for a desk accessory. The alternative way to set up the printer is to use BASIC to send sequences of CHR$ statements to the printer.

To make our application easy to use we'll use a "dialog box" for the input. What is the quickest and easiest method for creating this type of dialog box?

The Resource Construction Set (RCS), which is part of the Atari Development Package lets you easily create dialog boxes. With this utility program, all of the required menu structures can be created and later edited—in no time at all. The RCS creates .RSC files, which contain all of the specifications concering the dialog box and the required inputs. These specifications are loaded into memory by the rsrc_load(filename) function when the program is later executed.

The biggest advantage of using resource files is that they can be easily changed. This allows for quick translations of your application into a foreign language. To change the following application for use in Germany only the resource file would have to be edited and not the complete program.

Our application program sets several parameters for the Star SG-10 printer. To show the flexibility of resource files, we will later change the application to a desk accessory to work with an Epson FX-80 printer.

In the next section we'll show you all of the necessary steps for constructing the PRINIT.RSC file.

Figure 4-2

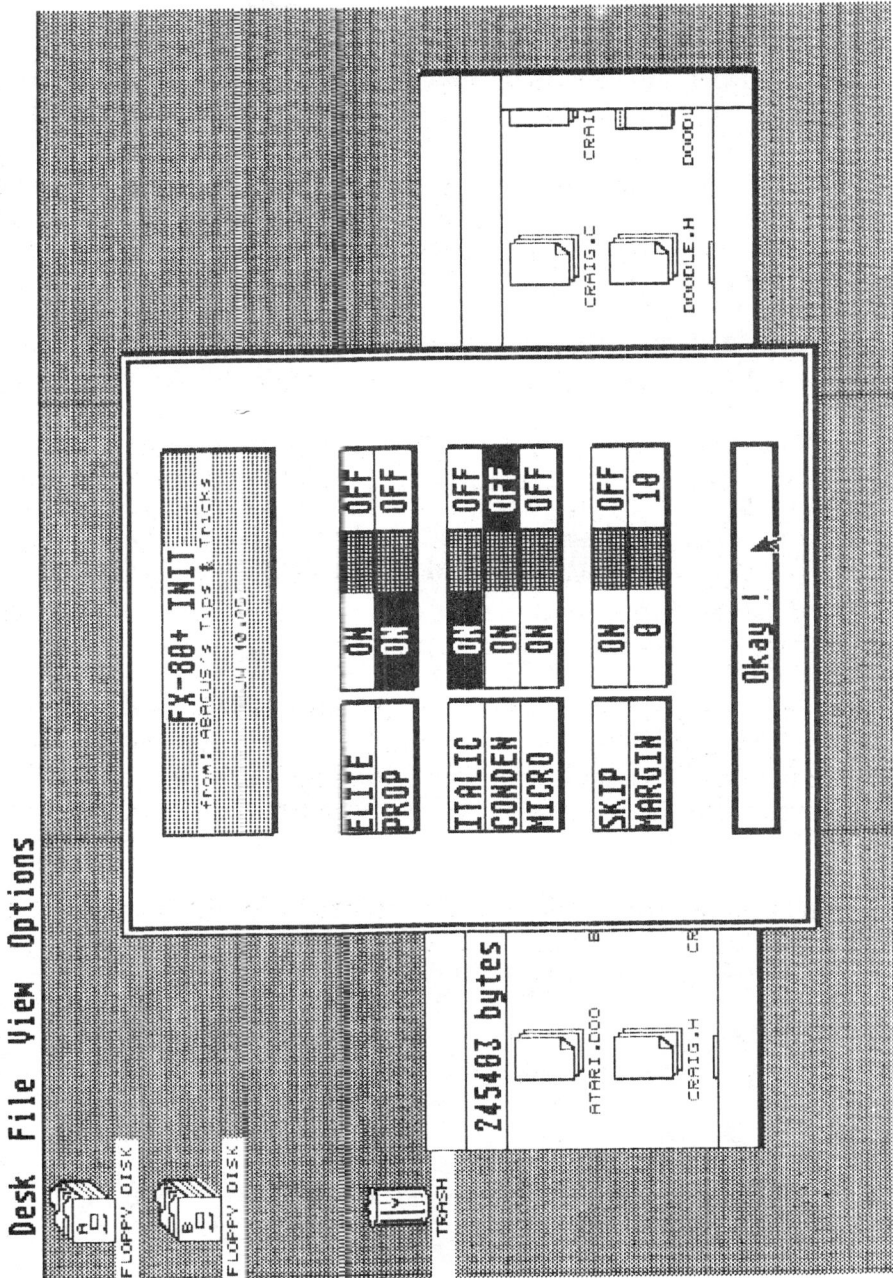

4.4 Building a RSC file

Start the Resource Construction Set from the ST Development System utilities disk. Two windows will appear on the screen. In the top one, the RESOURCE PARTBOX, all of the components available are pictured.

You must now decide if you want to build a MENU or a DIALOG tree, within which the user can select between several alternatives.

These two types are the most-used, but there is also the ALERT tree, which is very similar in structure to the DIALOG tree and is used to send messages to the user. In addition, the RCS recognizes the tree FREE, which places almost no restrictions on the programmer. The only condition that applies to this tree is that no object may extend outside of another, while the others must observe certain formatting rules.

The tree symbolized by a question mark is only a place holder until the programmer finally knows what it does and correspondingly, what to call it. If a tree of type unknown (?) is found within the resource file, you can rest assured that the program will crash.

To start building our tree, drag the icon for a DIALOG tree to the lower window. The RCS displays its own dialog box (Figure 4-3) and asks us to name this tree. Enter SGMENU (in uppercase) and press <RETURN> or click the OK box. The dialog box will disappear.

Next move the mouse pointer to the lower window. Then select the dialog box SGMENU and OPEN it from the FILE menu or by doubling clicking. A new window is opened on top of the lower window.

Select the component BOXTEXT from the upper window and drag a copy of it to the lower window, SGMENU. We will use BOXTEXT, a simple box containing text, in order to name the various print options (ELITE, ITALIC, ...); for our application we will need seven boxes of this type. We can use the copy operation to make this task easier. To do this select BOXTEXT in the lower window and drag it to the desired screen position, but this time holding down the <SHIFT> key. Repeat this procedure until you have the appropriate number of BOXTEXT boxes. See Figure 4-4 for the placement of the boxes. Now open each BOXTEXT and enter the following in the TEXT field: ELITE, PROPO, ITALICS, CONDEN, NLQ, SKIP, MARGIN.

Figure 4-3

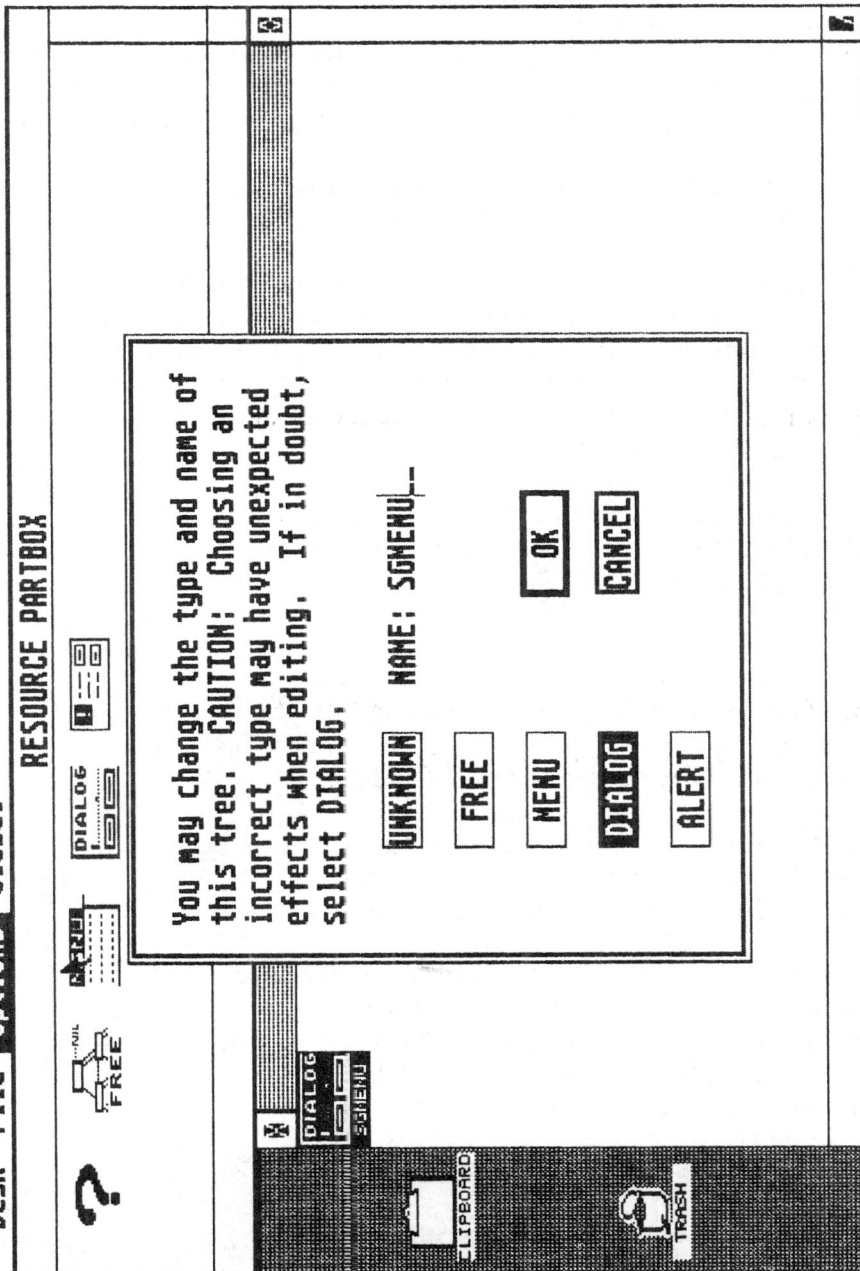

Figure 4-4

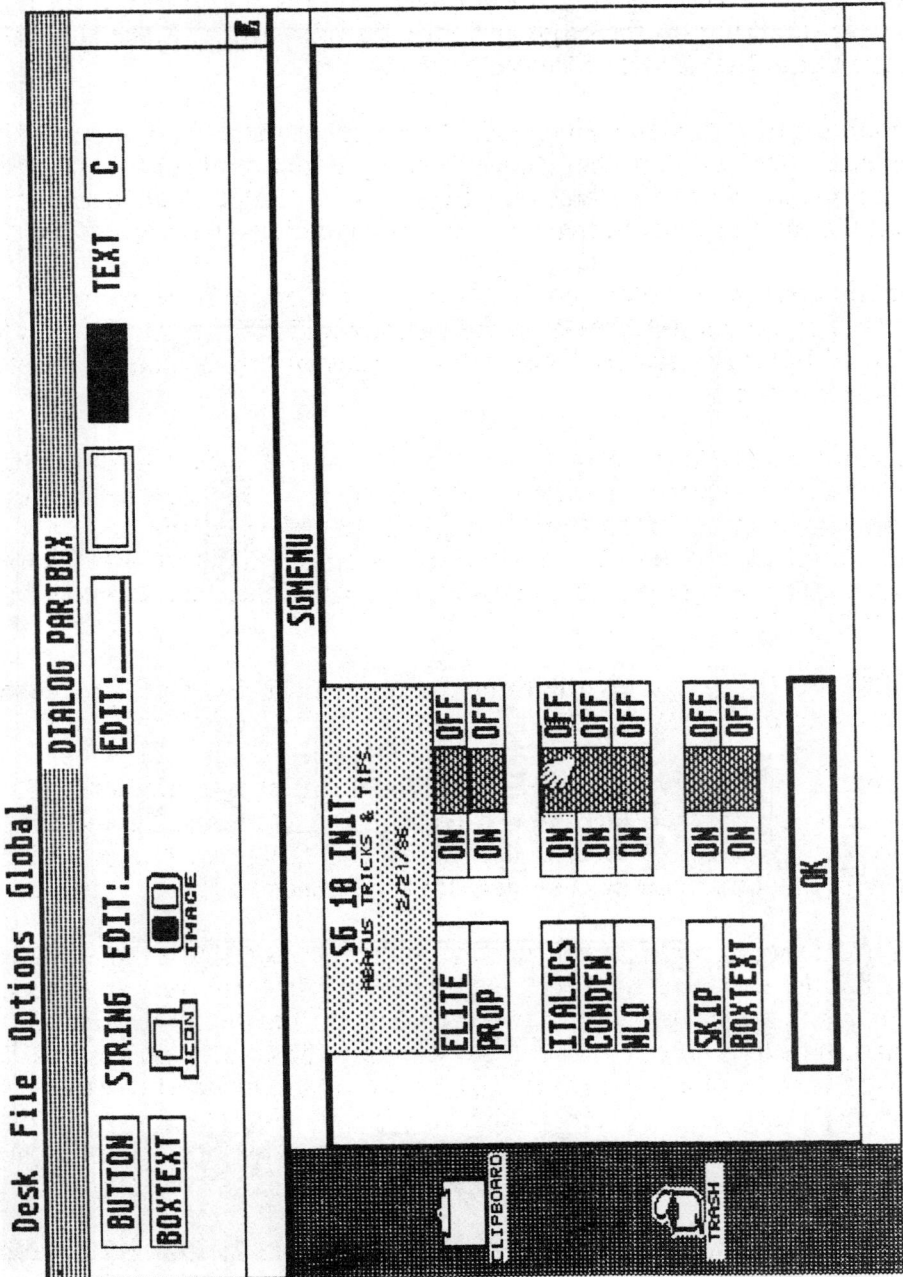

Each of the ON/OFF switches in the SGMENU (see Figure 4-2) is seperated by a shaded box (the third element from the right within the PARTBOX - see Figure 4-4). Drag it into the lower window and resize it to the desired size by clicking on the edge and moving the outline. Place this box to the right of the first BOXTEXT box.

Double click this box or select Open from the File menu. The RSC presents you with another dialog box, by which you set the parameters for the appearance of this box (see Figure 4-5.) Select a shaded background and the number 1 from the Background choices. Now press the OK box.

So that we may select each ON or OFF they will be represented by a BUTTON. Select a BUTTON in the partbox and position it to one side of the shaded box just created. Then move a copy of this button to the other side of the shaded box.

Open the left BUTTON with a double click and enter ON as the text. You should also select SELECTABLE and RADIO BUTN. Then press the OK box. Open the BUTTON on the right side and enter the text OFF. Select SELCTABLE and RADIO BUTN for this box (see Figure 4-6.) Resize these boxes for the most pleasing asppearence. Then place these boxes next to the first BOXTEXT.

After this is done, copy the three boxes for each BOXTEXT present. Edit the boxes next to MARGIN so that ON is 0 and OFF is 10.

The last important control element for you to create is another BUTTON with the text "OK" and define it as SELECTABLE, DEFAULT, and EXIT. Drag the BUTTON below the BOXTEXTs and OPEN it to make your choices. Resize this box to create a symerical appearence.

We're done, except for the title field, which consists of a large BOX outfitted with three elements of type TEXT. Select a box from the parts box and drag it into the lower window. Resize this box to fit, then open the box and add shading. Next select TEXT from the parts box and move it into the box. Copy text so you have three TEXTs in the box. Open the top TEXT and input SG10 INIT as text, select Lg Font. Select the second text, OPEN it and enter ABACUS Tricks and Tips. This time choose Sm Font. The third TEXT is opened and todays date is input as Sm Font.

Now OPEN the work window fully by clicking the box in the upper right hand corner. Then resize the large white box and repostion for appearence.

Now we must create the references so that our program later knows exactly which box has been selected. The function NAME within the OPTION menu of the title line serves this purpose.

You need to assign names only to objects which will be assigned a program function later. In our case we used the descriptions; ELITEIN, ELITEOUT, PROPIN, PROPOUT, ITALIN, ITALOUT, CONDENIN, CONDENOT, NLQIN, NLQOOT, SKIPIN, SKIPOUT, MARGIN0, MARGIN10, and EXIT for the OK field. Select each item (ON, OFF, 0, 10) and from the OPTIONS menu Name them accordingly.

Then click the close box on the window so that the DIALOG icon appears in the lower window. Next enter the File menu and tell the RCS to save the whole thing under the name "PRINIT.RSC" with the Save As option.

This will create the desired files, PRINIT.RSC, PRINIT.DEF and PRINIT.H. Then click the close field of the lower window so the RCS view window is empty again. Quit the RCS.

On your diskette you will find the following files:

PRINIT.RSC – the resource file for the following program
PRINIT.H   – an include file with all of the symbolic constants
PRINIT.DEF – an RCS file

Now that we have instructed you in the use of the RCS, here is a brief look at all of the components in the file as well as the optional parameters required for C programming.

The first thing listed is the object type. Most of the objects which you use for constructing your resources are of type BOX. They may be one of the following:

    G_IBOX, G_BOX   empty boxes
    G_BOXCHAR   contains a single character

If there are strings in the RSC file they are one of the following:

    G_STRING   a text string
    G_BUTTON   a string enclosed by a box
    G_TITLE   a string within a menu bar

Figure 4-5

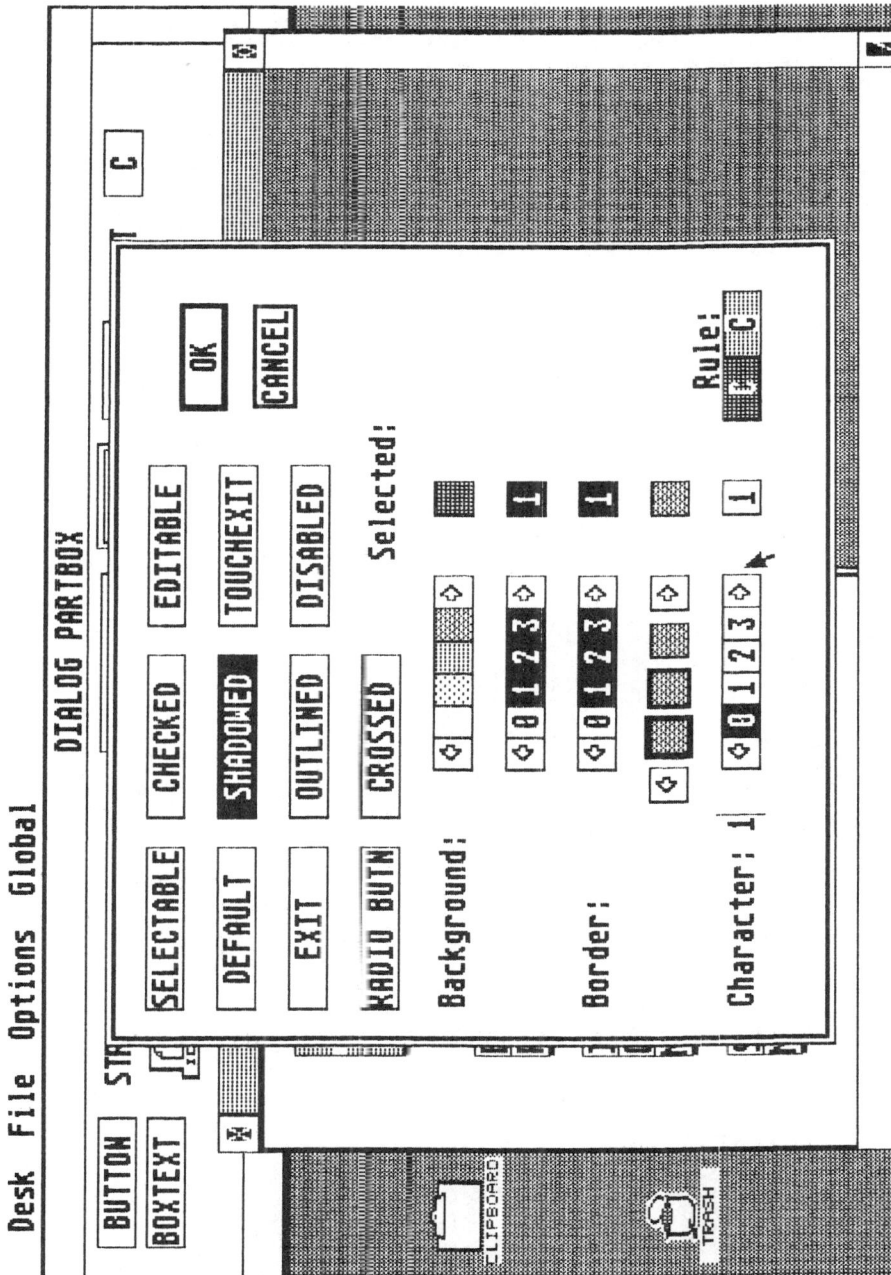

Figure 4-6

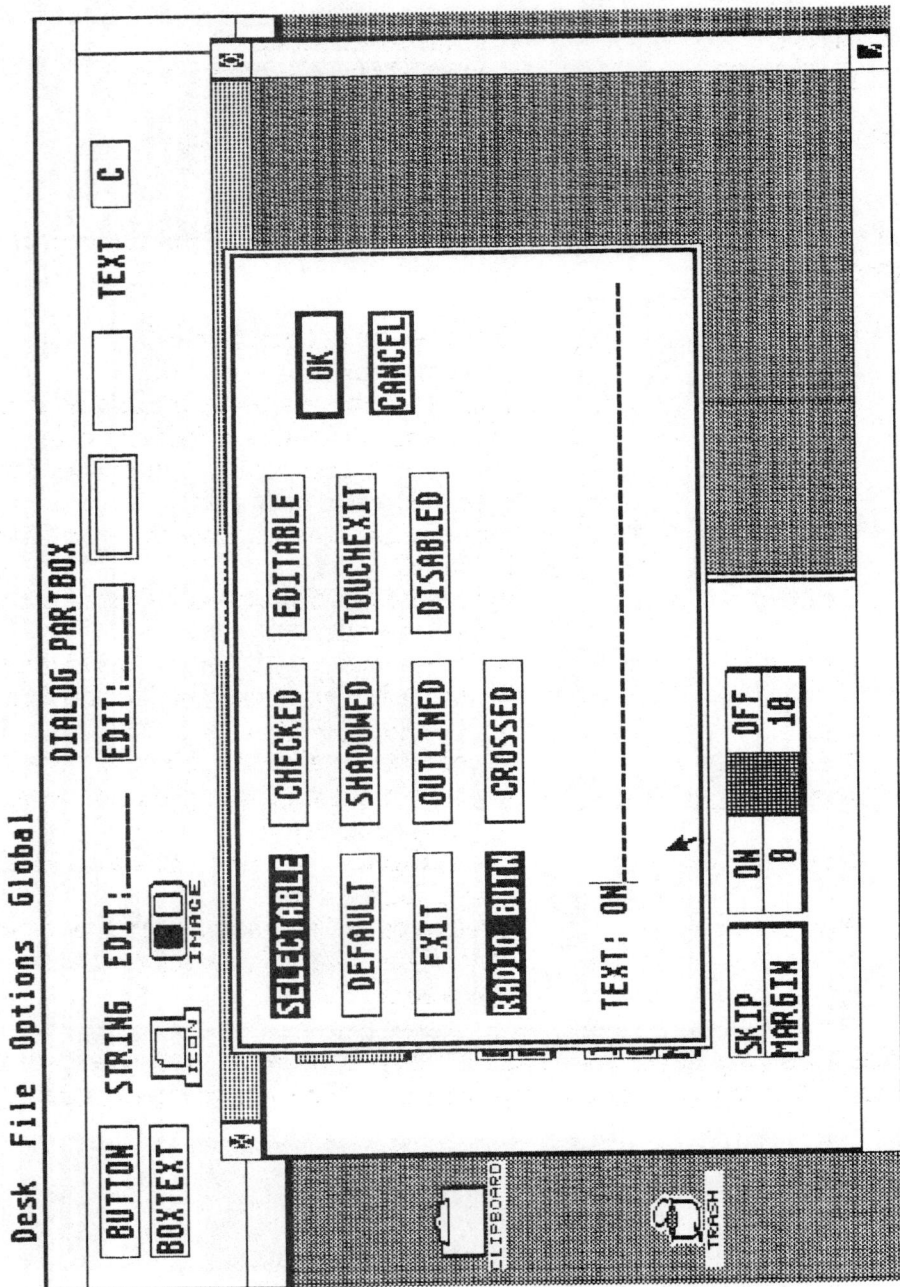

In addition, the RCS recognizes formatted text types, which are used for messages to be edited (such as in the file selection menu):

G_TEXT   is a formatted string
G_BOXTEXT   formatted string within a box
G_FTEXT   editable text
G_FBOXTEXT   editable text within a box

After putting the desired objects in the tree, you must set the object status and some flags:

Selected	draws an object in reverse
Crossed	crosses a box
Checked	displays a checkmark to the left of an object
Disabled	represents the object at half intensity
Outlined	the object contains another border (not together with Shadowed)
Shadowed	draws a shadow around the box (not with Outlined)
Selectable	the object can be activated during the course of the program
Default	pressing the <RETURN> key selects this object; it is display with a dark border
Exit	ends a dialog
Editable	the object contains editable text
Rbutton	the object belongs to a group of which only one can be selected
Hidetree	the object is not drawn with an Objc_Draw call
Touchexit	as soon as the mouse pointer is over such an object, the dialog is ended (without a clock operation)

On the following pages is a listing of the printer initialization program. Note that the .H file was merged into the main file by using a text editor.

If you have create a RSC file with the Resource Construction Set, note the values defined for each symbol so that these may be used in your C programs. For example, the value for the symbol EXIT is 5. The values in your .H file will differ from the ones in the following PRINT.H listing. Consult the .H file listing that you create and use these values in place of those below.

```
/********************************/
/* This file was created by the  */
/* authors using the RCS. The     */
/* values in your .H file will    */
/* differ from these. Substitute  */
/* the values from your listing   */
/* in the printer initialization  */
/* listing.                       */
/* PRINIT.H file  created by RCS  */
/********************************/

#define SGMENU 0          /* TREE */
#define EXIT 5            /* OBJECT in TREE #0 */
#define ELITEIN 7         /* OBJECT in TREE #0 */
#define PROPIN 10         /* OBJECT in TREE #0 */
#define PROPOUT 11        /* OBJECT in TREE #0 */
#define ITALIN 13         /* OBJECT in TREE #0 */
#define ITALOUT 14        /* OBJECT in TREE #0 */
#define CONENIN 16        /* OBJECT in TREE #0 */
#define CONDENOT 17       /* OBJECT in TREE #0 */
#define NLQIN 19          /* OBJECT in TREE #0 */
#define NLQOUT 20         /* OBJECT in TREE #0 */
#define SKIPIN 22         /* OBJECT in TREE #0 */
#define SKIPOUT 23        /* OBJECT in TREE #0 */
#define MARGIN0 26        /* OBJECT in TREE #0 */
#define MARGIN10 25       /* OBJECT in TREE #0 */
#define ELITEOUT 8        /* OBJECT in TREE #0 */
```

```
/***************************************************************/
/*              Printer initialization program            */
/*                  for STAR SG-10  printer               */
/***************************************************************/


/***************************************************************/
/* Use #include "PRINIT.H" or merge file into text using  your editor */
/* Your values from the RSC will be different from those listed below */
/***************************************************************/

#define SGMENU 0                 /* TREE                       */
#define EXIT 5                   /* OBJECT in TREE #0          */
#define ELITEIN 7                /* OBJECT in TREE #0          */
#define ELITEOUT 8               /* OBJECT in TREE #0          */
#define PROPIN 10                /* OBJECT in TREE #0          */
#define PROPOUT 11               /* OBJECT in TREE #0          */
#define ITALIN 13                /* OBJECT in TREE #0          */
#define ITALOUT 14               /* OBJECT in TREE #0          */
#define CONDENIN 16              /* OBJECT in TREE #0          */
#define CONDENOT 17              /* OBJECT in TREE #0          */
#define NLQIN 19                 /* OBJECT in TREE #0          */
#define NLQOUT 20                /* OBJECT in TREE #0          */
#define SKIPIN 22                /* OBJECT in TREE #0          */
#define SKIPOUT 23               /* OBJECT in TREE #0          */
#define MARGIN0 26               /* OBJECT in TREE #0          */
#define MARGIN10 25              /* OBJECT in TREE #0          */

long menu_tree;                  /* Address OF RSC-Objects     */

/***************************************************************/
/*                      Definition BUTTON in Menus       */
/***************************************************************/
#define SELECTED 0x0001
#define NORMAL 0x0000
#define WI_KIND 0x0001           /* Window has Name line       */
/***************************************************************/
/*                      Printer codes for                */
/*                          : STAR SG-10                 */
/***************************************************************/
#define RET 13                   /* Return                     */
#define ESC 27                   /* Escape                     */
#define BELL 7
#define SMALL 15                 /* Small print                */
#define SMALLOFF 18
#define ELITE 77                 /* Elite                      */
#define ELITEOFF 80
#define PROPORTIONAL 112         /* Proportional               */
```

```
#define PSET 1                    /* on                         */
#define PRESET 0                  /* off                        */
#define ITALIC 52                 /* Italic                     */
#define ITALICOFF 53
#define NLQ1 66                   /* NLQ mode                   */
#define NLQ2 4
#define NLQOFF 5
#define SKIP 78                   /* Skip over Perforation      */
#define SKIP1 6                   /* 6 lines                    */
#define SKIPOFF 79
#define LMARG 108                 /* left margin set            */
#define LMAROFF 0                 /*  left margin reset         */
#define POS10 10                  /*  Print at position  10     */

/*********************************************************************/
/*                          global Variables              */
/*********************************************************************/
int contrl[12];                   /* Controll-Arrays            */
int intin[128];
int ptsin[128];
int intout[128];
int ptsout[128];                  /* reserve space for all parameters */
int pxyarray[12];                 /* Array for x,y coordinates      */

int int_in[11];                   /* Input in GSX Array         */
int int_out[57];                  /* Output from GSX Array      */

int handle,i;                     /* virtual workstation handle */
int phys_handle;                  /* physical workstation handle */
int wi_handle;                    /* Window handle              */

int ap_id;                        /* Code number of application */

int gl_hchar, gl_wchar;           /* Height and widthof character */
int gl_wbox, gl_hbox;

int xwork,ywork,wwork,hwork;      /* dimensions of window       */
int xdesk,ydesk,wdesk,hdesk;      /* Desktop dimensions         */
int xold, yold, hold, wold;
                   /* temporary variables for window manipulation*/
int xobj,yobj,wobj,hobj;          /* coordinates of objects     */
int mausx, mausy;                 /* where was mouse when pressed?  */

int dummy;                        /* ... dummy parameter        */

int event;                        /* which event occured at the moment */
int title, item;                  /* Menu title and actual object   */
```

194

```
/*************************************************************************/
/*                              Window open, close                   */
/*************************************************************************/
open_window()
{
   wi_handle=wind_create(WI_KIND,xdesk,ydesk,wdesk,hdesk);
   graf_growbox(xdesk+wdesk/2,ydesk+hdesk/2,gl_wbox,gl_hbox,xdesk,
               ydesk,wdesk,hdesk);
   wind_open(wi_handle,xdesk,ydesk,wdesk,hdesk);
   wind_get(wi_handle,WF_WORKXYWH,&xwork,&ywork,&wwork,&hwork);
}


close_window()
{
   wind_close(wi_handle);
   graf_shrinkbox(xwork+wwork/2,ywork+hwork/2,gl_wbox,gl_hbox,xwork,
               ywork,wwork,hwork);
   wind_delete(wi_handle);
}


open_vwork()
{
int i;
      for (i = 1; i <10; i++){
        int_in[i] = 1;       /* init int_in array: line type, color,  */
        }                    /* fill styles usw.                      */
      int_in[10] = 2;        /* use RC - coordinates                  */
      handle=phys_handle;
      v_opnvwk(int_in, &handle, int_out); /* set window ...           */
}


/*************************************************************************/
/*                              Main program                         */
/*************************************************************************/
main()
{
int ende;                            /* is TRUE when EXIT box selected */
long   gemdos();                     /* for gemdos-call                */

      ap_id=appl_init();       /* initialize GEM AES Array-Structures */

      phys_handle=graf_handle(&gl_wchar,&gl_hchar,&gl_wbox,&gl_hbox);
                        /* Parameter for Desktop established         */
      wind_get(0,WF_WORKXYWH,&xdesk,&ydesk,&wdesk,&hdesk);
      open_vwork();                  /* Work station opened           */
```

```
        if(!rsrc_load(FILENAME))        /* RSC-file loaded               */
          {
   form_alert(1,"[3][Bad Copy?|PRINIT.RSC|could not be found.][Abort]");
        close_window;
        desktop();
        }
      if(rsrc_gaddr(0,0,&menu_tree)== 0)
          {
       form_alert(1,"[3] [Fatal error!|Resource File not OK.][Abort]");
        close_window;
        desktop();
        }
      rsrc_gaddr(R_TREE,SGMENU,&menu_tree);
      form_center(menu_tree,&xobj,&yobj,&wobj,&hobj);
      form_dial(0,xobj,yobj,wobj,hobj);
      form_dial(1,1,1,1,1,xobj,yobj,wobj,hobj);

      objc_draw(menu_tree,0,MAX_DEPTH,0,0,wdesk,hdesk);

      graf_mouse(3,&dummy);            /* Mouse = Hand                  */

      while (ende != TRUE){
          event=evnt_button(1,1,1,&mausx,&mausy,&dummy,&dummy);
                              /* Wait for left button click      */

          item=objc_find(menu_tree,SGMENU,13,mausx,mausy);
                          /* which object in menu_tree at Mouse position*/

          switch(item){
case    ELITEIN:
objc_change(menu_tree,ELITEIN,0,xwork,ywork,wwork,hwork,SELECTED,1);

objc_change(menu_tree,ELITEOUT,0,xwork,ywork,wwork,hwork,NORMAL,1);
              gemdos(0x5,ESC);
              gemdos(0x5,ELITE);
              gemdos(0x5,BELL);
              break;


case    ELITEOUT:
objc_change(menu_tree,ELITEOUT,0,xwork,ywork,wwork,hwork,SELECTED,1);

objc_change(menu_tree,ELITEIN,0,xwork,ywork,wwork,hwork,NORMAL,1);
              gemdos(0x5,ESC);
              gemdos(0x5,ELITEOFF);
              gemdos(0x5,BELL);
              break;
```

```
case    CONDENIN:
objc_change(menu_tree,CONDENIN,0,xwork,ywork,wwork,hwork,SELECTED,1);

objc_change(menu_tree,CONDENOT,0,xwork,ywork,wwork,hwork,NORMAL,1);
            gemdos(0x5,SMALL);
            gemdos(0x5,BELL);
            break;

case    CONDENOT:
objc_change(menu_tree,CONDENOT,0,xwork,ywork,wwork,hwork,SELECTED,1);

objc_change(menu_tree,CONDENIN,0,xwork,ywork,wwork,hwork,NORMAL,1);
            gemdos(0x5,SMALLOFF);
            gemdos(0x5,BELL);
            break;

case    PROPIN:
objc_change(menu_tree,PROPIN,0,xwork,ywork,wwork,hwork,SELECTED,1);

objc_change(menu_tree,PROPOUT,0,xwork,ywork,wwork,hwork,NORMAL,1);
            gemdos(0x5,ESC);
            gemdos(0x5,PROPORTIONAL);
            gemdos(0x5,PSET);
            gemdos(0x5,BELL);
            break;

    case    PROPOUT:
objc_change(menu_tree,PROPOUT,0,xwork,ywork,wwork,hwork,SELECTED,1);

objc_change(menu_tree,PROPIN,0,xwork,ywork,wwork,hwork,NORMAL,1);
            gemdos(0x5,ESC);
            gemdos(0x5,PROPORTIONAL);
            gemdos(0x5,PRESET);
            gemdos(0x5,BELL);
            break;

case    ITALIN:
objc_change(menu_tree,ITALIN,0,xwork,ywork,wwork,hwork,SELECTED,1);

objc_change(menu_tree,ITALOUT,0,xwork,ywork,wwork,hwork,NORMAL,1);
            gemdos(0x5,ESC);
            gemdos(0x5,ITALIC);
            gemdos(0x5,BELL);
            break;
```

```
case      ITALOUT:
objc_change(menu_tree,ITALOUT,0,xwork,ywork,wwork,hwork,SELECTED,1);

objc_change(menu_tree,ITALIN,0,xwork,ywork,wwork,hwork,NORMAL,1);
              gemdos(0x5,ESC);
              gemdos(0x5,ITALICOFF);
              gemdos(0x5,BELL);
              break;

case      NLQIN:
objc_change(menu_tree,NLQIN,0,xwork,ywork,wwork,hwork,SELECTED,1);

objc_change(menu_tree,NLQOUT,0,xwork,ywork,wwork,hwork,NORMAL,1);
              gemdos(0x5,ESC);
              gemdos(0x5,NLQ1);
              gemdos(0x5,NLQ2);
              gemdos(0x5,BELL);
              break;

case      NLQOUT:
objc_change(menu_tree,NLQOUT,0,xwork,ywork,wwork,hwork,SELECTED,1);

objc_change(menu_tree,NLQIN,0,xwork,ywork,wwork,hwork,NORMAL,1);
              gemdos(0x5,ESC);
              gemdos(0x5,NLQ1);
              gemdos(0x5,NLQOFF);
              gemdos(0x5,BELL);
              break;

case      SKIPIN:
objc_change(menu_tree,SKIPIN,0,xwork,ywork,wwork,hwork,SELECTED,1);

objc_change(menu_tree,SKIPOUT,0,xwork,ywork,wwork,hwork,NORMAL,1);
              gemdos(0x5,ESC);
              gemdos(0x5,SKIP);
              gemdos(0x5,SKIP1);
              gemdos(0x5,BELL);
              break;

case      SKIPOUT:
objc_change(menu_tree,SKIPOUT,0,xwork,ywork,wwork,hwork,SELECTED,1);

objc_change(menu_tree,SKIPIN,0,xwork,ywork,wwork,hwork,NORMAL,1);
              gemdos(0x5,ESC);
              gemdos(0x5,SKIPOFF);
              gemdos(0x5,BELL);
              break;
```

```
case    MARGIN0:
objc_change(menu_tree,MARGIN0,0,xwork,ywork,wwork,hwork,SELECTED,1);

objc_change(menu_tree,MARGIN10,0,xwork,ywork,wwork,hwork,NORMAL,1);
                gemdos(0x5,ESC);
                gemdos(0x5,LMARG);
                gemdos(0x5,LMAROFF);
                gemdos(0x5,BELL);
                break;

case    MARGIN10:
objc_change(menu_tree,MARGIN10,0,xwork,ywork,wwork,hwork,SELECTED,1);

objc_change(menu_tree,MARGIN0,0,xwork,ywork,wwork,hwork,NORMAL,1);
                gemdos(0x5,ESC);
                gemdos(0x5,LMARG);
                gemdos(0x5,POS10);
                gemdos(0x5,BELL);
                break;

case    EXIT:
objc_change(menu_tree,EXIT,0,xwork,ywork,wwork,hwork,SELECTED,1);
                gemdos(0x5,RET);
                form_dial(3,xobj,yobj,wobj,hobj);
                form_dial(2,1,1,1,1,xobj,yobj,wobj,hobj);
                ende=TRUE;
                break;

        } /* End switch  */

    } /* End while */
    desktop();

} /* End main() */

desktop()
{
   v_clsvwk();
   appl_exit();
}
```

If you don't have an SG-10 or Epson-compatible printer you will have to substitute the appropriate codes for your printer in the program.

Small changes, which provide only aesthetic changes are the calls to `graf_growbox` and `graf_shrinkbox` within the window routines. They cause the box to appear to grow and shrink.

Something new is the call to the RSC file. And since `rsrc_load()` is a function, it also returns a function value, namely TRUE or FALSE. In case of an error in the loading procedure, an alert tree can be displayed and program execution terminated.

An important call is to `rsrc_gaddr()`. This function returns a pointer to the object desired.

Example:

After the start of the program the entire tree must be displayed from first to last object. We must therefore find out where the root of the tree, in our case the SGMENU tree, is located in memory.

So we call `rsrc_gaddr()` and tell the AES what we're looking for: namely the object SGMENU is a tree (R_TREE). The address of SGMENU should be assigned to the pointer &menu_tree:

`rsrc_gaddr(R_TREE,SGMENU,&menu_tree);`

To display the tree or any other object, we call Object_Draw, a function which draws partial sections of a tree:

`objc_draw(menu_tree,0,MAX_DEPTH,0,0,wdesk,hdesk);`

The parameters, in order of their occurrence determine which tree is drawn, starting with which object (here zero, the first), up to `chich` (the maximum number can be read under INFO in the RCS), and finally a surface which will be prepared for this task.

The call to Object_Find within the main loop outputs the number of the object under the mouse pointer after entering the mouse position—which is given as the fourth and fifth parameters of `event_button`. This is then compared to all of our object numbers, for which the symbolic constants stand, in order, until a match is found and the corresponding action is carried out.

The Object_Change statements there have no other function then to make the object in question black.

The form_dial statemenrts in the program listing display the dialog box. They release the corresponding memory space—the underlying screen area must be saved—draw the growing or shrinking box, and then release the previously occupied memory area again.

For those of you who do not have a C compiler the following BASIC loaders will create the PRINIT.RCS and SGINIT.PRG programs on your disk.

```
100     rem BASIC loader to create PRINIT.RSC for SG10INIT.PRG
1000    open"R",1,"a:prinit.rsc",16
1010    field#1,16 as bin$
1020    a$="":for i=1 TO 16:read d$:if d$="*"then 1050
1030    a=val("&H"+d$):s=s+a:a$=a$+chr$(a):next
1040    lset bin$=a$:rec=rec+1:put 1,rec:goto 1020
1050    data 00,00,01,E4,C0,CC,00,CC,00,CC,00,00,00,24,00,CC
1060    data 00,00,05,14,C0,22,00,01,00,0A,00,00,00,00,00,00
1070    data 00,00,05,18,53,47,31,30,20,49,4E,49,54,00,00,00
1080    data 20,20,66,72,6F,6D,3A,20,41,42,41,43,55,53,BA,73
1090    data 20,54,69,70,73,20,26,20,54,72,69,63,6B,73,20,20
1100    data 00,00,00,4A,57,20,31,30,2E,38,35,00,00,00,4F,6B
1110    data 61,79,20,21,00,4F,4E,00,4F,46,46,00,4F,4E,00,4F
1120    data 46,46,00,4F,4E,00,4F,46,46,00,4F,4E,00,4F,46,46
1130    data 00,4F,4E,00,4F,46,46,00,4F,4E,00,4F,46,46,00,31
1140    data 30,00,20,30,00,45,4C,49,54,45,00,00,00,50,52,4F
1150    data 50,00,00,00,49,54,41,4C,49,43,00,00,00,43,4F,4E
1160    data 44,45,4E,00,00,00,4E,4C,51,00,00,00,53,4B,49,50
1170    data 00,00,00,4D,41,52,47,49,4E,00,00,00,00,00,00,24
1180    data 00,00,00,2E,00,00,00,2F,00,03,00,06,00,00,11,80
1190    data 00,00,FF,FF,00,0A,00,01,00,00,00,30,00,00,00,51
1200    data 00,00,00,52,00,05,00,06,00,02,11,A0,00,00,FF,FF
1210    data 00,21,00,01,00,00,00,53,00,00,00,5C,00,00,00,5D
1220    data 00,05,00,06,00,02,11,80,00,00,FF,FF,00,09,00,01
1230    data 00,00,00,95,00,00,00,9B,00,00,00,9C,00,03,00,06
1240    data 00,00,11,60,00,00,FF,FF,00,06,00,01,00,00,00,9D
```

```
1250   data 00,00,00,A2,00,00,00,A3,00,03,00,06,00,00,11,60
1260   data 00,00,FF,FF,00,05,00,01,00,00,00,A4,00,00,00,AB
1270   data 00,00,00,AC,00,03,00,06,00,00,11,60,00,00,FF,FF
1280   data 00,07,00,01,00,00,00,AD,00,00,00,B4,00,00,00,B5
1290   data 00,03,00,06,00,00,11,60,00,00,FF,FF,00,07,00,01
1300   data 00,00,00,B6,00,00,00,BA,00,00,00,BB,00,03,00,06
1310   data 00,00,11,60,00,00,FF,FF,00,04,00,01,00,00,00,BC
1320   data 00,00,00,C1,00,00,00,C2,00,03,00,06,00,00,11,60
1330   data 00,00,FF,FF,00,05,00,01,00,00,00,C3,00,00,00,CA
1340   data 00,00,00,CB,00,03,00,06,00,00,11,60,00,00,FF,FF
1350   data 00,07,00,01,FF,FF,00,01,00,21,00,14,00,00,00,10
1360   data 00,02,11,20,00,00,00,00,00,24,00,13,00,05,00,02
1370   data 00,04,00,14,00,00,00,20,00,FF,33,A2,00,06,00,01
1380   data 00,18,00,03,00,03,FF,FF,FF,FF,00,15,00,00,00,00
1390   data 00,00,00,CC,00,07,00,00,00,09,00,01,00,04,FF,FF
1400   data FF,FF,00,15,00,00,00,00,00,00,00,E8,00,00,00,01
1410   data 00,18,06,00,00,01,FF,FF,FF,FF,00,15,00,00,00,00
1420   data 00,00,01,04,00,09,00,02,00,06,06,00,00,06,FF,FF
1430   data FF,FF,00,1A,00,07,00,00,00,00,00,5E,00,06,00,11
1440   data 00,18,00,01,00,09,00,07,00,08,00,14,00,00,00,20
1450   data 31,FF,11,E1,00,0F,00,06,00,0F,00,01,00,08,FF,FF
1460   data FF,FF,00,1A,00,11,00,00,00,00,00,65,00,00,00,00
1470   data 00,06,00,01,00,06,FF,FF,FF,FF,00,1A,00,11,00,00
1480   data 00,00,00,68,00,0A,00,00,00,05,00,01,00,0C,00,0A
1490   data 00,0B,00,14,00,00,00,20,31,FF,11,61,00,0F,00,07
1500   data 00,0F,00,01,00,0B,FF,FF,FF,FF,00,1A,00,11,00,00
1510   data 00,00,00,6C,00,00,00,00,00,06,00,01,00,09,FF,FF
1520   data FF,FF,00,1A,00,11,00,00,00,00,00,6F,00,0A,00,00
1530   data 00,05,00,01,00,0F,00,0D,00,0E,00,14,00,00,00,20
1540   data 31,FF,11,61,00,0F,00,09,00,0F,00,01,00,0E,FF,FF
1550   data FF,FF,00,1A,00,01,00,00,00,00,00,73,00,00,00,00
1560   data 00,06,00,01,00,0C,FF,FF,FF,FF,00,1A,00,01,00,00
1570   data 00,00,00,76,00,0A,00,00,00,05,00,01,00,12,00,10
1580   data 00,11,00,14,00,00,00,20,31,FF,11,61,00,0F,00,0A
1590   data 00,0F,00,01,00,11,FF,FF,FF,FF,00,1A,00,11,00,00
1600   data 00,00,00,7A,00,00,00,00,00,06,00,01,00,0F,FF,FF
1610   data FF,FF,00,1A,00,11,00,00,00,00,00,7D,00,0A,00,00
1620   data 00,05,00,01,00,15,00,13,00,14,00,14,00,00,00,20
1630   data 31,FF,11,61,00,0F,00,0B,00,0F,00,01,00,14,FF,FF
1640   data FF,FF,00,1A,00,11,00,00,00,00,00,81,00,00,00,00
1650   data 00,06,00,01,00,12,FF,FF,FF,FF,00,1A,00,11,00,00
1660   data 00,00,00,84,00,0A,00,00,00,05,00,01,00,18,00,16
1670   data 00,17,00,14,00,00,00,20,31,FF,11,61,00,0F,00,0D
```

```
1680    data 00,0F,00,01,03,17,FF,FF,FF,FF,00,1A,00,11,00,00
1690    data 00,00,00,88,03,00,00,00,00,06,00,01,00,15,FF,FF
1700    data FF,FF,00,1A,00,11,00,00,00,00,00,8B,00,0A,00,00
1710    data 00,05,00,01,00,1A,00,19,00,19,00,14,00,00,00,20
1720    data 31,FF,11,61,00,0F,00,0E,00,0F,00,01,00,18,FF,FF
1730    data FF,FF,00,1A,00,01,00,00,00,00,00,8F,00,0A,00,00
1740    data 00,05,00,01,00,1B,FF,FF,FF,FF,00,1A,00,11,00,00
1750    data 00,00,00,92,00,0F,00,0E,00,06,00,01,00,1C,FF,FF
1760    data FF,FF,00,16,00,00,00,20,00,00,01,20,00,06,00,06
1770    data 00,08,00,01,00,1D,FF,FF,FF,FF,00,16,00,00,00,20
1780    data 00,00,01,3C,00,06,00,07,00,08,00,01,00,1E,FF,FF
1790    data FF,FF,00,16,00,00,00,20,00,00,01,58,00,06,00,09
1800    data 00,08,00,01,00,1F,FF,FF,FF,FF,00,16,00,00,00,20
1810    data 00,00,01,74,00,06,00,0A,00,08,00,01,00,20,FF,FF
1820    data FF,FF,00,16,00,00,00,20,00,00,01,90,00,06,00,0B
1830    data 00,08,00,01,00,21,FF,FF,FF,FF,00,16,00,00,00,20
1840    data 00,00,01,AC,00,06,00,0D,00,08,00,01,00,00,FF,FF
1850    data FF,FF,00,16,00,20,00,20,00,00,01,C8,00,06,00,0E
1860    data 00,08,00,01,00,00,01,E4,00,00,00,00,00,00,00,00
1870    data *
1880    close 1:if s<> 57208 then print"ERROR IN DATA!":end
1900    print "Ok."
```

```
100    rem BASIC loader to create SG10INIT.PRG
1000   open"R",1,"sg10init.prg",16
1010   field#1,16 as bin$
1020   a$="":for i=1 TO 16:read d$:if d$="*"then 1050
1030   a=val("&H"+d$):s=s+a:a$=a$+chr$(a):next
1040   lset bin$=a$:rec=rec+1:put 1,rec:goto 1020
1050   data 60,1A,00,00,14,30,00,00,02,24,00,00,09,70,00,00
1060   data 00,00,00,00,00,00,00,00,00,00,00,00,2A,4F,2E,7C
1070   data 00,00,1A,54,2A,6D,00,04,20,2D,00,0C,D0,AD,00,14
1080   data D0,AD,00,1C,D0,BC,00,00,01,00,2F,00,2F,0D,3F,00
1090   data 3F,3C,00,4A,4E,41,DF,FC,00,00,00,0C,4E,B9,00,00
1100   data 02,00,2F,3C,00,00,00,00,4E,41,22,2F,00,04,30,3C
1110   data 00,C8,4E,42,4E,75,4E,56,FF,FC,3E,B9,00,00,1F,92
1120   data 3F,39,00,00,1F,BA,3F,39,00,00,1F,C2,3F,39,00,00
1130   data 1F,C0,3F,3C,00,01,4E,B9,00,00,13,36,50,8F,33,C0
1140   data 00,00,1F,B8,3E,B9,00,00,1F,92,3F,39,00,00,1F,BA
1150   data 3F,39,00,00,1F,C2,3F,39,00,00,1F,C0,3F,39,00,00
1160   data 1C,74,3F,39,00,00,1E,A2,30,39,00,00,1F,92,48,C0
1170   data 81,FC,00,02,3F,00,30,39,00,00,1F,C2,D1,57,30,39
1180   data 00,00,1F,BA,48,C0,81,FC,00,02,3F,00,30,39,00,00
1190   data 1F,C0,D1,57,4E,B9,00,00,11,02,DF,FC,00,00,00,0E
1200   data 3E,B9,00,00,1F,92,3F,39,00,00,1F,BA,3F,39,00,00
1210   data 1F,C2,3F,39,00,00,1F,C0,3F,39,00,00,1F,B8,4E,B9
1220   data 00,00,13,70,50,8F,2E,BC,00,00,1C,98,2F,3C,00,00
1230   data 1E,D2,2F,3C,00,00,1E,D6,2F,3C,00,00,1E,D4,3F,3C
1240   data 00,04,3F,39,00,00,1F,B8,4E,B9,00,00,13,DE,DF,FC
1250   data 00,00,00,10,4E,5E,4E,75,4E,56,FF,FC,3E,B9,00,00
1260   data 1F,B8,4E,B9,00,00,13,AA,3E,B9,00,00,1C,98,3F,39
1270   data 00,00,1E,D2,3F,39,00,00,1E,D6,3F,39,00,00,1E,D4
1280   data 3F,39,00,00,1C,74,3F,39,00,00,1E,A2,30,39,00,00
1290   data 1C,98,48,C0,81,FC,00,02,3F,00,30,39,00,00,1E,D6
1300   data D1,57,30,39,00,00,1E,D2,48,C0,81,FC,00,02,3F,00
1310   data 30,39,00,00,1E,D4,D1,57,4E,B9,00,00,11,54,DF,FC
1320   data 00,00,00,0E,3E,B9,00,00,1F,B8,4E,B9,00,00,13,C4
1330   data 4E,5E,4E,75,4E,56,FF,FA,3D,7C,00,01,FF,FE,60,14
1340   data 30,6E,FF,FE,D1,C8,D1,FC,00,00,1E,DA,30,BC,00,01
1350   data 52,6E,FF,FE,0C,6E,00,0A,FF,FE,6D,E4,33,FC,00,02
1360   data 00,00,1E,EE,33,F9,00,00,1C,96,00,00,1C,94,2E,BC
1370   data 00,00,1E,FA,2F,3C,00,00,1C,94,2F,3C,00,00,1E,DA
1380   data 4E,B9,00,00,0E,3E,50,8F,4E,5E,4E,75,4E,56,FF,FA
1390   data 4E,B9,00,00,0F,6E,33,C0,00,00,1E,D8,2E,BC,00,00
1400   data 1C,74,2F,3C,00,00,1E,A2,2F,3C,00,00,1F,74,2F,3C
1410   data 00,00,1F,B6,4E,B9,00,00,11,A6,DF,FC,00,00,00,0C
```

```
1420    data 33,C0,00,00,1C,96,2E,BC,00,00,1F,92,2F,3C,00,00
1430    data 1F,BA,2F,3C,00,00,1F,C2,2F,3C,00,00,1F,C0,3F,3C
1440    data 00,04,42,67,4E,B9,00,00,13,DE,DF,FC,00,00,00,10
1450    data 61,00,FF,42,2E,BC,00,00,15,E4,4E,B9,00,00,12,E8
1460    data 4A,40,66,1C,2E,BC,00,00,15,EF,3F,3C,00,01,4E,B9
1470    data 00,00,10,96,54,8F,20,3C,00,00,01,2C,61,00,0B,6E
1480    data 2E,BC,00,00,1E,CE,42,67,42,67,4E,B9,00,00,13,02
1490    data 58,8F,4A,40,66,1C,2E,BC,00,00,16,24,3F,3C,00,01
1500    data 4E,B9,00,00,1C,96,54,8F,20,3C,00,00,01,2C,61,00
1510    data 0B,3C,2E,BC,00,00,1E,CE,42,67,42,67,4E,B9,00,00
1520    data 13,02,58,8F,2E,BC,00,00,1C,76,2F,3C,00,00,1E,A4
1530    data 2F,3C,00,00,1E,C6,2F,3C,00,00,1E,C4,2F,39,00,00
1540    data 1E,CE,4E,B9,00,00,10,B8,DF,FC,00,00,00,10,3E,B9
1550    data 00,00,1C,76,3F,39,00,00,1E,A4,3F,39,00,00,1E,C6
1560    data 3F,39,00,00,1E,C4,42,67,4E,B9,00,00,10,3C,50,8F
1570    data 3E,B9,00,00,1C,76,3F,39,00,00,1E,A4,3F,39,00,00
1580    data 1E,C6,3F,39,00,00,1E,C4,3F,3C,00,01,3F,3C,00,01
1590    data 3F,3C,00,01,3F,3C,00,01,3F,3C,00,01,4E,B9,00,00
1600    data 10,3C,DF,FC,00,00,00,10,3E,B9,00,00,1F,92,3F,39
1610    data 00,00,1F,BA,42,67,42,67,3F,3C,00,22,42,67,2F,39
1620    data 00,00,1E,CE,4E,B9,00,00,12,0A,DF,FC,00,00,00,0E
1630    data 2E,BC,00,00,1C,9A,3F,3C,00,03,4E,B9,00,00,11,E8
1640    data 54,8F,60,00,0A,58,2E,BC,00,00,1C,9A,2F,3C,00,00
1650    data 1C,9A,2F,3C,00,00,1E,9E,2F,3C,00,00,1D,9C,3F,3C
1660    data 00,01,3F,3C,00,01,3F,3C,00,01,4E,B9,00,00,0F,E2
1670    data DF,FC,00,00,00,12,33,C0,00,00,1B,70,3E,B9,00,00
1680    data 1E,9E,3F,39,00,00,1D,9C,3F,3C,00,0D,42,67,2F,39
1690    data 00,00,1E,CE,4E,B9,00,00,12,54,DF,FC,00,00,00,0A
1700    data 33,C0,00,00,1E,A0,30,39,00,00,1E,A0,60,00,09,D8
1710    data 3E,BC,00,01,3F,3C,00,01,3F,39,00,00,1C,98,3F,39
1720    data 00,00,1E,D2,3F,39,00,00,1E,D6,3F,39,00,00,1E,D4
1730    data 42,67,3F,3C,00,07,2F,39,00,00,1E,CE,4E,B9,00,00
1740    data 12,8E,DF,FC,00,00,00,12,3E,BC,00,01,42,67,3F,39
1750    data 00,00,1C,98,3F,39,00,00,1E,D2,3F,39,00,00,1E,D6
1760    data 3F,39,00,00,1E,D4,42,67,3F,3C,00,08,2F,39,00,00
1770    data 1E,CE,4E,B9,00,00,12,8E,DF,FC,00,00,00,12,3E,BC
1780    data 00,1B,3F,3C,00,05,4E,B9,00,00,0E,F4,54,8F,3E,BC
1790    data 00,4D,3F,3C,00,05,4E,B9,00,00,0E,F4,54,8F,3E,BC
1800    data 00,07,3F,3C,00,05,4E,B9,00,00,0E,F4,54,8F,60,00
1810    data 09,4C,3E,BC,00,01,3F,3C,00,01,3F,39,00,00,1C,98
1820    data 3F,39,00,00,1E,D2,3F,39,00,00,1E,D6,3F,39,00,00
1830    data 1E,D4,42,67,3F,3C,00,08,2F,39,00,00,1E,CE,4E,B9
1840    data 00,00,12,8E,DF,FC,00,00,00,12,3E,BC,00,01,42,67
```

```
1850   data 3F,39,00,00,1C,98,3F,39,00,00,1E,D2,3F,39,00,00
1860   data 1E,D6,3F,39,00,00,1E,D4,42,67,3F,3C,00,07,2F,39
1870   data 00,00,1E,CE,4E,B9,00,00,12,8E,DF,FC,00,00,00,12
1880   data 3E,BC,00,1B,3F,3C,00,05,4E,B9,00,00,0E,F4,54,8F
1890   data 3E,BC,00,50,3F,3C,00,05,4E,B9,00,00,0E,F4,54,8F
1900   data 3E,BC,00,07,3F,3C,00,05,4E,B9,00,00,0E,F4,54,8F
1910   data 60,00,08,AA,3E,BC,00,01,3F,3C,00,01,3F,39,00,00
1920   data 1C,98,3F,39,00,00,1E,D2,3F,39,00,00,1E,D6,3F,39
1930   data 00,00,1E,D4,42,67,3F,3C,00,10,2F,39,00,00,1E,CE
1940   data 4E,B9,00,00,12,8E,DF,FC,00,00,00,12,3E,BC,00,01
1950   data 42,67,3F,39,00,00,1C,98,3F,39,00,00,1E,D2,3F,39
1960   data 00,00,1E,D6,3F,39,00,00,1E,D4,42,67,3F,3C,00,11
1970   data 2F,39,00,00,1E,CE,4E,B9,00,00,12,8E,DF,FC,00,00
1980   data 00,12,3E,BC,00,0F,3F,3C,00,05,4E,B9,00,00,0E,F4
1990   data 54,8F,3E,BC,00,07,3F,3C,00,05,4E,B9,00,00,0E,F4
2000   data 54,8F,60,00,08,18,3E,BC,00,01,3F,3C,00,01,3F,39
2010   data 00,00,1C,98,3F,39,00,00,1E,D2,3F,39,00,00,1E,D6
2020   data 3F,39,00,00,1E,D4,42,67,3F,3C,00,11,2F,39,00,00
2030   data 1E,CE,4E,B9,00,00,12,8E,DF,FC,00,00,00,12,3E,BC
2040   data 00,01,42,67,3F,39,00,00,1C,98,3F,39,00,00,1E,D2
2050   data 3F,39,00,00,1E,D6,3F,39,00,00,1E,D4,42,67,3F,3C
2060   data 00,10,2F,39,00,00,1E,CE,4E,B9,00,00,12,8E,DF,FC
2070   data 00,00,00,12,3E,BC,00,12,3F,3C,00,05,4E,B9,00,00
2080   data 0E,F4,54,8F,3E,BC,00,07,3F,3C,00,05,4E,B9,00,00
2090   data 0E,F4,54,8F,60,00,07,86,3E,BC,00,01,3F,3C,00,01
2100   data 3F,39,00,00,1C,98,3F,39,00,00,1E,D2,3F,39,00,00
2110   data 1E,D6,3F,39,00,00,1E,D4,42,67,3F,3C,00,0A,2F,39
2120   data 00,00,1E,CE,4E,B9,00,00,12,8E,DF,FC,00,00,00,12
2130   data 3E,BC,00,01,42,67,3F,39,00,00,1C,98,3F,39,00,00
2140   data 1E,D2,3F,39,00,00,1E,D6,3F,39,00,00,1E,D4,42,67
2150   data 3F,3C,00,0B,2F,39,00,00,1E,CE,4E,B9,00,00,12,8E
2160   data DF,FC,00,00,00,12,3E,BC,00,1B,3F,3C,00,05,4E,B9
2170   data 00,00,0E,F4,54,8F,3E,BC,00,70,3F,3C,00,05,4E,B9
2180   data 00,00,0E,F4,54,8F,3E,BC,00,01,3F,3C,00,05,4E,B9
2190   data 00,00,0E,F4,54,8F,3E,BC,00,07,3F,3C,00,05,4E,B9
2200   data 00,00,0E,F4,54,8F,60,00,06,D4,3E,BC,00,01,3F,3C
2210   data 00,01,3F,39,00,00,1C,98,3F,39,00,00,1E,D2,3F,39
2220   data 00,00,1E,D6,3F,39,00,00,1E,D4,42,67,3F,3C,00,0B
2230   data 2F,39,00,00,1E,CE,4E,B9,00,00,12,8E,DF,FC,00,00
2240   data 00,12,3E,BC,00,01,42,67,3F,39,00,00,1C,98,3F,39
2250   data 00,00,1E,D2,3F,39,00,00,1E,D6,3F,39,00,00,1E,D4
2260   data 42,67,3F,3C,00,0A,2F,39,00,00,1E,CE,4E,B9,00,00
2270   data 12,8E,DF,FC,00,00,00,12,3E,BC,00,1B,3F,3C,00,05
```

```
2280   data 4E,B9,00,00,0E,F4,54,8F,3E,BC,00,70,3F,3C,00,05
2290   data 4E,B9,00,00,0E,F4,54,8F,42,57,3F,3C,00,05,4E,B9
2300   data 00,00,0E,F4,54,8F,3E,BC,00,07,3F,3C,00,05,4E,B9
2310   data 00,00,0E,F4,54,8F,60,00,06,24,3E,BC,00,01,3F,3C
2320   data 00,01,3F,39,00,00,1C,98,3F,39,00,00,1E,D2,3F,39
2330   data 00,00,1E,D6,3F,39,00,00,1E,D4,42,67,3F,3C,00,0D
2340   data 2F,39,00,00,1E,CE,4E,B9,00,00,12,8E,DF,FC,00,00
2350   data 00,12,3E,BC,00,01,42,67,3F,39,00,00,1C,98,3F,39
2360   data 00,00,1E,D2,3F,39,00,00,1E,D6,3F,39,00,00,1E,D4
2370   data 42,67,3F,3C,00,0E,2F,39,00,00,1E,CE,4E,B9,00,00
2380   data 12,8E,DF,FC,00,00,00,12,3E,BC,00,1B,3F,3C,00,05
2390   data 4E,B9,00,00,0E,F4,54,8F,3E,BC,00,34,3F,3C,00,05
2400   data 4E,B9,00,00,0E,F4,54,8F,3E,BC,00,07,3F,3C,00,05
2410   data 4E,B9,00,00,0E,F4,54,8F,60,00,05,82,3E,BC,00,01
2420   data 3F,3C,00,01,3F,39,00,00,1C,98,3F,39,00,00,1E,D2
2430   data 3F,39,00,00,1E,D6,3F,39,00,00,1E,D4,42,67,3F,3C
2440   data 00,0E,2F,39,00,00,1E,CE,4E,B9,00,00,12,8E,DF,FC
2450   data 00,00,00,12,3E,BC,00,01,42,67,3F,39,00,00,1C,98
2460   data 3F,39,00,00,1E,D2,3F,39,00,00,1E,D6,3F,39,00,00
2470   data 1E,D4,42,67,3F,3C,00,0D,2F,39,00,00,1E,CE,4E,B9
2480   data 00,00,12,8E,DF,FC,00,00,00,12,3E,BC,00,1B,3F,3C
2490   data 00,05,4E,B9,00,00,0E,F4,54,8F,3E,BC,00,35,3F,3C
2500   data 00,05,4E,B9,00,00,0E,F4,54,8F,3E,BC,00,07,3F,3C
2510   data 00,05,4E,B9,00,00,0E,F4,54,8F,60,00,04,E0,3E,BC
2520   data 00,01,3F,3C,00,01,3F,39,00,00,1C,98,3F,39,00,00
2530   data 1E,D2,3F,39,00,00,1E,D6,3F,39,00,00,1E,D4,42,67
2540   data 3F,3C,00,13,2F,39,00,00,1E,CE,4E,B9,00,00,12,8E
2550   data DF,FC,00,00,00,12,3E,BC,00,01,42,67,3F,39,00,00
2560   data 1C,98,3F,39,00,00,1E,D2,3F,39,00,00,1E,D6,3F,39
2570   data 00,00,1E,D4,42,67,3F,3C,00,14,2F,39,00,00,1E,CE
2580   data 4E,B9,00,00,12,8E,DF,FC,00,00,00,12,3E,BC,00,1B
2590   data 3F,3C,00,05,4E,B9,00,00,0E,F4,54,8F,3E,BC,00,42
2600   data 3F,3C,00,05,4E,B9,00,00,0E,F4,54,8F,3E,BC,00,04
2610   data 3F,3C,00,05,4E,B9,00,00,0E,F4,54,8F,3E,BC,00,07
2620   data 3F,3C,00,05,4E,B9,00,00,0E,F4,54,8F,60,00,04,2E
2630   data 3E,BC,00,01,3F,3C,00,01,3F,39,00,00,1C,98,3F,39
2640   data 00,00,1E,D2,3F,39,00,00,1E,D6,3F,39,00,00,1E,D4
2650   data 42,67,3F,3C,00,14,2F,39,00,00,1E,CE,4E,B9,00,00
2660   data 12,8E,DF,FC,00,00,00,12,3E,BC,00,01,42,67,3F,39
2670   data 00,00,1C,98,3F,39,00,00,1E,D2,3F,39,00,00,1E,D6
2680   data 3F,39,00,00,1E,D4,42,67,3F,3C,00,13,2F,39,00,00
2690   data 1E,CE,4E,B9,00,00,12,8E,DF,FC,00,00,00,12,3E,BC
2700   data 00,1B,3F,3C,00,05,4E,B9,00,00,0E,F4,54,8F,3E,BC
```

207

```
2710  data 00,42,3F,3C,00,05,4E,B9,00,00,0E,F4,54,8F,3E,BC
2720  data 00,05,3F,3C,00,05,4E,B9,00,00,0E,F4,54,8F,3E,BC
2730  data 00,07,3F,3C,00,05,4E,B9,00,00,0E,F4,54,8F,60,00
2740  data 03,7C,3E,BC,00,01,3F,3C,00,01,3F,39,00,00,1C,98
2750  data 3F,39,00,00,1E,D2,3F,39,00,00,1E,D6,3F,39,00,00
2760  data 1E,D4,42,67,3F,3C,00,16,2F,39,00,00,1E,CE,4E,B9
2770  data 00,00,12,8E,DF,FC,00,00,00,12,3E,BC,00,01,42,67
2780  data 3F,39,00,00,1C,98,3F,39,00,00,1E,D2,3F,39,00,00
2790  data 1E,D6,3F,39,00,00,1E,D4,42,67,3F,3C,00,17,2F,39
2800  data 00,00,1E,CE,4E,B9,00,00,12,8E,DF,FC,00,00,00,12
2810  data 3E,BC,00,1B,3F,3C,00,05,4E,B9,00,00,0E,F4,54,8F
2820  data 3E,BC,00,4E,3F,3C,00,05,4E,B9,00,00,0E,F4,54,8F
2830  data 3E,BC,00,06,3F,3C,00,05,4E,B9,00,00,0E,F4,54,8F
2840  data 3E,BC,00,07,3F,3C,00,05,4E,B9,00,00,0E,F4,54,8F
2850  data 60,00,02,CA,3E,BC,00,01,3F,3C,00,01,3F,39,00,00
2860  data 1C,98,3F,39,00,00,1E,D2,3F,39,00,00,1E,D6,3F,39
2870  data 00,00,1E,D4,42,67,3F,3C,00,17,2F,39,00,00,1E,CE
2880  data 4E,B9,00,00,12,8E,DF,FC,00,00,00,12,3E,BC,00,01
2890  data 42,67,3F,39,00,00,1C,98,3F,39,00,00,1E,D2,3F,39
2900  data 00,00,1E,D6,3F,39,00,00,1E,D4,42,67,3F,3C,00,16
2910  data 2F,39,00,00,1E,CE,4E,B9,00,00,12,8E,DF,FC,00,00
2920  data 00,12,3E,BC,00,1B,3F,3C,00,05,4E,B9,00,00,0E,F4
2930  data 54,8F,3E,BC,00,4F,3F,3C,00,05,4E,B9,00,00,0E,F4
2940  data 54,8F,3E,BC,00,07,3F,3C,00,05,4E,B9,00,00,0E,F4
2950  data 54,8F,60,00,02,28,3E,BC,00,01,3F,3C,00,01,3F,39
2960  data 00,00,1C,98,3F,39,00,00,1E,D2,3F,39,00,00,1E,D6
2970  data 3F,39,00,00,1E,D4,42,67,3F,3C,00,1A,2F,39,00,00
2980  data 1E,CE,4E,B9,00,00,12,8E,DF,FC,00,00,00,12,3E,BC
2990  data 00,01,42,67,3F,39,00,00,1C,98,3F,39,00,00,1E,D2
3000  data 3F,39,00,00,1E,D6,3F,39,00,00,1E,D4,42,67,3F,3C
3010  data 00,19,2F,39,00,00,1E,CE,4E,B9,00,00,12,8E,DF,FC
3020  data 00,00,00,12,3E,BC,00,1B,3F,3C,00,05,4E,B9,00,00
3030  data 0E,F4,54,8F,3E,BC,00,6C,3F,3C,00,05,4E,B9,00,00
3040  data 0E,F4,54,8F,42,57,3F,3C,00,05,4E,B9,00,00,0E,F4
3050  data 54,8F,3E,BC,00,07,3F,3C,00,05,4E,B9,00,00,0E,F4
3060  data 54,8F,60,00,01,78,3E,BC,00,01,3F,3C,00,01,3F,39
3070  data 00,00,1C,98,3F,39,00,00,1E,D2,3F,39,00,00,1E,D6
3080  data 3F,39,00,00,1E,D4,42,67,3F,3C,00,19,2F,39,00,00
3090  data 1E,CE,4E,B9,00,00,12,8E,DF,FC,00,00,00,12,3E,BC
3100  data 00,01,42,67,3F,39,00,00,1C,98,3F,39,00,00,1E,D2
3110  data 3F,39,00,00,1E,D6,3F,39,00,00,1E,D4,42,67,3F,3C
3120  data 00,1A,2F,39,00,00,1E,CE,4E,B9,00,00,12,8E,DF,FC
3130  data 00,00,00,12,3E,BC,00,1B,3F,3C,00,05,4E,B9,00,00
```

208

```
3140    data 0E,F4,54,8F,3E,BC,00,6C,3F,3C,00,05,4E,B9,00,00
3150    data 0E,F4,54,8F,3E,BC,00,05,3F,3C,00,05,4E,B9,00,00
3160    data 0E,F4,54,8F,3E,BC,00,07,3F,3C,00,05,4E,B9,00,00
3170    data 0E,F4,54,8F,60,00,00,C6,3E,BC,00,01,3F,3C,00,01
3180    data 3F,39,00,00,1C,98,3F,39,00,00,1E,D2,3F,39,00,00
3190    data 1E,D6,3F,39,00,00,1E,D4,42,67,3F,3C,00,05,2F,39
3200    data 00,00,1E,CE,4E,B9,00,00,12,8E,DF,FC,00,00,00,12
3210    data 3E,BC,00,0D,3F,3C,00,05,4E,B9,00,00,0E,F4,54,8F
3220    data 3E,B9,00,00,1C,76,3F,39,00,00,1E,A4,3F,39,00,00
3230    data 1E,C6,3F,39,00,00,1E,C4,3F,3C,00,03,4E,B9,00,00
3240    data 10,3C,50,8F,3E,B9,00,00,1C,76,3F,39,00,00,1E,A4
3250    data 3F,39,00,00,1E,C6,3F,39,00,00,1E,C4,3F,3C,00,01
3260    data 3F,3C,00,01,3F,3C,00,01,3F,3C,00,01,3F,3C,00,02
3270    data 4E,B9,00,00,10,3C,DF,FC,00,00,00,10,3D,7C,00,01
3280    data FF,FE,60,18,60,16,5B,40,B0,7C,00,15,62,0E,E5,40
3290    data 30,40,D1,FC,00,00,15,8C,20,50,4E,D0,0C,6E,00,01
3300    data FF,FE,66,00,F5,A2,61,04,4E,5E,4E,75,4E,56,FF,FC
3310    data 4E,B9,00,00,0E,14,4E,B9,00,00,0F,D0,4E,5E,4E,75
3320    data 4E,56,FF,FC,33,FC,00,65,00,00,1F,96,42,79,00,00
3330    data 1F,98,42,79,00,00,1F,9C,33,EE,00,08,00,00,1F,A2
3340    data 4E,B9,00,00,0E,BE,4E,5E,4E,75,4E,56,FF,FC,23,EE
3350    data 00,08,00,00,1A,5C,23,EE,00,10,00,00,1A,64,20,2E
3360    data 00,10,D0,BC,00,00,00,5A,23,C0,00,00,1A,68,33,FC
3370    data 00,64,00,00,1F,96,42,79,00,00,1F,98,33,FC,00,0B
3380    data 00,00,1F,9C,20,6E,00,0C,33,D0,00,00,1F,A2,4E,B9
3390    data 00,00,0E,BE,20,6E,00,0C,30,B9,00,00,1F,A2,23,FC
3400    data 00,00,1A,70,00,00,1A,5C,23,FC,00,00,1B,74,00,00
3410    data 1A,64,23,FC,00,00,1D,9E,00,00,1A,68,23,FC,00,00
3420    data 1C,9C,00,00,1A,60,4E,5E,4E,75,23,FC,00,00,1F,96
3430    data 00,00,1A,58,22,3C,00,00,1A,58,70,73,4E,42,4E,75
3440    data 23,DF,00,00,1A,6C,4E,4E,2F,39,00,00,1A,6C,4E,75
3450    data 23,DF,00,00,1A,6C,4E,4D,2F,39,00,00,1A,6C,4E,75
3460    data 23,DF,00,00,1A,6C,4E,41,2F,39,00,00,1A,6C,4E,75
3470    data 4E,56,FF,F6,33,EE,00,08,00,00,1F,6C,30,2E,00,08
3480    data D0,7C,FF,F6,C1,FC,00,03,48,C0,D0,BC,00,00,14,30
3490    data 2D,40,FF,FA,3D,7C,00,01,FF,FE,60,1E,20,6E,FF,FA
3500    data 10,10,48,80,32,6E,FF,FE,D3,C9,D3,FC,00,00,1F,6C
3510    data 32,80,52,AE,FF,FA,52,6E,FF,FE,0C,6E,00,04,FF,FE
3520    data 6D,DA,2E,B9,00,00,1F,8E,4E,B9,00,00,00,3E,42,40
3530    data 30,39,00,00,1E,FA,4E,5E,4E,75,4E,56,FF,FA,23,FC
3540    data 00,00,1F,6C,00,00,1C,78,23,FC,00,00,1E,A6,00,00
3550    data 1C,7C,23,FC,00,00,1E,DA,00,00,1C,80,23,FC,00,00
3560    data 1E,FA,00,00,1C,84,23,FC,00,00,1F,AE,00,00,1C,88
```

```
3570    data 23,FC,00,00,1F,BC,00,00,1C,8C,23,FC,00,00,1C,78
3580    data 00,00,1F,8E,3E,BC,00,0A,61,00,FF,46,33,F9,00,00
3590    data 1E,FA,00,00,1F,94,70,01,4E,5E,4E,75,4E,56,FF,FC
3600    data 3E,BC,00,13,61,00,FF,2A,70,01,4E,5E,4E,75,4E,56
3610    data FF,FC,33,EE,00,08,00,00,1E,DA,33,EE,00,0A,00,00
3620    data 1E,DC,33,EE,00,0C,00,00,1E,DE,3E,BC,00,15,4E,B9
3630    data 00,00,0F,04,20,6E,00,0E,30,B9,00,00,1E,FC,20,6E
3640    data 00,12,30,B9,00,00,1E,FE,20,6E,00,16,30,B9,00,00
3650    data 1F,00,20,6E,00,1A,30,B9,00,00,1F,02,42,40,30,39
3660    data 00,00,1E,FA,4E,5E,4E,75,4E,56,FF,FC,33,EE,00,08
3670    data 00,00,1E,DA,33,EE,00,0A,00,00,1E,DC,33,EE,00,0C
3680    data 00,00,1E,DE,33,EE,00,0E,00,00,1E,E0,33,EE,00,10
3690    data 00,00,1E,E2,33,EE,00,12,00,00,1E,E4,33,EE,00,14
3700    data 00,00,1E,E6,33,EE,00,16,00,00,1E,E8,33,EE,00,18
3710    data 00,00,1E,EA,3E,BC,00,33,4E,B9,00,00,0F,04,4E,5E
3720    data 4E,75,4E,56,FF,FC,33,EE,00,08,00,00,1E,DA,23,EE
3730    data 00,0A,00,00,1F,AE,3E,BC,00,34,4E,B9,00,00,0F,04
3740    data 4E,5E,4E,75,4E,56,FF,FC,23,EE,00,08,00,00,1F,AE
3750    data 3E,BC,00,36,4E,B9,00,00,0F,04,20,6E,00,0C,30,B9
3760    data 00,00,1E,FC,20,6E,00,10,30,B9,00,00,1E,FE,20,6E
3770    data 00,14,30,B9,00,00,1F,00,20,6E,00,18,30,B9,00,00
3780    data 1F,02,42,40,30,39,00,00,1E,FA,4E,5E,4E,75,4E,56
3790    data FF,FC,33,EE,00,08,00,00,1E,DA,33,EE,00,0A,00,00
3800    data 1E,DC,33,EE,00,0C,00,00,1E,DE,33,EE,00,0E,00,00
3810    data 1E,E0,33,EE,00,10,00,00,1E,E2,33,EE,00,12,00,00
3820    data 1E,E4,33,EE,00,14,00,00,1E,E6,33,EE,00,16,00,00
3830    data 1E,E8,3E,BC,00,49,4E,B9,00,00,0F,04,4E,5E,4E,75
3840    data 4E,56,FF,FC,33,EE,00,08,00,00,1E,DA,33,EE,00,0A
3850    data 00,00,1E,DC,33,EE,00,0C,00,00,1E,DE,33,EE,00,0E
3860    data 00,00,1E,E0,33,EE,00,10,00,00,1E,E2,33,EE,00,12
3870    data 00,00,1E,E4,33,EE,00,14,00,00,1E,E6,33,EE,00,16
3880    data 00,00,1E,E8,3E,BC,00,4A,4E,B9,00,00,0F,04,4E,5E
3890    data 4E,75,4E,56,FF,FC,3E,BC,00,4D,4E,B9,00,00,0F,04
3900    data 20,6E,00,08,30,B9,00,00,1E,FC,20,6E,00,0C,30,B9
3910    data 00,00,1E,FE,20,6E,00,10,30,B9,00,00,1F,00,20,6E
3920    data 00,14,30,B9,00,00,1F,02,42,40,30,39,00,00,1E,FA
3930    data 4E,5E,4E,75,4E,56,FF,FC,33,EE,00,08,00,00,1E,DA
3940    data 23,EE,00,0A,00,00,1F,AE,3E,BC,00,4E,4E,B9,00,00
3950    data 0F,04,4E,5E,4E,75,4E,56,FF,FC,23,EE,00,08,00,00
3960    data 1F,AE,33,EE,00,0C,00,00,1E,DA,33,EE,00,0E,00,00
3970    data 1E,DC,33,EE,00,10,00,00,1E,DE,33,EE,00,12,00,00
3980    data 1E,E0,33,EE,00,14,00,00,1E,E2,33,EE,00,16,00,00
3990    data 1E,E4,3E,BC,00,2A,4E,B9,00,00,0F,04,4E,5E,4E,75
```

```
4000    data 4E,56,FF,FC,23,EE,00,08,00,00,1F,AE,33,EE,00,0C
4010    data 00,00,1E,DA,33,EE,00,0E,00,00,1E,DC,33,EE,00,10
4020    data 00,00,1E,DE,33,EE,00,12,00,00,1E,E0,3E,BC,00,2B
4030    data 4E,B9,00,00,0F,04,4E,5E,4E,75,4E,56,FF,FC,23,EE
4040    data 00,08,00,00,1F,AE,33,EE,00,0C,00,00,1E,DA,33,EE
4050    data 00,0E,00,00,1E,DC,33,EE,00,10,00,00,1E,DE,33,EE
4060    data 00,12,00,00,1E,E0,33,EE,00,14,00,00,1E,E2,33,EE
4070    data 00,16,00,00,1E,E4,33,EE,00,18,00,00,1E,E6,33,EE
4080    data 00,1A,00,00,1E,E8,3E,BC,00,2F,4E,B9,00,00,0F,04
4090    data 4E,5E,4E,75,4E,56,FF,FC,23,EE,00,08,00,00,1F,AE
4100    data 3E,BC,00,6E,4E,B9,00,00,0F,04,4E,5E,4E,75,4E,56
4110    data FF,FC,33,EE,00,08,00,00,1E,DA,33,EE,00,0A,00,00
4120    data 1E,DC,3E,BC,00,70,4E,B9,00,00,0F,04,20,6E,00,0C
4130    data 20,B9,00,00,1F,BC,42,40,30,39,00,00,1E,FA,4E,5E
4140    data 4E,75,4E,56,FF,FC,33,EE,00,08,00,00,1E,DA,33,EE
4150    data 00,0A,00,00,1E,DC,33,EE,00,0C,00,00,1E,DE,33,EE
4160    data 00,0E,00,00,1E,E0,33,EE,00,10,00,00,1E,E2,3E,BC
4170    data 00,64,4E,B9,00,00,0F,04,4E,5E,4E,75,4E,56,FF,FC
4180    data 33,EE,00,08,00,00,1E,DA,33,EE,00,0A,00,00,1E,DC
4190    data 33,EE,00,0C,00,00,1E,DE,33,EE,00,0E,00,00,1E,E0
4200    data 33,EE,00,10,00,00,1E,E2,3E,BC,00,65,4E,B9,00,00
4210    data 0F,04,4E,5E,4E,75,4E,56,FF,FC,33,EE,00,08,00,00
4220    data 1E,DA,3E,BC,00,66,4E,B9,00,00,0F,04,4E,5E,4E,75
4230    data 4E,56,FF,FC,33,EE,00,08,00,00,1E,DA,3E,BC,00,67
4240    data 4E,B9,00,00,0F,04,4E,5E,4E,75,4E,56,FF,FC,33,EE
4250    data 00,08,00,00,1E,DA,33,EE,00,0A,00,00,1E,DC,3E,BC
4260    data 00,68,4E,B9,00,00,0F,04,20,6E,00,0C,30,B9,00,00
4270    data 1E,FC,20,6E,00,10,30,B9,00,00,1E,FE,20,6E,00,14
4280    data 30,B9,00,00,1F,00,20,6E,00,18,30,B9,00,00,1F,02
4290    data 42,40,30,39,00,00,1E,FA,4E,5E,4E,75,00,01,00,02
4300    data 01,01,02,01,01,00,01,01,02,01,01,01,01,01,00,00
4310    data 00,00,00,00,00,00,00,00,01,00,00,01,00,03,05,00
4320    data 05,05,00,00,01,01,02,01,00,10,07,01,02,01,00,00
4330    data 00,00,00,00,00,00,00,00,01,01,01,02,01,01,02,01
4340    data 01,02,01,01,01,01,02,01,01,01,00,00,00,00,00,00
4350    data 00,00,00,00,00,00,02,01,01,01,01,01,06,01,01,04
4360    data 01,01,01,03,01,02,01,01,04,02,01,08,01,01,00,00
4370    data 00,00,00,00,01,01,01,09,01,01,01,01,01,01,01,00
4380    data 00,05,01,00,00,00,00,00,00,00,00,00,00,00,00,00
4390    data 00,00,00,00,00,00,00,00,00,00,00,00,00,00,00,00
4400    data 00,00,00,00,00,00,00,00,00,00,00,00,00,00,00,00
4410    data 04,03,00,08,03,00,06,01,00,08,01,00,08,01,00,04
4420    data 01,01,03,01,01,00,05,00,01,01,01,00,05,00,00,01
```

211

```
4430   data 01,00,01,01,00,00,00,00,00,00,00,00,00,00,00,00
4440   data 00,00,00,00,00,00,00,00,00,00,00,00,00,02,02,00
4450   data 00,00,00,00,00,00,00,00,00,00,00,00,00,00,00,00
4460   data 00,00,00,00,00,00,00,00,00,00,05,01,00,05,01,00
4470   data 01,01,00,01,01,00,02,05,00,06,01,00,02,01,00,01
4480   data 01,00,06,05,00,00,00,00,00,01,01,00,01,00,02,01
4490   data 00,02,01,01,01,01,01,00,00,00,00,00,00,00,00,00
4500   data 00,00,00,00,00,00,00,01,02,03,01,02,01,01,01,01
4510   data 01,01,00,01,01,00,01,02,00,00,0D,2C,00,00,0D,F0
4520   data 00,00,04,04,00,00,04,A6,00,00,0D,F0,00,00,06,6C
4530   data 00,00,07,1E,00,00,0D,F0,00,00,07,CE,00,00,08,70
4540   data 00,00,0D,F0,00,00,05,48,00,00,05,DA,00,00,0D,F0
4550   data 00,00,09,12,00,00,09,C4,00,00,0D,F0,00,00,0A,76
4560   data 00,00,0B,28,00,00,0D,F0,00,00,0C,7A,00,00,0B,CA
4570   data 50,52,49,4E,49,54,2E,52,53,43,00,5B,33,5D,5B,42
4580   data 61,64,20,43,6F,70,79,3F,7C,50,52,49,4E,49,54,2E
4590   data 52,53,43,7C,63,6F,75,6C,64,20,6E,6F,74,20,62,65
4600   data 20,66,6F,75,6E,64,2E,5D,5B,41,62,6F,72,74,5D,00
4610   data 5B,33,5D,20,5B,46,61,74,61,6C,20,65,72,72,6F,72
4620   data 21,7C,52,65,73,6F,75,72,63,65,20,46,69,6C,65,20
4630   data 6E,6F,74,20,4F,4B,2E,5D,5B,41,62,6F,72,74,5D,00
4640   data 00,00,00,04,2E,1E,06,06,06,0A,08,06,06,06,06,06
4650   data 06,06,0E,08,0E,08,0C,06,06,06,06,06,08,06,06,06
4660   data 0A,06,14,06,06,06,06,06,06,06,0E,08,0E,08,0C
4670   data 06,1C,18,06,04,06,06,06,06,10,06,06,06,06,06,06
4680   data 0C,06,06,06,06,0C,10,06,0A,0A,08,0A,0A,0C,0A,08
4690   data 0A,0A,08,06,06,06,06,06,0C,06,06,06,08,08,06,06
4700   data 06,1A,0C,06,10,06,0C,0A,0C,06,06,06,12,0C,06,06
4710   data 0C,06,0C,06,12,06,06,06,0C,06,12,06,06,06,0C,06
4720   data 14,10,10,14,06,06,06,0C,06,12,06,06,06,0C,06,14
4730   data 10,10,14,06,06,06,0C,06,12,06,06,06,0C,06,14,10
4740   data 14,06,06,06,0C,06,12,06,06,06,0C,06,14,10,14,06
4750   data 06,06,0C,06,12,06,06,06,0C,06,14,10,10,10,14,06
4760   data 06,06,0C,06,12,06,06,06,0C,06,14,10,0E,10,14,06
4770   data 06,06,0C,06,12,06,06,06,0C,06,14,10,10,14,06,06
4780   data 06,0C,06,12,06,06,06,0C,06,14,10,10,14,06,06,06
4790   data 0C,06,12,06,06,06,0C,06,14,10,10,10,14,06,06,06
4800   data 0C,06,12,06,06,06,0C,06,14,10,10,10,14,06,06,06
4810   data 0C,06,12,06,06,06,0C,06,14,10,10,10,14,06,06,06
4820   data 0C,06,12,06,06,06,0C,06,14,10,10,14,06,06,06,0C
4830   data 06,12,06,06,06,0C,06,14,10,0E,10,14,06,06,06,0C
4840   data 06,12,06,06,06,0C,06,14,10,10,10,14,06,06,06,0C
4850   data 06,14,08,06,06,06,0A,08,06,06,06,1A,22,1E,06,10
```

212

```
4860   data 06,06,08,06,10,08,10,08,06,08,0A,06,0A,06,04,06
4870   data 04,06,04,06,04,0A,04,06,0C,08,08,08,08,08,0E,14
4880   data 20,18,06,08,0E,04,06,04,06,04,06,04,06,04,06,04
4890   data 06,04,0E,04,24,08,08,0A,0A,0A,0A,0A,08,10,08,08
4900   data 08,08,08,08,08,08,0A,10,08,0A,10,0A,0A,0A,0A,0A
4910   data 08,10,08,08,08,08,08,08,08,0A,10,0E,08,08,08,08
4920   data 08,08,0A,12,0A,0A,0A,0A,08,10,08,0A,10,08,08,08
4930   data 08,08,08,0A,10,08,08,08,08,0A,10,0E,08,08,08,08
4940   data 08,08,08,0A,10,0A,10,08,0A,0A,08,10,08,08,08,08
4950   data 0A,10,08,08,08,08,0A,10,0A,10,0A,10,08,0A,0A,0A
4960   data 0A,0A,08,01,66,04,04,04,04,04,04,04,04,04,04,04
4970   data 04,04,04,04,04,04,04,04,04,04,00,00,00,00,00,00
4980   data *
4990   close 1:if s<> 371988 then print"ERROR IN DATA!":end
5010   print "Ok."
```

4.5 PRINIT as a desk accessory

To install the application as an accessory, a number of changes are necessary. This desk accessory program sets several parameters for an Epson FX-80 printer. An accessory should limit itself to one window, and it should not be larger than the actual dialog box. It doesn't matter much if the accessory can be moved around the screen since it is called for only a short time. This saves some programming work, memory space and loading time. The only function calls we need in the `open_window` area are `wind_create` and `wind_get`. For those who would really like to have a window, the necessary source code is included in the listing as comment lines.

To make an accessory accessable from the desk menu, the procedure `menu_register` is used. As parameters it requires the ID code of the application (from `appl_init`) and a string under which the program is to appear on the menu. As the result, `menu_register` returns a number between zero and five, which corresponds to an accessory ID code.

But in order to get this far, the program must be started. This takes place after loading the operating system. The user doesn't notice this because the workstation has not yet been opened.

After this phase of the intitialization, the accessory issues an `evnt_multi` for all events, so as not to interfere with the main program. There it waits for a message event to return the actual accessory ID in the message buffer.

As we explained before, the code of the calling application is in `msgbuff(4)`, that is, if the condition,

```
if (msgbuff(4) == menu_id)
```

returns TRUE, the user has called the accessory in question.

Now the workstation and the window are opened and a branch made to the actual program (here `output();`). This corresponds to a normal application. The only thing to note is to declare the termination as FALSE; this can happen before the program is exited (not ended!), or at the beginning of the main loop, or else it would be possible to call the accessory again.

The most important thing to remember is that execution of an accessory is never ended, and you will never find an `appl_exit`. Accessories always run under multi-tasking operation, that is, every accessory is placed on the *ready* list and the `evnt_multi` takes care of each accessory.

The structure of such an `event_multi` call looks like this:

```
while (TRUE)
    ... event_multi /* read event */
    ... Message_event /* for this accessory? */
        ... if yes: is it actual menu_id ?
            ... if yes: start function
        ... if no: keep waiting for Message_event
    ... if no: keep waiting for Message_event
... /* end while */
```

There may never be a statement within all of the program code that could interrupt this loop. This is why the condition is just TRUE, which is naturally always the case! For an accessory the `evnt_multi` call must always be available.

Next you must change the resource file using the RSC. Rename the dialog tree to FXMENU. Change the NLQIN and NLQOUT to MICROIN and MICROOUT. Change the text NLQ to MICRO. We will substitute the super script feature of the FX-80 instead of the near letter quality mode of the SG-10. By comparing the printer initialization listings in the two C programs you should be able to adapt these programs to any printer.

In the desk accessory the dialog box is handled with the `form_do` function. This function gives control to the AES and monitors all input to the dialog box. The `form_do` function only returns a value on an *exit* so change the ON, OFF, 0, 10 buttons in the resource file to SELECTED, RADIO BUTN and TOUCHEXIT. Now we can replace our `event_button` call with the `form_do` function. This allows input only in the dialog box making sure that our desk accessory does not allow windows to be opened over it.

The printer's bell has also been removed for silent operation of the accessory.

```
/**********************************************************************/
/******               PROGRAM: PR-INIT                 *********/
/****** Initialize ACCESSORY for printer in parallel port  **********/
/******      (c) J. Walkowiak, 4. November 1985              ********/
/**********************************************************************/
#include "obdefs.h"               /* Object definitions        */
#include "gemdefs.h"              /* Definitions for  GEM      */
#include "define.h"
#include "gembind.h"
#include "vdibind.h"


/**********************************************************************/
/*                              Definitions for RSC-File       */
/**********************************************************************/
#define FILENAME "PRINIT.RSC"     /* Name of RSC-file           */
#define MAX_DEPTH 34              /* Number of all objects, Char. depth */
#define FXMENU 0                  /* TREE                       */
#define EXIT 5                    /* OBJECT in TREE #0          */
#define ELITEIN 7                 /* OBJECT in TREE #0          */
#define ELITEOUT 8                /* OBJECT in TREE #0          */
#define PROPIN 10                 /* OBJECT in TREE #0          */
#define PROPOUT 11                /* OBJECT in TREE #0          */
#define ITALIN 13                 /* OBJECT in TREE #0          */
#define ITALOUT 14                /* OBJECT in TREE #0          */
#define CONDENIN 16               /* OBJECT in TREE #0          */
#define CONDENOT 17               /* OBJECT in TREE #0          */
#define MICROIN 19                /* OBJECT in TREE #0          */
#define MICROOUT 20               /* OBJECT in TREE #0          */
#define SKIPIN 22                 /* OBJECT in TREE #0          */
#define SKIPOUT 23                /* OBJECT in TREE #0          */
#define MARG0 26                  /* OBJECT in TREE #0          */
#define MARG10 25                 /* OBJECT in TREE #0          */

long menu_tree;                   /* Address of desired RSC-Object */

/**********************************************************************/
/*                    Definitions of BUTTON-types in Menu      */
/**********************************************************************/
#define SELECTED 0x0001
#define NORMAL 0x0000



/**********************************************************************/
/*                              Printer control codes          */
/*                              here: EPSON FX-80+             */
/**********************************************************************/
```

```
#define RET 13                  /* Return                        */
#define ESC 27                  /* Escape                        */
#define SMALL 15                /* Condensed type                */
#define SMALLOFF 18
#define ELITE 77                /* Elite                         */
#define ELITEOFF 80
#define PROPORTIONAL 112        /* Proportional type:            */
#define PSET 1                  /*  on                           */
#define PRESET 0                /*  off                          */
#define ITALIC 52               /* Italics                       */
#define ITALICOFF 53
#define MICRO1 83               /* Super script1                 */
#define MICRO2 0
#define MICROOFF 84
#define SKIP 78                 /* Skip over Perforation         */
#define SKIP1 6                 /* skip 6 lines       */
#define SKIPOFF 79
#define LMARG 108               /* Set left margin               */
#define LMAROFF 0               /*  Count from the right         */
#define POS10 10                /*  Print at position 10         */

#define NO_WINDOW (-1)

#define MIN_WIDTH (2*gl_wbox)
#define MIN_HEIGHT (3*gl_box)

/********************************************************************/
/*                   global variables                             */
/********************************************************************/
int contrl(12);                      */ control arrays           */
int intin[128];
int ptsin[128];
int intout[128];
int ptsout[128];        /* Sufficient memory for all circumstances*/
int pxyarray[12];       /* Array for x,y coordinates         */

int work_in[11];        /* Input in GSX array                 */
int work_out[57];       /* Output from GSX array              */


int handle,i;           /* virtual workstation handle         */
int phys_handle;        /* physical workstation handle        */
int wi_handle;          /* Window handle                      */

extern gl_apid;         /* Application identifier             */
extern long gemdos();   /* for GEMDOS-Call                    */
```

217

```
int menu_id;                /* Accessory marker in Desk menu        */

int gl_hchar, gl_wchar;  /* Character height & width              */
int gl_wbox, gl_hbox;

int xwork,ywork,wwork,hwork;      /* Size of working window         */
int xdesk,ydesk,wdesk,hdesk;      /* Size of desktop                */
int xold, yold, hold, wold;  /* Help variables by window  manipulation*/
int xobj,yobj,wobj,hobj;          /* Size of an object              */
int mausx, mausy;                 /* Where is the mouse ?           */

int dummy;                        /* ... for dummy parameter        */

int event;                        /* Which input device             */
int msgbuff[8];
int title, item;                  /* Menu title and current object   */

int ende;



int    top_window;    /* handle of topped window */

int    keycode;       /* keycode returned by event-keyboard */
int    mx,my;         /* mouse x and y pos. */
int    butdown;       /* button state tested for, UP/DOWN */
int    ret;           /* dummy return variable */

int    hidden;        /* current state of cursor */

int    fulled;        /* current state of window */


/***************************************************************/
/* open virtual workstation                                  */
/***************************************************************/
open_vwork()
{
int i;
   for(i=0;i<10;work_in[i++]=1);
   work_in[10]=2;
   handle=phys_handle;
   v_opnvwk(work_in,&handle,work_out);
}
```

```
/*******************************************************************/
/* open window                                                    */
/*******************************************************************/
open_window()
{
   wi_handle=wind_create(0x00C),xobj,yobj,wobj,hobj);
                              /* Window only as big as dialog box  (obj)*/

/*    wind_set(wi_handle, WF_KAME," name goes here ",0,0);   only when
window w/ title line

graf_growbox(xdesk+wdesk/2,ydesk+hdesk/2,gl_wbox,gl_hbox,xdesk,ydesk,wde
sk,hdesk);*/

   wind_open(wi_handle,xobj,ycbj,wobj,hobj);
                              /* Open work window                 */
   wind_get(wi_handle,WF_WORKXYWH,&xwork,&ywork,&wwork,&hwork);
}



/*******************************************************************/
/*      Accessory Init. Until First Event_Multi                  */
/*******************************************************************/
main()
{
   appl_init();
   phys_handle=graf_handle(&gl_wchar,&gl_hchar,&gl_wbox,&gl_hbox);
   menu_id=menu_register(gl_ap_d,"  FX-80+ INIT");
   wind_get(0, WF_WORKXYWH, &xdesk, &ydesk, &wdesk, &hdesk);

      if(!rsrc_load(FILENAME))      /* Load RSC-file                 */
         {
             form_alert(1,"[3][Bad  copy?  |PRINIT.RSC|  couldn't  be
found!][Cancel]");
         }
      if(rsrc_gaddr(0,0,&menu_tree)== 0)
         {
             form_alert(1,'[3]  [Fatal  error!!|Resource  File  not
OK.][Cancel]");
         }

      rsrc_gaddr(R_TREE,FXMENU,&menu_tree);
      form_center(menu_tree,&xobj,&yobj,&wobj,&hobj);

   multi();
}
```

```
    while (TRUE) {
        event = evnt_multi (MU_MESAG | MU_BUTTON | MU_KEYBD,
            1,1,1,
            0,0,0,0,0,
            0,0,0,0,0,
            msgbuff,0,0,&mausx,&mausy,&dummy,&dummy,
            &dummy,&dummy);


    if (event & MU_MESAG)
        switch (msgbuff[0]) {

            case AC_OPEN:
                if (msgbuff[4] == menu_id) {
                    open_vwork();
                    open_window();
                    output();
                    wind_close(wi_handle);
                    wind_delete(wi_handle);
                    v_clsvwk(handle);
                }
                break;
        }   /* switch */
    } /*while TRUE */
}

output()
{
        rsrc_gaddr(R_TREE,FXMENU,&menu_tree);
        form_center(menu_tree,&xobj,&yobj,&wobj,&hobj);
        form_dial(0,xobj,yobj,wobj,hobj);
        form_dial(1,1,1,1,1,xobj,yobj,wobj,hobj);

        objc_draw(menu_tree,0,MAX_DEPTH,0,0,wdesk,hdesk);

        ende = FALSE;                  /* Otherwise, just one run       */
        while (ende != TRUE){

                item = form_do(menu_tree,FXMENU);
                        /*returns obj. number on exit*/

/* removed to use form_do all selected objects must be TOUCHEXIT or EXIT
        event=evnt_button(1,1,1,&mausx,&mausy,&dummy,&dummy);
          item=objc_find(menu_tree,FXMENU,13,mausx,mausy);
                    which object in menu_tree is at mouse pos */
```

```
            switch(item){

case      ELITEIN:
objc_change(menu_tree,ELITEIN,C,xobj,yobj,wobj,hobj,SELECTED,1);

objc_change(menu_tree,ELITEOUT,0,xobj,yobj,wobj,hobj,NORMAL,1);
            gemdos(0x5,ESC);
            gemdos(0x5,ELITE);
            break;

case      ELITEOUT:
objc_change(menu_tree,ELITEOUT,0,xwork,ywork,wwork,hwork,SELECTED,1);

objc_change(menu_tree,ELITEIN,0,xwork,ywork,wwork,hwork,NORMAL,1);
            gemdos(0x5,ESC);
            gemdos(0x5,ELITEOFF);
            break;

case      CONDENIN:
objc_change(menu_tree,CONDENIN,0,xwork,ywork,wwork,hwork,SELECTED,1);

objc_change(menu_tree,CONDENOT,0,xwork,ywork,wwork,hwork,NORMAL,1);
            gemdos(0x5,SMALL);
            break;

case      CONDENOT:
objc_change(menu_tree,CONDENOT,0,xwork,ywork,wwork,hwork,SELECTED,1);

objc_change(menu_tree,CONDENIN,0,xwork,ywork,wwork,hwork,NORMAL,1);
            gemdos(0x5,SMALLOFF);
            break;

    case      PROPIN:
objc_change(menu_tree,PROPIN,0,xwork,ywork,wwork,hwork,SELECTED,1);

objc_change(menu_tree,PROPOUT,C,xwork,ywork,wwork,hwork,NORMAL,1);
            gemdos(0x5,ESC);
            gemdos(0x5,PROPORTIONAL);
            gemdos(0x5,PSET);
            break;

case      PROPOUT:
objc_change(menu_tree,PROPOUT,C,xwork,ywork,wwork,hwork,SELECTED,1);

objc_change(menu_tree,PROPIN,0,xwork,ywork,wwork,hwork,NORMAL,1);
            gemdos(0x5,ESC);
            gemdos(0x5,PROPORTIONAL);
```

```
                gemdos(0x5,PRESET);
                break;


case        ITALIN:
objc_change(menu_tree,ITALIN,0,xwork,ywork,wwork,hwork,SELECTED,1);

objc_change(menu_tree,ITALOUT,0,xwork,ywork,wwork,hwork,NORMAL,1);
                gemdos(0x5,ESC);
                gemdos(0x5,ITALIC);
                break;

case        ITALOUT:
objc_change(menu_tree,ITALOUT,0,xwork,ywork,wwork,hwork,SELECTED,1);

objc_change(menu_tree,ITALIN,0,xwork,ywork,wwork,hwork,NORMAL,1);
                gemdos(0x5,ESC);
                gemdos(0x5,ITALICOFF);
                break;

case        MICROIN:
objc_change(menu_tree,MICROIN,0,xwork,ywork,wwork,hwork,SELECTED,1);

objc_change(menu_tree,MICROOUT,0,xwork,ywork,wwork,hwork,NORMAL,1);
                gemdos(0x5,ESC);
                gemdos(0x5,MICRO1);
                gemdos(0x5,MICRO2);
                break;

case        MICROOUT:
objc_change(menu_tree,MICROOUT,0,xwork,ywork,wwork,hwork,SELECTED,1);

objc_change(menu_tree,MICROIN,0,xwork,ywork,wwork,hwork,NORMAL,1);
                gemdos(0x5,ESC);
                gemdos(0x5,MICROOFF);
                break;

case        SKIPIN:
objc_change(menu_tree,SKIPIN,0,xwork,ywork,wwork,hwork,SELECTED,1);

objc_change(menu_tree,SKIPOUT,0,xwork,ywork,wwork,hwork,NORMAL,1);
                gemdos(0x5,ESC);
                gemdos(0x5,SKIP);
                gemdos(0x5,SKIP1);
                break;
```

```
case      SKIPOUT:
objc_change(menu_tree,SKIPOUT,0,xwork,ywork,wwork,hwork,SELECTED,1);

objc_change(menu_tree,SKIPIN,0,xwork,ywork,wwork,hwork,NORMAL,1);
            gemdos(0x5,ESC);
            gemdos(0x5,SKIPOFF);
            break;

case      MARG0:
objc_change(menu_tree,MARG0,0,xwork,ywork,wwork,hwork,SELECTED,1);

objc_change(menu_tree,MARG10,0,xwork,ywork,wwork,hwork,NORMAL,1);
            gemdos(0x5,ESC);
            gemdos(0x5,LMARG);
            gemdos(0x5,LMAROFF);
            break;

case      MARG10:
objc_change(menu_tree,MARG10,0,xwork,ywork,wwork,hwork,SELECTED,1);

objc_change(menu_tree,MARG0,0,xwork,ywork,wwork,hwork,NORMAL,1);
            gemdos(0x5,ESC);
            gemdos(0x5,LMARG);
            gemdos(0x5,POS10);
            break;

case      EXIT:
objc_change(menu_tree,EXIT,0,xwork,ywork,wwork,hwork,SELECTED,1);
            gemdos(0x5,RET);
            form_dial(2,xobj,yobj,wobj,hobj);
            form_dial(3,1,1,1,1,xobj,yobj,wobj,hobj);
            ende=TRUE;

objc_change(menu_tree,EXIT,0,xwork,ywork,wwork,hwork,NORMAL,1);
        /* Return; otherwise, a break on the next accessory call      */
            break;

        } /* End switch  */

    } /* End while */
}
```

For those of you who don't have a C compiler, the following BASIC
loaders will create the files PRINIT.RSC and FX80INIT.ACC on your
disk.

```
100    ' BASIC loader to create PRINIT.RSC for FX80INIT.ACC
1000   open"R",1,"a:prinit.rsc",16
1010   field#1,16 as bin$
1020   a$="":for i=1 TO 16:read d$:if d$="*"then 1050
1030   a=val("&H"+d$):s=s+a:a$=a$+chr$(a):next
1040   lset bin$=a$:rec=rec+1:put 1,rec:goto 1020
1050   data 00,00,01,E8,00,D0,00,D0,00,D0,00,00,00,24,00,D0
1060   data 00,00,05,18,00,22,00,01,00,0A,00,00,00,00,00,00
1070   data 00,00,05,1C,46,58,2D,38,30,2B,20,49,4E,49,54,00
1080   data 00,00,20,20,66,72,6F,6D,3A,20,41,42,41,43,55,53
1090   data BA,73,20,54,69,70,73,20,26,20,54,72,69,63,6B,73
1100   data 20,20,00,00,00,4A,57,20,31,30,2E,38,35,00,00,00
1110   data 4F,6B,61,79,20,21,00,4F,4E,00,4F,46,46,00,4F,4E
1120   data 00,4F,46,46,00,4F,4E,00,4F,46,46,00,4F,4E,00,4F
1130   data 46,46,00,4F,4E,00,4F,46,46,00,4F,4E,00,4F,46,46
1140   data 00,31,30,00,20,30,00,45,4C,49,54,45,00,00,00,50
1150   data 52,4F,50,00,00,00,49,54,41,4C,49,43,00,00,00,43
1160   data 4F,4E,44,45,4E,00,00,00,4D,49,43,52,4F,00,00,00
1170   data 53,4B,49,50,00,00,00,4D,41,52,47,49,4E,00,00,00
1180   data 00,00,00,24,00,00,00,30,00,00,00,31,00,03,00,06
1190   data 00,00,11,80,00,00,FF,FF,00,0C,00,01,00,00,00,32
1200   data 00,00,00,53,00,00,00,54,00,05,00,06,00,02,11,A0
1210   data 00,00,FF,FF,00,21,00,01,00,00,00,55,00,00,00,5E
1220   data 00,00,00,5F,00,05,00,06,00,02,11,80,00,00,FF,FF
1230   data 00,09,00,01,00,00,00,97,00,00,00,9D,00,00,00,9E
1240   data 00,03,00,06,00,00,11,60,00,00,FF,FF,00,06,00,01
1250   data 00,00,00,9F,00,00,00,A4,00,00,00,A5,00,03,00,06
1260   data 00,00,11,60,00,00,FF,FF,00,05,00,01,00,00,00,A6
1270   data 00,00,00,AD,00,00,00,AE,00,03,00,06,00,00,11,60
1280   data 00,00,FF,FF,00,07,00,01,00,00,00,AF,00,00,00,B6
1290   data 00,00,00,B7,00,03,00,06,00,00,11,60,00,00,FF,FF
1300   data 00,07,00,01,00,00,00,B8,00,00,00,BE,00,00,00,BF
1310   data 00,03,00,06,00,00,11,60,00,00,FF,FF,00,06,00,01
1320   data 00,00,00,C0,00,00,00,C5,00,00,00,C6,00,03,00,06
1330   data 00,00,11,60,00,00,FF,FF,00,05,00,01,00,00,00,C7
1340   data 00,00,00,CE,00,00,00,CF,00,03,00,06,00,00,11,60
1350   data 00,00,FF,FF,00,07,00,01,FF,FF,00,01,00,21,00,14
1360   data 00,00,00,10,00,02,11,20,00,00,00,00,00,24,00,13
1370   data 00,05,00,02,00,04,00,14,00,00,00,20,00,FF,33,A2
```

```
1380  data 00,06,00,01,00,18,00,03,00,03,FF,FF,FF,FF,00,15
1390  data 00,00,00,00,00,00,00,D0,00,07,00,00,00,0B,00,01
1400  data 00,04,FF,FF,FF,FF,00,15,00,00,00,00,00,00,00,EC
1410  data 00,00,00,01,00,18,06,00,00,01,FF,FF,FF,FF,00,15
1420  data 00,00,00,00,00,00,01,08,00,09,00,02,00,06,06,00
1430  data 00,06,FF,FF,FF,FF,00,1A,00,07,00,00,00,00,00,60
1440  data 00,06,00,11,00,18,00,01,00,09,00,07,00,08,00,14
1450  data 00,00,00,20,31,FF,11,E1,00,0F,00,06,00,0F,00,01
1460  data 00,08,FF,FF,FF,FF,00,1A,00,51,00,00,00,00,00,67
1470  data 00,00,00,00,00,06,00,01,00,06,FF,FF,FF,FF,00,1A
1480  data 00,51,00,00,00,00,00,6A,00,0A,00,00,00,05,00,01
1490  data 00,0C,00,0A,00,0B,00,14,00,00,00,20,31,FF,11,61
1500  data 00,0F,00,07,00,0F,00,01,00,0B,FF,FF,FF,FF,00,1A
1510  data 00,51,00,00,00,00,00,6E,00,00,00,00,00,06,00,01
1520  data 00,09,FF,FF,FF,FF,00,1A,00,51,00,00,00,00,00,71
1530  data 00,0A,00,00,00,05,00,01,00,0F,00,0D,00,0E,00,14
1540  data 00,00,00,20,31,FF,11,61,00,0F,00,09,00,0F,00,01
1550  data 00,0E,FF,FF,FF,FF,00,1A,00,51,00,00,00,00,00,75
1560  data 00,00,00,00,00,06,00,01,00,0C,FF,FF,FF,FF,00,1A
1570  data 00,51,00,00,00,00,00,78,00,0A,00,00,00,05,00,01
1580  data 00,12,00,10,00,11,00,14,00,00,00,20,31,FF,11,61
1590  data 00,0F,00,0A,00,0F,00,01,00,11,FF,FF,FF,FF,00,1A
1600  data 00,51,00,00,00,00,00,7C,00,00,00,00,00,06,00,01
1610  data 00,0F,FF,FF,FF,FF,00,1A,00,51,00,00,00,00,00,7F
1620  data 00,0A,00,00,00,05,00,01,00,15,00,13,00,14,00,14
1630  data 00,00,00,20,31,FF,11,61,00,0F,00,0B,00,0F,00,01
1640  data 00,14,FF,FF,FF,FF,00,1A,00,51,00,00,00,00,00,83
1650  data 00,00,00,00,00,06,00,01,00,12,FF,FF,FF,FF,00,1A
1660  data 00,51,00,00,00,00,00,86,00,0A,00,00,00,05,00,01
1670  data 00,18,00,16,00,17,00,14,00,00,00,20,31,FF,11,61
1680  data 00,0F,00,0D,00,0F,00,01,00,17,FF,FF,FF,FF,00,1A
1690  data 00,51,00,00,00,00,00,8A,00,00,00,00,00,06,00,01
1700  data 00,15,FF,FF,FF,FF,00,1A,00,51,00,00,00,00,00,8D
1710  data 00,0A,00,00,00,05,00,01,00,1A,00,19,00,19,00,14
1720  data 00,00,00,20,31,FF,11,61,00,0F,00,0E,00,0F,00,01
1730  data 00,18,FF,FF,FF,FF,00,1A,00,51,00,00,00,00,00,91
1740  data 00,0A,00,00,00,05,00,01,00,1B,FF,FF,FF,FF,00,1A
1750  data 00,51,00,00,00,00,00,94,00,0F,00,0E,00,06,00,01
1760  data 00,1C,FF,FF,FF,FF,00,16,00,00,00,20,00,00,01,24
1770  data 00,06,00,06,00,08,00,01,00,1D,FF,FF,FF,FF,00,16
1780  data 00,00,00,20,00,00,01,40,00,06,00,07,00,08,00,01
1790  data 00,1E,FF,FF,FF,FF,00,16,00,00,00,20,00,00,01,5C
1800  data 00,06,00,09,00,08,00,01,00,1F,FF,FF,FF,FF,00,16
```

```
1810    data 00,00,00,20,00,00,01,78,00,06,00,0A,00,08,00,01
1820    data 00,20,FF,FF,FF,FF,00,16,00,00,00,20,00,00,01,94
1830    data 00,06,00,0B,00,08,00,01,00,21,FF,FF,FF,FF,00,16
1840    data 00,00,00,20,00,00,01,B0,00,06,00,0D,00,08,00,01
1850    data 00,00,FF,FF,FF,FF,00,16,00,20,00,20,00,00,01,CC
1860    data 00,06,00,0E,00,08,00,01,00,00,01,E8,00,00,00,00
1870    data *
1880    close 1:if s<> 58576 then print"ERROR IN DATA!":end
1900    print "Ok."
```

```
1000   open"R",1,"c:fx80acc.acc",16
1010   field#1,16 as bin$
1020   a$="":for i=1 TO 16:read d$:if d$="*"then 1050
1030   a=val("&H"+d$):s=s+a:a$=a$+chr$(a):next
1040   lset bin$=a$:rec=rec+1:put 1,rec:goto 1020
1050   data 60,1A,00,00,12,DC,00,00,02,36,00,00,09,BA,00,00
1060   data 00,00,00,00,00,00,00,00,00,00,00,00,2E,7C,00,00
1070   data 19,16,4E,B9,00,00,00,FA,2E,BC,00,00,00,00,4E,41
1080   data 22,2F,00,04,30,3C,00,C8,4E,42,4E,75,4E,56,FF,FA
1090   data 42,6E,FF,FE,60,14,30,6E,FF,FE,D1,C8,D1,FC,00,00
1100   data 1D,AE,30,BC,00,01,52,6E,FF,FE,0C,6E,00,0A,FF,FE
1110   data 6D,E4,33,FC,00,02,00,00,1D,C2,33,F9,00,00,1B,70
1120   data 00,00,1B,6E,2E,BC,00,00,1E,06,2F,3C,00,00,1B,6E
1130   data 2F,3C,00,00,1D,AE,4E,B9,00,00,0D,22,50,8F,4E,5E
1140   data 4E,75,4E,56,FF,FC,3E,B9,00,00,1B,3A,3F,39,00,00
1150   data 1D,80,3F,39,00,00,1D,A2,3F,39,00,00,1D,A0,42,67
1160   data 4E,B9,00,00,11,B2,50,8F,33,C0,00,00,1E,BE,3E,B9
1170   data 00,00,1B,3A,3F,39,00,00,1D,80,3F,39,00,00,1D,A2
1180   data 3F,39,00,00,1D,A0,3F,39,00,00,1E,BE,4E,B9,00,00
1190   data 11,EC,50,8F,2E,BC,00,00,1B,72,2F,3C,00,00,1D,C4
1200   data 2F,3C,00,00,1D,C8,2F,3C,00,00,1D,C6,3F,3C,00,04
1210   data 3F,39,00,00,1E,BE,4E,B9,00,00,12,5A,DF,FC,00,00
1220   data 00,10,4E,5E,4E,75,4E,56,FF,FC,4E,B9,00,00,0E,22
1230   data 2E,BC,00,00,1B,38,2F,3C,00,00,1D,7E,2F,3C,00,00
1240   data 1E,78,2F,3C,00,00,1E,BC,4E,B9,00,00,10,5C,DF,FC
1250   data 00,00,00,0C,33,C0,00,00,1B,70,2E,BC,00,00,14,90
1260   data 3F,39,00,00,1E,9A,4E,B9,00,00,10,9E,54,8F,33,C0
1270   data 00,00,1A,32,2E,BC,00,00,1E,98,2F,3C,00,00,1E,C2
1280   data 2F,3C,00,00,1E,CA,2F,3C,00,00,1E,C8,3F,3C,00,04
1290   data 42,67,4E,B9,00,00,12,5A,DF,FC,00,00,00,10,2E,BC
1300   data 00,00,14,9E,4E,B9,00,00,11,64,4A,40,66,12,2E,BC
1310   data 00,00,14,A9,3F,3C,00,01,4E,B9,00,00,0F,F0,54,8F
1320   data 2E,BC,00,00,1D,AA,42,67,42,67,4E,B9,00,00,11,7E
1330   data 58,8F,4A,40,66,12,2E,BC,00,00,14,E0,3F,3C,00,01
1340   data 4E,B9,00,00,0F,F0,54,8F,2E,BC,00,00,1D,AA,42,67
1350   data 42,67,4E,B9,00,00,11,7E,58,8F,2E,BC,00,00,1B,3A
1360   data 2F,3C,00,00,1D,80,2F,3C,00,00,1D,A2,2F,3C,00,00
1370   data 1D,A0,2F,39,00,00,1D,AA,4E,B9,00,00,10,12,DF,FC
1380   data 00,00,00,10,61,04,4E,5E,4E,75,4E,56,FF,FC,60,00
1390   data 00,BE,2E,BC,00,00,1B,74,2F,3C,00,00,1B,74,2F,3C
1400   data 00,00,1B,74,2F,3C,00,00,1B,74,2F,3C,00,00,1D,7A
1410   data 2F,3C,00,00,1C,78,42,67,42,67,2F,3C,00,00,1B,5E
1420   data 42,67,42,67,42,67,42,67,42,67,42,67,42,67,42,67
```

227

```
1430   data  42,67,42,67,3F,3C,00,01,3F,3C,00,01,3F,3C,00,01
1440   data  3F,3C,00,13,4E,B9,00,00,0E,96,DF,FC,00,00,00,38
1450   data  33,C0,00,00,1A,34,08,39,00,04,00,00,1A,35,67,4E
1460   data  30,39,00,00,1B,5E,60,40,30,39,00,00,1B,66,B0,79
1470   data  00,00,1A,32,66,2E,61,00,FD,94,61,00,FD,E6,61,36
1480   data  3E,B9,00,00,1E,BE,4E,B9,00,00,12,26,3E,B9,00,00
1490   data  1E,BE,4E,B9,00,00,12,40,3E,B9,00,00,1B,6E,4E,B9
1500   data  00,00,0C,F8,60,08,60,06,B0,7C,00,28,67,BA,60,00
1510   data  FF,42,4E,5E,4E,75,4E,56,FF,FC,2E,BC,00,00,1D,AA
1520   data  42,67,42,67,4E,B9,00,00,11,7E,58,8F,2E,BC,00,00
1530   data  1B,3A,2F,3C,00,00,1D,80,2F,3C,00,00,1D,A2,2F,3C
1540   data  00,00,1D,A0,2F,39,00,00,1D,AA,4E,B9,00,00,10,12
1550   data  DF,FC,00,00,00,10,3E,B9,00,00,1B,3A,3F,39,00,00
1560   data  1D,80,3F,39,00,00,1D,A2,3F,39,00,00,1D,A0,42,67
1570   data  4E,B9,00,00,0F,96,50,8F,3E,B9,00,00,1B,3A,3F,39
1580   data  00,00,1D,80,3F,39,00,00,1D,A2,3F,39,00,00,1D,A0
1590   data  3F,3C,00,01,3F,3C,00,01,3F,3C,00,01,3F,3C,00,01
1600   data  3F,3C,00,01,4E,B9,00,00,0F,96,DF,FC,00,00,00,10
1610   data  3E,B9,00,00,1E,98,3F,39,00,00,1E,C2,42,67,42,67
1620   data  3F,3C,00,22,42,67,2F,39,00,00,1D,AA,4E,B9,00,00
1630   data  10,C0,DF,FC,00,00,00,0E,42,79,00,00,1E,C0,60,00
1640   data  09,54,42,57,2F,39,00,00,1D,AA,4E,B9,00,00,0F,74
1650   data  58,8F,33,C0,00,00,1D,7C,30,39,00,00,1D,7C,60,00
1660   data  09,1E,3E,BC,00,01,3F,3C,00,01,3F,39,00,00,1B,3A
1670   data  3F,39,00,00,1D,80,3F,39,00,00,1D,A2,3F,39,00,00
1680   data  1D,A0,42,67,3F,3C,00,07,2F,39,00,00,1D,AA,4E,B9
1690   data  00,00,11,0A,DF,FC,00,00,00,12,3E,BC,00,01,42,67
1700   data  3F,39,00,00,1B,3A,3F,39,00,00,1D,80,3F,39,00,00
1710   data  1D,A2,3F,39,00,00,1D,A0,42,67,3F,3C,00,08,2F,39
1720   data  00,00,1D,AA,4E,B9,00,00,11,0A,DF,FC,00,00,00,12
1730   data  3E,BC,00,1B,3F,3C,00,05,4E,B9,00,00,12,CC,54,8F
1740   data  3E,BC,00,4D,3F,3C,00,05,4E,B9,00,00,12,CC,54,8F
1750   data  60,00,08,A2,3E,BC,00,01,3F,3C,00,01,3F,39,00,00
1760   data  1B,72,3F,39,00,00,1D,C4,3F,39,00,00,1D,C8,3F,39
1770   data  00,00,1D,C6,42,67,3F,3C,00,08,2F,39,00,00,1D,AA
1780   data  4E,B9,00,00,11,0A,DF,FC,00,00,00,12,3E,BC,00,01
1790   data  42,67,3F,39,00,00,1B,72,3F,39,00,00,1D,C4,3F,39
1800   data  00,00,1D,C8,3F,39,00,00,1D,C6,42,67,3F,3C,00,07
1810   data  2F,39,00,00,1D,AA,4E,B9,00,00,11,0A,DF,FC,00,00
1820   data  00,12,3E,BC,00,1B,3F,3C,00,05,4E,B9,00,00,12,CC
1830   data  54,8F,3E,BC,00,50,3F,3C,00,05,4E,B9,00,00,12,CC
1840   data  54,8F,60,00,08,10,3E,BC,00,01,3F,3C,00,01,3F,39
1850   data  00,00,1B,72,3F,39,00,00,1D,C4,3F,39,00,00,1D,C8
```

```
1860    data 3F,39,00,00,1D,C6,42,67,3F,3C,00,10,2F,39,00,00
1870    data 1D,AA,4E,B9,00,00,11,0A,DF,FC,00,00,00,12,3E,BC
1880    data 00,01,42,67,3F,39,00,00,1B,72,3F,39,00,00,1D,C4
1890    data 3F,39,00,00,1D,C8,3F,39,00,00,1D,C6,42,67,3F,3C
1900    data 00,11,2F,39,00,00,1D,AA,4E,B9,00,00,11,0A,DF,FC
1910    data 00,00,00,12,3E,BC,00,0F,3F,3C,00,05,4E,B9,00,00
1920    data 12,CC,54,8F,60,00,07,8E,3E,BC,00,01,3F,3C,00,01
1930    data 3F,39,00,00,1B,72,3F,39,00,00,1D,C4,3F,39,00,00
1940    data 1D,C8,3F,39,00,00,1D,C6,42,67,3F,3C,00,11,2F,39
1950    data 00,00,1D,AA,4E,B9,00,00,11,0A,DF,FC,00,00,00,12
1960    data 3E,BC,00,01,42,67,3F,39,00,00,1B,72,3F,39,00,00
1970    data 1D,C4,3F,39,00,00,1D,C8,3F,39,00,00,1D,C6,42,67
1980    data 3F,3C,00,10,2F,39,00,00,1D,AA,4E,B9,00,00,11,0A
1990    data DF,FC,00,00,00,12,3E,BC,00,12,3F,3C,00,05,4E,B9
2000    data 00,00,12,CC,54,8F,60,00,07,0C,3E,BC,00,01,3F,3C
2010    data 00,01,3F,39,00,00,1B,72,3F,39,00,00,1D,C4,3F,39
2020    data 00,00,1D,C8,3F,39,00,00,1D,C6,42,67,3F,3C,00,0A
2030    data 2F,39,00,00,1D,AA,4E,B9,00,00,11,0A,DF,FC,00,00
2040    data 00,12,3E,BC,00,01,42,67,3F,39,00,00,1B,72,3F,39
2050    data 00,00,1D,C4,3F,39,00,00,1D,C8,3F,39,00,00,1D,C6
2060    data 42,67,3F,3C,00,0B,2F,39,00,00,1D,AA,4E,B9,00,00
2070    data 11,0A,DF,FC,00,00,00,12,3E,BC,00,1B,3F,3C,00,05
2080    data 4E,B9,00,00,12,CC,54,8F,3E,BC,00,70,3F,3C,00,05
2090    data 4E,B9,00,00,12,CC,54,8F,3E,BC,00,01,3F,3C,00,05
2100    data 4E,B9,00,00,12,CC,54,8F,60,00,06,6A,3E,BC,00,01
2110    data 3F,3C,00,01,3F,39,00,00,1B,72,3F,39,00,00,1D,C4
2120    data 3F,39,00,00,1D,C8,3F,39,00,00,1D,C6,42,67,3F,3C
2130    data 00,0B,2F,39,00,00,1D,AA,4E,B9,00,00,11,0A,DF,FC
2140    data 00,00,00,12,3E,BC,00,01,42,67,3F,39,00,00,1B,72
2150    data 3F,39,00,00,1D,C4,3F,39,00,00,1D,C8,3F,39,00,00
2160    data 1D,C6,42,67,3F,3C,00,0A,2F,39,00,00,1D,AA,4E,B9
2170    data 00,00,11,0A,DF,FC,00,00,00,12,3E,BC,00,1B,3F,3C
2180    data 00,05,4E,B9,00,00,12,CC,54,8F,3E,BC,00,70,3F,3C
2190    data 00,05,4E,B9,00,00,12,CC,54,8F,42,57,3F,3C,00,05
2200    data 4E,B9,00,00,12,CC,54,8F,60,00,05,CA,3E,BC,00,01
2210    data 3F,3C,00,01,3F,39,00,00,1B,72,3F,39,00,00,1D,C4
2220    data 3F,39,00,00,1D,C8,3F,39,00,00,1D,C6,42,67,3F,3C
2230    data 00,0D,2F,39,00,00,1D,AA,4E,B9,00,00,11,0A,DF,FC
2240    data 00,00,00,12,3E,BC,00,01,42,67,3F,39,00,00,1B,72
2250    data 3F,39,00,00,1D,C4,3F,39,00,00,1D,C8,3F,39,00,00
2260    data 1D,C6,42,67,3F,3C,00,0E,2F,39,00,00,1D,AA,4E,B9
2270    data 00,00,11,0A,DF,FC,00,00,00,12,3E,BC,00,1B,3F,3C
2280    data 00,05,4E,B9,00,00,12,CC,54,8F,3E,BC,00,34,3F,3C
```

```
2290    data 00,05,4E,B9,00,00,12,CC,54,8F,60,00,05,38,3E,BC
2300    data 00,01,3F,3C,00,01,3F,39,00,00,1B,72,3F,39,00,00
2310    data 1D,C4,3F,39,00,00,1D,C8,3F,39,00,00,1D,C6,42,67
2320    data 3F,3C,00,0E,2F,39,00,00,1D,AA,4E,B9,00,00,11,0A
2330    data DF,FC,00,00,00,12,3E,BC,00,01,42,67,3F,39,00,00
2340    data 1B,72,3F,39,00,00,1D,C4,3F,39,00,00,1D,C8,3F,39
2350    data 00,00,1D,C6,42,67,3F,3C,00,0D,2F,39,00,00,1D,AA
2360    data 4E,B9,00,00,11,0A,DF,FC,00,00,00,12,3E,BC,00,1B
2370    data 3F,3C,00,05,4E,B9,00,00,12,CC,54,8F,3E,BC,00,35
2380    data 3F,3C,00,05,4E,B9,00,00,12,CC,54,8F,60,00,04,A6
2390    data 3E,BC,00,01,3F,3C,00,01,3F,39,00,00,1B,72,3F,39
2400    data 00,00,1D,C4,3F,39,00,00,1D,C8,3F,39,00,00,1D,C6
2410    data 42,67,3F,3C,00,13,2F,39,00,00,1D,AA,4E,B9,00,00
2420    data 11,0A,DF,FC,00,00,00,12,3E,BC,00,01,42,67,3F,39
2430    data 00,00,1B,72,3F,39,00,00,1D,C4,3F,39,00,00,1D,C8
2440    data 3F,39,00,00,1D,C6,42,67,3F,3C,00,14,2F,39,00,00
2450    data 1D,AA,4E,B9,00,00,11,0A,DF,FC,00,00,00,12,3E,BC
2460    data 00,1B,3F,3C,00,05,4E,B9,00,00,12,CC,54,8F,3E,BC
2470    data 00,53,3F,3C,00,05,4E,B9,00,00,12,CC,54,8F,42,57
2480    data 3F,3C,00,05,4E,B9,00,00,12,CC,54,8F,60,00,04,06
2490    data 3E,BC,00,01,3F,3C,00,01,3F,39,00,00,1B,72,3F,39
2500    data 00,00,1D,C4,3F,39,00,00,1D,C8,3F,39,00,00,1D,C6
2510    data 42,67,3F,3C,00,14,2F,39,00,00,1D,AA,4E,B9,00,00
2520    data 11,0A,DF,FC,00,00,00,12,3E,BC,00,01,42,67,3F,39
2530    data 00,00,1B,72,3F,39,00,00,1D,C4,3F,39,00,00,1D,C8
2540    data 3F,39,00,00,1D,C6,42,67,3F,3C,00,13,2F,39,00,00
2550    data 1D,AA,4E,B9,00,00,11,0A,DF,FC,00,00,00,12,3E,BC
2560    data 00,1B,3F,3C,00,05,4E,B9,00,00,12,CC,54,8F,3E,BC
2570    data 00,54,3F,3C,00,05,4E,B9,00,00,12,CC,54,8F,60,00
2580    data 03,74,3E,BC,00,01,3F,3C,00,01,3F,39,00,00,1B,72
2590    data 3F,39,00,00,1D,C4,3F,39,00,00,1D,C8,3F,39,00,00
2600    data 1D,C6,42,67,3F,3C,00,16,2F,39,00,00,1D,AA,4E,B9
2610    data 00,00,11,0A,DF,FC,00,00,00,12,3E,BC,00,01,42,67
2620    data 3F,39,00,00,1B,72,3F,39,00,00,1D,C4,3F,39,00,00
2630    data 1D,C8,3F,39,00,00,1D,C6,42,67,3F,3C,00,17,2F,39
2640    data 00,00,1D,AA,4E,B9,00,00,11,0A,DF,FC,00,00,00,12
2650    data 3E,BC,00,1B,3F,3C,00,05,4E,B9,00,00,12,CC,54,8F
2660    data 3E,BC,00,4E,3F,3C,00,05,4E,B9,00,00,12,CC,54,8F
2670    data 3E,BC,00,06,3F,3C,00,05,4E,B9,00,00,12,CC,54,8F
2680    data 60,00,02,D2,3E,BC,00,01,3F,3C,00,01,3F,39,00,00
2690    data 1B,72,3F,39,00,00,1D,C4,3F,39,00,00,1D,C8,3F,39
2700    data 00,00,1D,C6,42,67,3F,3C,00,17,2F,39,00,00,1D,AA
2710    data 4E,B9,00,00,11,0A,DF,FC,00,00,00,12,3E,BC,00,01
```

```
2720    data 42,67,3F,39,00,00,1B,72,3F,39,00,00,1D,C4,3F,39
2730    data 00,00,1D,C8,3F,39,00,00,1D,C6,42,67,3F,3C,00,16
2740    data 2F,39,00,00,1D,AA,4E,B9,00,00,11,0A,DF,FC,00,00
2750    data 00,12,3E,BC,00,1B,3F,3C,00,05,4E,B9,00,00,12,CC
2760    data 54,8F,3E,BC,00,4F,3F,3C,00,05,4E,B9,00,00,12,CC
2770    data 54,8F,60,00,02,40,3E,BC,00,01,3F,3C,00,01,3F,39
2780    data 00,00,1B,72,3F,39,00,00,1D,C4,3F,39,00,00,1D,C8
2790    data 3F,39,00,00,1D,C6,42,67,3F,3C,00,1A,2F,39,00,00
2800    data 1D,AA,4E,B9,00,00,11,0A,DF,FC,00,00,00,12,3E,BC
2810    data 00,01,42,67,3F,39,00,00,1B,72,3F,39,00,00,1D,C4
2820    data 3F,39,00,00,1D,C8,3F,39,00,00,1D,C6,42,67,3F,3C
2830    data 00,19,2F,39,00,00,1D,AA,4E,B9,00,00,11,0A,DF,FC
2840    data 00,00,00,12,3E,BC,00,1B,3F,3C,00,05,4E,B9,00,00
2850    data 12,CC,54,8F,3E,BC,00,6C,3F,3C,00,05,4E,B9,00,00
2860    data 12,CC,54,8F,42,57,3F,3C,00,05,4E,B9,00,00,12,CC
2870    data 54,8F,60,00,01,A0,3E,BC,00,01,3F,3C,00,01,3F,39
2880    data 00,00,1B,72,3F,39,00,00,1D,C4,3F,39,00,00,1D,C8
2890    data 3F,39,00,00,1D,C6,42,67,3F,3C,00,19,2F,39,00,00
2900    data 1D,AA,4E,B9,00,00,11,0A,DF,FC,00,00,00,12,3E,BC
2910    data 00,01,42,67,3F,39,00,00,1B,72,3F,39,00,00,1D,C4
2920    data 3F,39,00,00,1D,C8,3F,39,00,00,1D,C6,42,67,3F,3C
2930    data 00,1A,2F,39,00,00,1D,AA,4E,B9,00,00,11,0A,DF,FC
2940    data 00,00,00,12,3E,BC,00,1B,3F,3C,00,05,4E,B9,00,00
2950    data 12,CC,54,8F,3E,BC,00,6C,3F,3C,00,05,4E,B9,00,00
2960    data 12,CC,54,8F,3E,BC,00,0A,3F,3C,00,05,4E,B9,00,00
2970    data 12,CC,54,8F,60,00,00,FE,3E,BC,00,01,3F,3C,00,01
2980    data 3F,39,00,00,1B,72,3F,39,00,00,1D,C4,3F,39,00,00
2990    data 1D,C8,3F,39,00,00,1D,C6,42,67,3F,3C,00,05,2F,39
3000    data 00,00,1D,AA,4E,B9,00,00,11,0A,DF,FC,00,00,00,12
3010    data 3E,BC,00,0D,3F,3C,00,05,4E,B9,00,00,12,CC,54,8F
3020    data 3E,B9,00,00,1B,3A,3F,39,00,00,1D,80,3F,39,00,00
3030    data 1D,A2,3F,39,00,00,1D,A0,3F,3C,00,02,4E,B9,00,00
3040    data 0F,96,50,8F,3E,B9,00,00,1B,3A,3F,39,00,00,1D,80
3050    data 3F,39,00,00,1D,A2,3F,39,00,00,1D,A0,3F,3C,00,01
3060    data 3F,3C,00,01,3F,3C,00,01,3F,3C,00,01,3F,3C,00,03
3070    data 4E,B9,00,00,0F,96,DF,FC,00,00,00,10,33,FC,00,01
3080    data 00,00,1E,C0,3E,BC,00,01,42,67,3F,39,00,00,1B,72
3090    data 3F,39,00,00,1D,C4,3F,39,00,00,1D,C8,3F,39,00,00
3100    data 1D,C6,42,67,3F,3C,00,05,2F,39,00,00,1D,AA,4E,B9
3110    data 00,00,11,0A,DF,FC,00,00,00,12,60,18,60,16,5B,40
3120    data B0,7C,00,15,62,0E,E5,40,30,40,D1,FC,00,00,14,38
3130    data 20,50,4E,D0,0C,79,00,01,00,00,1E,C0,66,00,F6,A4
3140    data 4E,5E,4E,75,4E,56,FF,FC,33,FC,00,65,00,00,1E,9C
```

231

```
3150    data 42,79,00,00,1E,9E,42,79,00,00,1E,A2,33,EE,00,08
3160    data 00,00,1E,A8,4E,B9,00,00,0D,A2,4E,5E,4E,75,4E,56
3170    data FF,FC,23,EE,00,08,00,00,19,1E,23,EE,00,10,00,00
3180    data 19,26,20,2E,00,10,D0,BC,00,00,00,5A,23,C0,00,00
3190    data 19,2A,33,FC,00,64,00,00,1E,9C,42,79,00,00,1E,9E
3200    data 33,FC,00,0B,00,00,1E,A2,20,6E,00,0C,33,D0,00,00
3210    data 1E,A8,4E,B9,00,00,0D,A2,20,6E,00,0C,30,B9,00,00
3220    data 1E,A8,23,FC,00,00,19,32,00,00,19,1E,23,FC,00,00
3230    data 1A,38,00,00,19,26,23,FC,00,00,1C,7A,00,00,19,2A
3240    data 23,FC,00,00,1B,78,00,00,19,22,4E,5E,4E,75,23,FC
3250    data 00,00,1E,9C,00,00,19,1A,22,3C,00,00,19,1A,70,73
3260    data 4E,42,4E,75,4E,56,FF,F6,33,EE,00,08,00,00,1D,CE
3270    data 30,2E,00,08,D0,7C,FF,F6,C1,FC,00,03,48,C0,D0,BC
3280    data 00,00,12,DC,2D,40,FF,FA,3D,7C,00,01,FF,FE,60,1E
3290    data 20,6E,FF,FA,10,10,48,80,32,6E,FF,FE,D3,C9,D3,FC
3300    data 00,00,1D,CE,32,80,52,AE,FF,FA,52,6E,FF,FE,0C,6E
3310    data 00,04,FF,FE,6D,DA,2E,B9,00,00,1E,92,4E,B9,00,00
3320    data 00,14,42,40,30,39,00,00,1D,F6,4E,5E,4E,75,4E,56
3330    data FF,FA,23,FC,00,00,1D,CE,00,00,1B,3E,23,FC,00,00
3340    data 1D,82,00,00,1B,42,23,FC,00,00,1D,D6,00,00,1B,46
3350    data 23,FC,00,00,1D,F6,00,00,1B,4A,23,FC,00,00,1E,B4
3360    data 00,00,1B,4E,23,FC,00,00,1E,C4,00,00,1B,52,23,FC
3370    data 00,00,1B,3E,00,00,1E,92,3E,BC,00,0A,61,00,FF,46
3380    data 33,F9,00,00,1D,F6,00,00,1E,9A,70,01,4E,5E,4E,75
3390    data 4E,56,FF,FC,3E,BC,00,13,61,00,FF,2A,70,01,4E,5E
3400    data 4E,75,4E,56,FF,FC,33,EE,00,08,00,00,1D,D6,33,EE
3410    data 00,0A,00,00,1D,D8,33,EE,00,0C,00,00,1D,DA,33,EE
3420    data 00,0E,00,00,1D,DC,33,EE,00,10,00,00,1D,DE,33,EE
3430    data 00,12,00,00,1D,E0,33,EE,00,14,00,00,1D,E2,33,EE
3440    data 00,16,00,00,1D,E4,33,EE,00,18,00,00,1D,E6,33,EE
3450    data 00,1A,00,00,1D,E8,33,EE,00,1C,00,00,1D,EA,33,EE
3460    data 00,1E,00,00,1D,EC,33,EE,00,20,00,00,1D,EE,33,EE
3470    data 00,22,00,00,1D,F0,23,EE,00,24,00,00,1E,B4,33,EE
3480    data 00,28,00,00,1D,F2,33,EE,00,2A,00,00,1D,F4,3E,BC
3490    data 00,19,4E,B9,00,00,0D,B8,20,6E,00,2C,30,B9,00,00
3500    data 1D,F8,20,6E,00,30,30,B9,00,00,1D,FA,20,6E,00,34
3510    data 30,B9,00,00,1D,FC,20,6E,00,38,30,B9,00,00,1D,FE
3520    data 20,6E,00,3C,30,B9,00,00,1E,00,20,6E,00,40,30,B9
3530    data 00,00,1E,02,42,40,30,39,00,00,1D,F6,4E,5E,4E,75
3540    data 4E,56,FF,FC,23,EE,00,08,00,00,1E,B4,33,EE,00,0C
3550    data 00,00,1D,D6,3E,BC,00,32,4E,B9,00,00,0D,B8,4E,5E
3560    data 4E,75,4E,56,FF,FC,33,EE,00,08,00,00,1D,D6,33,EE
3570    data 00,0A,00,00,1D,D8,33,EE,00,0C,00,00,1D,DA,33,EE
```

```
3580    data 00,0E,00,00,1D,DC,33,EE,00,10,00,00,1D,DE,33,EE
3590    data 00,12,00,00,1D,E0,33,EE,00,14,00,00,1D,E2,33,EE
3600    data 00,16,00,00,1D,E4,33,EE,00,18,00,00,1D,E6,3E,BC
3610    data 00,33,4E,B9,00,00,0D,B8,4E,5E,4E,75,4E,56,FF,FC
3620    data 33,EE,00,08,00,00,1D,D6,23,EE,00,0A,00,00,1E,B4
3630    data 3E,BC,00,34,4E,B9,00,00,0D,B8,4E,5E,4E,75,4E,56
3640    data FF,FC,23,EE,00,08,00,00,1E,B4,3E,BC,00,36,4E,B9
3650    data 00,00,0D,B8,20,6E,00,0C,30,B9,00,00,1D,F8,20,6E
3660    data 00,10,30,B9,00,00,1D,FA,20,6E,00,14,30,B9,00,00
3670    data 1D,FC,20,6E,00,18,30,B9,00,00,1D,FE,42,40,30,39
3680    data 00,00,1D,F6,4E,5E,4E,75,4E,56,FF,FC,3E,BC,00,4D
3690    data 4E,B9,00,00,0D,B8,20,6E,00,08,30,B9,00,00,1D,F8
3700    data 20,6E,00,0C,30,B9,00,00,1D,FA,20,6E,00,10,30,B9
3710    data 00,00,1D,FC,20,6E,00,14,30,B9,00,00,1D,FE,42,40
3720    data 30,39,00,00,1D,F6,4E,5E,4E,75,4E,56,FF,FC,33,EE
3730    data 00,08,00,00,1D,D6,23,EE,00,0A,00,00,1E,B4,3E,BC
3740    data 00,23,4E,B9,00,00,0D,B8,4E,5E,4E,75,4E,56,FF,FC
3750    data 23,EE,00,08,00,00,1E,B4,33,EE,00,0C,00,00,1D,D6
3760    data 33,EE,00,0E,00,00,1D,D8,33,EE,00,10,00,00,1D,DA
3770    data 33,EE,00,12,00,00,1D,DC,33,EE,00,14,00,00,1D,DE
3780    data 33,EE,00,16,00,00,1D,E0,3E,BC,00,2A,4E,B9,00,00
3790    data 0D,B8,4E,5E,4E,75,4E,56,FF,FC,23,EE,00,08,00,00
3800    data 1E,B4,33,EE,00,0C,00,00,1D,D6,33,EE,00,0E,00,00
3810    data 1D,D8,33,EE,00,10,00,00,1D,DA,33,EE,00,12,00,00
3820    data 1D,DC,33,EE,00,14,00,00,1D,DE,33,EE,00,16,00,00
3830    data 1D,E0,33,EE,00,18,00,00,1D,E2,33,EE,00,1A,00,00
3840    data 1D,E4,3E,BC,00,2F,4E,B9,00,00,0D,B8,4E,5E,4E,75
3850    data 4E,56,FF,FC,23,EE,00,08,00,00,1E,B4,3E,BC,00,6E
3860    data 4E,B9,00,00,0D,B8,4E,5E,4E,75,4E,56,FF,FC,33,EE
3870    data 00,08,00,00,1D,D6,33,EE,00,0A,00,00,1D,D8,3E,BC
3880    data 00,70,4E,B9,00,00,0D,B8,20,6E,00,0C,20,B9,00,00
3890    data 1E,C4,42,40,30,39,00,00,1D,F6,4E,5E,4E,75,4E,56
3900    data FF,FC,33,EE,00,08,00,00,1D,D6,33,EE,00,0A,00,00
3910    data 1D,D8,33,EE,00,0C,00,00,1D,DA,33,EE,00,0E,00,00
3920    data 1D,DC,33,EE,00,10,00,00,1D,DE,3E,BC,00,64,4E,B9
3930    data 00,00,0D,B8,4E,5E,4E,75,4E,56,FF,FC,33,EE,00,08
3940    data 00,00,1D,D6,33,EE,00,0A,00,00,1D,D8,33,EE,00,0C
3950    data 00,00,1D,DA,33,EE,00,0E,00,00,1D,DC,33,EE,00,10
3960    data 00,00,1D,DE,3E,BC,00,65,4E,B9,00,00,0D,B8,4E,5E
3970    data 4E,75,4E,56,FF,FC,33,EE,00,08,00,00,1D,D6,3E,BC
3980    data 00,66,4E,B9,00,00,0D,B8,4E,5E,4E,75,4E,56,FF,FC
3990    data 33,EE,00,08,00,00,1D,D6,3E,BC,00,67,4E,B9,00,00
4000    data 0D,B8,4E,5E,4E,75,4E,56,FF,FC,33,EE,00,08,00,00
```

```
4010    data  1D,D6,33,EE,00,0A,00,00,1D,D8,3E,BC,00,68,4E,B9
4020    data  00,00,0D,B8,20,6E,00,0C,30,B9,00,00,1D,F8,20,6E
4030    data  00,10,30,B9,00,00,1D,FA,20,6E,00,14,30,B9,00,00
4040    data  1D,FC,20,6E,00,18,30,B9,00,00,1D,FE,42,40,30,39
4050    data  00,00,1D,F6,4E,5E,4E,75,23,DF,00,00,19,2E,4E,4E
4060    data  2F,39,00,00,19,2E,4E,75,23,DF,00,00,19,2E,4E,4D
4070    data  2F,39,00,00,19,2E,4E,75,23,DF,00,00,19,2E,4E,41
4080    data  2F,39,00,00,19,2E,4E,75,00,01,00,02,01,01,02,01
4090    data  01,00,01,01,02,01,01,01,01,01,00,00,00,00,00,00
4100    data  00,00,00,00,01,00,00,01,00,03,05,00,05,05,00,00
4110    data  01,01,02,01,00,10,07,01,02,01,01,00,00,00,00,00
4120    data  00,00,00,00,01,01,01,02,01,01,02,01,01,02,01,01
4130    data  01,01,02,01,01,01,00,00,00,00,00,00,00,00,00,00
4140    data  00,00,02,01,01,01,01,01,06,01,01,04,01,01,01,03
4150    data  01,02,01,01,04,02,01,08,01,01,00,00,00,00,00,00
4160    data  01,01,01,09,01,01,01,01,01,01,01,01,00,00,05,01,00
4170    data  00,00,00,00,00,00,00,00,00,00,00,00,00,00,00,00
4180    data  00,00,00,00,00,00,00,00,00,00,00,00,00,00,00,00
4190    data  00,00,00,00,00,00,00,00,00,00,00,00,04,03,00,08
4200    data  03,00,06,01,00,08,01,00,08,01,00,04,01,01,03,01
4210    data  01,00,05,00,01,01,01,00,05,00,00,01,01,00,01,01
4220    data  00,00,00,00,00,00,00,00,00,00,00,00,00,00,00,00
4230    data  00,00,00,00,00,00,00,00,00,02,02,00,00,00,00,00
4240    data  00,00,00,00,00,00,00,00,00,00,00,00,00,00,00,00
4250    data  00,00,00,00,00,00,05,01,00,05,01,00,01,01,00,01
4260    data  01,00,02,05,00,06,01,00,02,01,00,01,01,00,06,05
4270    data  00,00,00,00,00,01,01,00,01,00,02,01,00,02,01,01
4280    data  01,01,01,00,00,00,00,00,00,00,00,00,00,00,00,00
4290    data  00,00,00,01,02,03,01,02,01,01,01,01,01,01,00,01
4300    data  01,00,01,02,00,00,0B,EC,00,00,0C,E8,00,00,03,B6
4310    data  00,00,04,48,00,00,0C,E8,00,00,05,DE,00,00,06,80
4320    data  00,00,0C,E8,00,00,07,20,00,00,07,B2,00,00,0C,E8
4330    data  00,00,04,DA,00,00,05,5C,00,00,0C,E8,00,00,08,44
4340    data  00,00,08,E4,00,00,0C,E8,00,00,09,76,00,00,0A,18
4350    data  00,00,0C,E8,00,00,0B,4A,00,00,0A,AA,20,20,46,58
4360    data  2D,38,30,2B,20,49,4E,49,54,00,50,52,49,4E,49,54
4370    data  2E,52,53,43,00,5B,33,5D,5B,42,61,64,20,63,6F,70
4380    data  79,3F,20,7C,50,52,49,4E,49,54,2E,52,53,43,7C,20
4390    data  63,6F,75,6C,64,6E,27,74,20,62,65,20,66,6F,75,6E
4400    data  64,21,5D,5B,43,61,6E,63,65,6C,5D,00,5B,33,5D,20
4410    data  5B,46,61,74,61,6C,20,65,72,72,6F,72,21,21,7C,52
4420    data  65,73,6F,75,72,63,65,20,46,69,6C,65,20,6E,6F,74
4430    data  20,4F,4B,2E,5D,5B,43,61,6E,63,65,6C,5D,00,00,00
```

234

```
4440  data 00,02,06,2A,18,06,04,06,06,06,06,10,06,06,06,08
4450  data 08,06,06,06,06,06,06,08,06,06,06,0A,06,14,06,06
4460  data 06,06,06,0C,06,06,06,08,06,06,06,06,0C,0C,06,0A
4470  data 0A,08,0A,0C,0A,08,0A,08,06,06,06,06,06,1A,06,06
4480  data 06,06,06,0A,2A,0C,08,08,08,06,12,06,06,06,06,06
4490  data 1C,0A,08,06,06,06,06,06,0C,06,06,06,08,08,06,06
4500  data 06,1A,0C,06,10,06,0C,0C,06,08,06,12,06,06,06,0C
4510  data 06,12,06,06,06,0C,06,14,10,14,06,06,06,0C,06,12
4520  data 06,06,06,0C,06,14,10,14,06,06,06,0C,06,12,06,06
4530  data 06,0C,06,14,14,06,06,06,0C,06,12,06,06,06,0C,06
4540  data 14,14,06,06,06,0C,06,12,06,06,06,0C,06,14,10,10
4550  data 14,06,06,06,0C,06,12,06,06,06,0C,06,14,10,0E,14
4560  data 06,06,06,0C,06,12,06,06,06,0C,06,14,10,14,06,06
4570  data 06,0C,06,12,06,06,06,0C,06,14,10,14,06,06,06,0C
4580  data 06,12,06,06,06,0C,06,14,10,0E,14,06,06,06,0C,06
4590  data 12,06,06,06,0C,06,14,10,14,06,06,06,0C,06,12,06
4600  data 06,06,0C,06,14,10,10,14,06,06,06,0C,06,12,06,06
4610  data 06,0C,06,14,10,14,06,06,06,0C,06,12,06,06,06,0C
4620  data 06,14,10,0E,14,06,06,06,0C,06,12,06,06,06,0C,06
4630  data 14,10,10,14,06,06,06,0C,06,14,08,06,06,06,0A,08
4640  data 06,06,06,1A,0E,0C,06,06,06,0C,06,1C,0C,14,06,06
4650  data 08,06,10,08,10,08,06,08,0A,06,0A,06,04,06,04,06
4660  data 04,06,04,0A,04,06,12,14,20,18,06,08,0E,04,06,04
4670  data 06,04,06,04,06,04,06,04,06,04,0E,04,24,08,08,08
4680  data 08,08,08,08,08,08,08,08,08,08,08,08,08,0A,0A,0A
4690  data 0A,0A,0A,0A,08,10,08,0A,10,08,08,08,08,08,08,08
4700  data 08,0A,10,08,0A,10,0A,0A,0A,0A,0A,08,12,0A,0A,0A
4710  data 0A,08,10,08,0A,10,08,08,08,08,08,08,0A,10,08,08
4720  data 08,08,08,08,08,08,0A,10,0A,10,08,0A,0A,08,10,08
4730  data 08,08,08,0A,10,08,08,08,08,0A,10,0A,10,0A,10,08
4740  data 0A,0A,0A,0A,0A,08,0A,08,08,08,08,08,01,64,04,04
4750  data 04,04,04,04,04,04,04,04,04,04,04,04,04,04,04,04
4760  data 04,04,04,00,00,00,00,00,00,00,00,00,00,00,00,00
4770  data *
4780  close 1:if s<> 340260 then print"ERROR IN DATA!":end
4800  print "Ok."
```

Calling All Authors

We hope you've enjoyed reading Atari ST Tricks and Tips, one of the many books in the Abacus ST Reference library. If you have any comments, suggestions or technical questions about the material, please let us know.

If you are a writer of books or articles for the ST and want to work with Abacus, a trusted and well-known publisher, please send an outline to us. We'll pay you for published submissions based on length and content or based on royalties.

Here are the guidelines for submissions:

- Programs should be on 3 1/2" ST formatted micro-floppy.

- Text should be on 3 1/2" diskette in ASCII format, or double-spaced typewritten.

- A cover letter with your name, address, phone number, and short description of your submission

- Self-addressed stamped envelope

Send to:

Abacus Software, Inc.
Product Development
Attn: Jim D'Haem
P.O. Box 7219
Grand Rapids, MI 49510

APPENDICES

Appendix A

The following program creates a table of the Atari ST character set. To use the table, choose the character you want to display. For example, let's use the copyright symbol (©). In the table, find the row (B) and column (D) in which it appears. This yeilds a hexadecimal nymber ($BD). To display it, we use the CHR$ function, so :o print the copyright symbol to the screen type:

```
print chr$(&hBD)
```

The &h tells the computer this is a hexadecimal number.

Perhaps you might want to printout a formula such as: $x^2y + xy^3 = 0$. We would need to look up the values for the superscripted 2 and 3. These are FD and FE. To display these, type the following:

```
print "x"chr$(&hFD)"y + xy"chr$(&hFE)" = 0"
```

By using the table, you can display characters not easily accessible from the keyboard.

BASIC program to create a character set table for the ST

```
1000 fullw 2:clearw 2
1010 print"     ";:for j%=0 to 15 'create column #s
1020 print hex$(j%)" ";
1030 next j%
1040 print:print"    ";:for j%=1 to 32
1050 print chr$(&h2d); '2d is chr code for dash
1060 next j%
1070 print
1080 for i%=0 to 15
1090 print " "hex$(i%)chr$(&h7c)" "; '7c code for vert bar
1100 for j%=0 to 15
1110 c% = i% * 16 + j% 'calculate char number
1120 if c%=7 or c%=10 or c%=13 then print"  ";:goto 1140
```

```
1130 print chr$(c%)" ";
1140 next j%:print
1150 next i%
1160 print "07=Bell 0A=LF 0D=CR" 'remove on color monitor
1170 poke 1262,0 'hardcopy to printer
1180 end
```

ST character set table

Appendix B

The following is a list of the commands available in ST BASIC.

ABS	ALL	AND
AS	ASC	ATN
AUTO	BASE	BLOAD
BREAK	BSAVE	CALL
CBDL	CHAIN	CHR$
CINT	CIRCLE	CLEAR
CLEARW	CLOSE	CLOSEW
COLOR	COMMON	CONT
CONTROL	COS	CSNG
CVD	CVI	CVS
DATA	DEF FN	DEF SEG
DEFFBL	DEFINT	DEFSNG
DEFSTR	DELETE	DIM
DIR	ED	EDIT
ELLIPSE	ELSE	END
EOF	EQF	ERA
ERASE	ERL	ERR
ERROR	EXP	FIELD
FIELD#	FILL	FIX
FLOAT	FOLLOW	FOR
FRE	FULLW	GEMSYS
GB	GET	GET#
GO	GOSUB	GOTO
GOTOXY	HEX$	IF
IMP	INKEY$	INP
INPUT	INPUT#	INPUT$
INSTR	INTIN	INTOUT
KILL	LEFT$	LEN
LET	LINE INPUT	LINE INPUT#
LINEF	LIST	LLIST
LOAD	LOC	LOF
LOG10	LPOS	LPRINT
LSET	MERGE	MID$

MKD$	MKS$	MOD
NAME	MEW	MEXT
NOT	OCT$	OLD
ON	OPEN	OPENW
OPTION	OR	OUT
PCIRCLE	PEEK	PELLIPSE
POKE	POS	PRINT
PRINT#	PRINT USING	PTSIN
PTSOUT	PUT	QUIT
RANDOMIZE	READ	REM
RENUM	REPLACE	RESET
RESTORE	RESUME	RETURN
RIGHT$	RND	RSET
RUN	SAVE	SGN
SIN	SOUND	SPACE$
SPC	SQR	STEP
STOP	STR$	STRING$
SWAP	SYSDBG	SYSTAB
SYSTEM	TAB	TAN
THEN	TO	TRACE
TROFF	TRON	UNBREAK
UNFOLLOW	UNTRACE	USING
VAL	VARPTR	VDISYS
WAIT	WAVE	WEND
WHILE	WIDTH	WRITE
WRITE#	XOR	

Index

P

R

S

W

window creation, 169-171
write modes, 40
workstation (GEM), 163-165
XOR mode, 40

Y

YM-2149, 13

Optional Diskette

Atari ST
TRICKS & TIPS
Optional Diskette

For your convenience, the program listings contained in this book are available on an SF354 formatted floppy disk. You should order the diskette if you want to use the programs, but don't want to type them in from the listings in the book.

All programs on the diskette have been fully tested. You can change the programs for your particular needs. The diskette is available for $14.95 plus $2.00 ($5.00 foreign) for postage and handling.

When ordering, please give your name and shipping address. Enclose a check, money order or credit card information. Mail your order to:

Abacus
5370 52nd Street SE
Grand Rapids, MI 49508

Or for *fast* service, call **616/698-0330**.

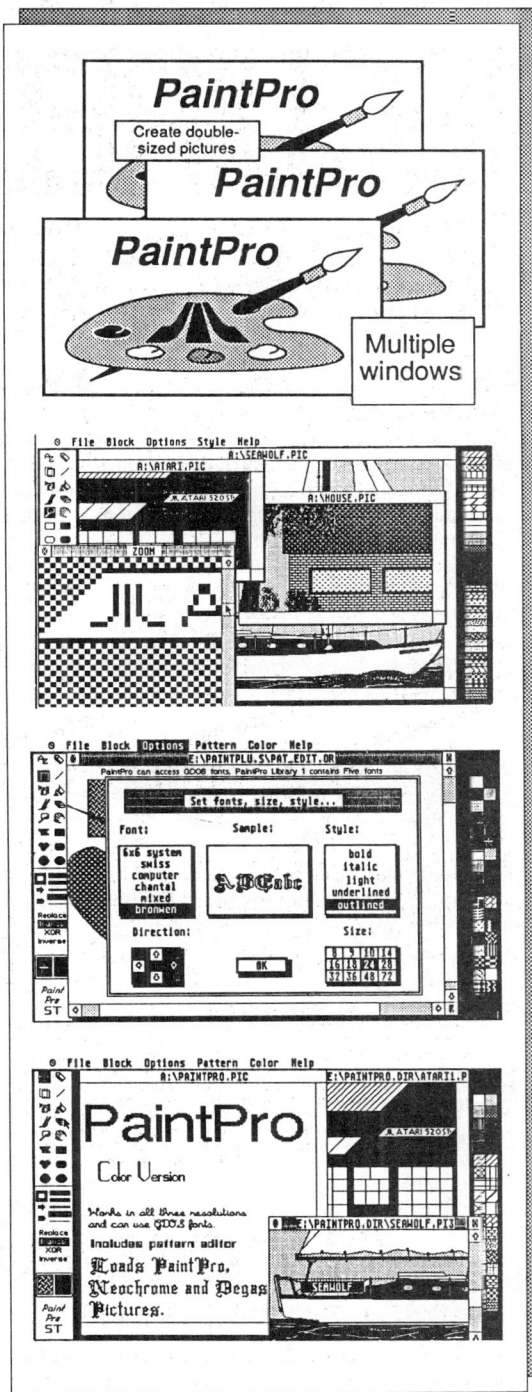

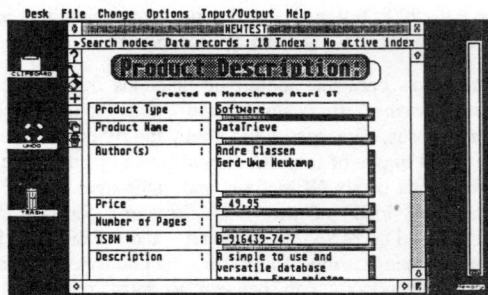